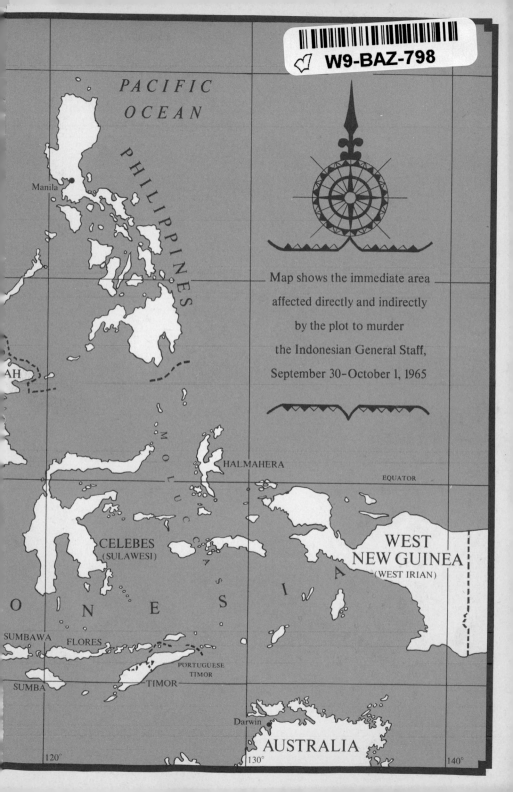

PACIFIC
OCEAN

PHILIPPINES

Manila

AH

MOLUCCAS

HALMAHERA

EQUATOR

CELEBES
(SULAWESI)

WEST
NEW GUINEA
(WEST IRIAN)

O   I   N   E   S   I   A

SUMBAWA   FLORES

SUMBA   TIMOR

PORTUGUESE
TIMOR

Darwin

AUSTRALIA

120°   130°   140°

Map shows the immediate area
affected directly and indirectly
by the plot to murder
the Indonesian General Staff,
September 30–October 1, 1965

THE COMMUNIST COLLAPSE IN INDONESIA

THE COMMUNIST COLLAPSE

IN INDONESIA

Arnold C. Brackman

W · W · Norton & Company · Inc ·  *New York*

To Sutan Sjahrir,
WHO, DYING AND UNABLE TO WRITE OR SPEAK,
LIVED TO SEE A DAWN.

Contents

THE COMMUNIST COLLAPSE IN INDONESIA

Introduction: The Time Frame

ON THE EVENING OF SEPTEMBER 30, 1965, one of the most bizarre and grisly events in contemporary Asian affairs began to unfold in the world's largest archipelago, on the periphery of Vietnam. It was Indonesia's self-styled night of the generals, the abortive Gestapu affair.* One consequence was the destruction of the Indonesian Communist Party (PKI), at the time the largest Communist movement in the non-Communist world.

In perspective, what transpired in Indonesia that night—not the massive United States intervention in Vietnam earlier in the year—was perhaps the most epochal event in Asia since Mao's rise to power on the Chinese mainland in 1949. Indeed, as observed later, the American intervention partly grew out of the situation which had been rapidly developing in Indonesia in the months preceding the September 30 "coup."

The word "coup" is used here circumspectly; for what transpired in Indonesia that night was not a coup in the generally accepted sense of the word. The Communists did not plan to overthrow the existing Sukarno regime. On the contrary, Indonesia's President-for-Life was privy to the plot. Sukarno and the PKI shared a relatively uncomplicated objective: The wholesale purge of the Army general staff, the only effectively organized group standing between Sukarno and the Communists and their desire to establish a "socialist" state.

In a series of coordinated, lightning raids, six Army generals were murdered shortly before dawn on October 1. The

---

* The code name for the plot was "September 30 movement"—*Gerakan Tigapuluh September*—which the Indonesian penchant for acronyms and hypocoristics has reduced to *Gestapu*. It is also frequently referred to as G. 30. S.

plot misfired when a seventh victim, the most important on the list, escaped in the confusion. He was General Abdul Haris Nasution, the minister/coordinator for defense and security and the armed forces chief of staff. Sukarno sensed that something had gone awry. Abruptly, he sought to change course in midstream. It was too late. He was too deeply compromised. The Army regrouped itself under the command of General Suharto and mounted a counterthrust. With popular support, generated especially by intellectuals, academicians, and students, the Communist Party leadership was largely liquidated and its mass base shattered. In the process, thousands of persons, Communists and non-Communists alike, were massacred in reprisals as the country, in the literal sense, ran amok—a Malay word, incidentally, which originated in the islands to describe a nervous seizure which leads to murderous frenzy.

The collapse of the third largest Communist Party in the world would be a major event by any measure, the more so when the party in question is not in a country which is contiguous to either the Soviet Union or China, the rival Communist strongholds. Indeed, Indonesia was not only outside the Eurasian heartland, but embraced 580,000 square miles along the strategically placed East Asian insular chain which stretches from the Kuriles to New Zealand. Thus, unquestionably, the Gestapu affair ranks in history with such Asian events in this century as the Russo-Japanese War, the Chinese Revolution, the Marco Polo Bridge, Pearl Harbor, and Hiroshima, the partition of the Indo-Pakistan subcontinent, the Communist triumph in China, and the limited wars on the Korean and Indo-Chinese peninsulas.

Indonesia—together with Japan, and China—ranks as one of Asia's Big Three. In strategic terms, its importance transcends that of China proper, which is impoverished, overpopulated, and on the Asian mainland. By itself, the Indonesian archipelago constitutes the fifth largest nation in the world. Its population of 110 million is almost equal in size to that of the whole of Southeast Asia. Moreover, Indonesia's natural wealth far exceeds that of any other Asian power.

Together with Malaysia and the Philippines, Indonesia forms a massive Malay bloc which stands racially apart from the rest of Asia. As a French diplomat, Claude Cheysson, has observed, whatever happens in Indonesia must inexorably have an impact not only on Asia, but also on the world at large. Malaysia's prime minister, characteristically, has expressed it more bluntly. The region's destiny—the destiny of the Malay world—is tied to Indonesia, Abdul Rahman has said, adding, "If it were to fall to the Communists then it would be a question of time before the Communists would take over the whole of Southeast Asia." [1]

In 1965, Indonesia tottered on the brink of the Communist abyss. "The odds favored a Communist Indonesia by the end of 1966," according to an official United States assessment, an estimate which was widely shared in Singapore, Canberra, Manila, and Kuala Lumpur.[2] For that matter, Peking and Hanoi felt similarly. The Russians, however, were less confident. The Russians were more cautious not only hopefully because the PKI was then siding with China in the Moscow-Peking polemic, but also because of the Kremlin's past miscalculations about Indonesia. The Russians had been burned as crisply in Indonesia in 1948 for triggering a premature Communist coup at Madiun as the United States was to be singed a decade later when the Central Intelligence Agency underwrote an abortive rebellion against the Sukarno regime. Here, then, we have a rare case of inverse parallelism. Moscow's estimate of Communist strength in Indonesia in 1965 was tempered by its past failure. The Washington estimate was tempered by the apparent weakness of the anti-Sukarno and anti-PKI forces in 1958—it's past failure.

But the most important readings of the situation in 1964–65—the critical years—were made by the Indonesians themselves. Invariably, educated, articulate, and politically sophisticated Indonesians feared a Communist takeover with the PKI catapulting itself into power not on its own strength but through its alliance with Sukarno.[3] The President, it should be stressed, was never a Communist himself—merely a neofascist dictator allied to Moscow and Peking as it suited his interests. Toward that end, he became increasingly convinced that only the Indonesian Communist Party possessed the machinery and mass base necessary to harness and exploit Indonesia's potential and thereby elevate her to the status of a first-class power. Accordingly, the wonder is not that the Gestapu affair came within a hairsbreadth of success, but that it failed.

It failed for two fundamental reasons. One determinant was sheer stupidity: Communist dependence on Sukarno, whose political biography is an open ledger of playing factions, personalities, and ideologies against one another in a notorious, albeit brilliant, fashion. As Sukarno himself once defined politics, "Politics is a game of survival." [4]

Self-deception was the other ingredient in the Communist failure. The PKI was a victim of its own "big lie" technique. The Communists, who effectively controlled Indonesia's mass media by 1965, made the fatal error of believing their own press notices. The PKI leadership was influenced by its own rhetoric and that of Sukarno's.

From whichever direction one studies the Gestapu affair, whether in an Indonesian, regional Southeast Asian, or global time frame, the debacle of the Indonesian Communists ranks as perhaps the most historic turning point in Asia in this decade. The estimate is not overdrawn. Consider some of the consequences:

In one fell swoop a major Communist movement foundered; a burgeoning Jakarta-Peking Axis collapsed; Sukarno's war against Malaysia and Singapore terminated; direct pressure on Australia and indirect pressure on the Philippines dissipated. In short, Southeast Asia's second front caved in: the Communist design to seize Vietnam's rear, an objective manifested in the sixties by the Brunei revolt; the emergence of Thai, Malayan, and Bornean national liberation fronts on the Viet Cong model; Indonesia's headlong slide toward communism in 1964–65; and the emergence of a self-proclaimed Jakarta-Peking Axis on the eve of the Gestapu affair.

Within Indonesia itself, the repressive atmosphere of the corrupt Sukarno regime was lifted. Sukarno himself was dropped into the dustbin of history and, in the bargain, many of his camp followers joined him. The country's political prisoners, largely drawn from the ranks of moderate Moslem and democratic socialist leaders, were liberated from jail—including cabinet ministers, economists, academicians, and writers. The Indonesian dream of representative government and civil liberties, manifest during the war for independence, 1945–49, was recharged.

So much for the brighter side of the ledger. But Indonesia was forced to pay a ghastly price for the follies of Sukarno and the PKI. The country's economy was wracked, the military came to power, and, worse, the nation underwent a night of the long knives, a bloodbath claiming thousands of lives.

Had the plot succeeded as originally envisioned, Indonesia would have accelerated her slide toward becoming a "People's Democracy." Jakarta would have entered the Asian Communist fold. The Jakarta-Peking Axis would have become an awesome reality. The consolidation of the Axis would have inaugurated a new era in the Pacific. It would have set up a chain of authoritarian, expansionist powers from Korea to New Guinea—the range of the Japanese Empire at its zenith. Such an alliance would doom South Vietnam, Thailand, Laos, Cambodia, Malaysia, and Singapore. It would threaten the security of Korea, the Philippines, Australia, and New Zealand. The balance of power in Asia would have inexorably tilted against the non-Communist world.

In this situation, the three primary maritime powers of this century—Japan, Britain, and the United States—would have found themselves in an extraordinary predicament.

Japan would have found herself isolated in Asia. Should the Indonesian rimland fall to the Communists, Dr. Yoshitaka Hirouchi, the economist, once observed, Japan would succumb in a matter of time. As for the Anglo-American powers, in 1965 they were pinned back-to-back along the coastlines of the South China Sea. The British were in Malaysian Borneo holding the line against the expansionism of Sukarno's Communist-backed regime. The Americans were in Vietnam on the short end of a struggle to maintain a viable, non-Communist South. In point of fact, the Jakarta-Hanoi military campaigns to "liberate" Malaysia and South Vietnam were a striking manifestation of things to come.

Nor would the repercussions of a Communist Indonesia

be confined to Asia. By 1965, for example, Indonesia had already withdrawn from the United Nations and, in collaboration with Peking, Hanoi, and Pyongyang, was laboring to construct a rival world organization composed of what Sukarno characterized as "the new emerging forces" (NEFO). Indeed, a conference of such forces was already in the preparatory stage when the September 30 affair unwound.

The events surrounding that night raise many questions. What prompted the Communists to strike when they did? Why were they in a hurry when everything appeared to be effortlessly moving their way? Why did the Communist mass movement virtually collapse overnight? Why did Indonesia run amok? What was Peking's role in the affair? What link is there, if any, between the Communist failure in Indonesia and the ensuing Cultural Revolution in China? Why have some Western academicians attempted to whitewash the roles of Sukarno and the Indonesian Communist Party in the affair? How did Moscow react to the debacle? What is the relationship between events in Indonesia and the American intervention in Vietnam earlier that year?

The last inquiry gives rise to a logical and very controversial question: Did American intervention in Southeast Asia buy time for Indonesia? This subject has been touched on very lightly, if at all, by doves and hawks alike in the interminable literature on Vietnam. Indeed, many of the "authoritative" writers and analysts on Vietnam seem oblivious to Indonesia's existence. Yet a strong case can be made for the view that the United States fought in Vietnam for time, not space. And, after all is said and done, in the long-term Indonesia—as a principal steppingstone along the East Asian insular barrier— is of far greater strategic importance to the United States and the non-Communist world generally than the Indo-Chinese peninsula. But if this assessment is reasonably correct, the Vietnam intervention paid off long ago. The shift in fortunes in Southeast Asia's island belt, the dissolution of the "second front," placed Vietnam in a new setting and, justifiably, set the stage for a phased de-escalation of the Vietnam conflict probably as early as 1966, not 1968.

These are some of the questions which I shall attempt to

explore in this book. In early 1968 I returned to Southeast Asia in pursuit of the answers. The quest took me from Indonesia to Vietnam, and in between. Some of the answers I found readily, others with some difficulty, and some not at all.

My revisit to Indonesia was personally exhilarating since I had been barred from the country by Sukarno's "Old Order," as the Indonesians now call it. Not only was I warmly welcomed on my return, but I was overwhelmed by assistance. Most important of all, I had the opportunity to renew intimate personal friendships with Indonesians of many political persuasions whom I had known since the days when I covered the Indonesian war for independence in the field as a correspondent. The following pages are drawn largely from these primary sources of information. Among the Indonesian leaders there is no uniform essay of the Gestapu affair. Indeed, sometimes their interpretations of events are in conflict. This is how it should be and, I hope that from this diversity will emerge a sense of unity.

Jakarta, Java 1968
Brookfield Center, Connecticut 1969

1

The Mephitic Climate

IN THE SIXTIES, THE MEPHITIC ATMO-
sphere in Jakarta superficially resembled Rome in the heyday
of fascism. Torchlight parades, emotionally charged rallies,
the inevitable slogans, the myriad of flags and banners, the
paper broadsides—all the trappings of the authoritarian state
were on display. Inevitably, too, the regime's superstructure
was capped by the omnipresent portraits of the omnipotent
"Great Leader of the Revolution" in homes and offices, in the
villages, and on side streets.

The Institute for Building the Revolutionary Spirit fab-
ricated for Sukarno an endless stream of slogans and symbols.
All newspapers, weeklies, and monthlies were authorized to
reserve columns for the propagation of Sukarno's "teachings"
or face charges of counterrevolutionary activity. Sukarno naturally judged who was, and who was not, a revolutionary
according to his own dictates. His definition constantly shifted
in favor of the Communist Party. The whole shaky edifice was
erected on Sukarno's spellbinding oratory. The impoverished,
credulous masses listened with awe and rapture as Sukarno
exhorted them to ignore the squalor around them and reach
for the stars to create a Greater Indonesia.[1] His speeches were
laced with acronyms and learned quotations from the original
Dutch, English, or French (invariably a Western language
sometimes spiced with Sanskrit). Most of his listeners had only
a hazy concept of what he was talking about—if they had one
at all—but he put on a spectacular show and, most important,
it was effective. Increasingly, Sukarno turned his appeals on
narrow nationalism and the arousing of base emotions as he
constantly delivered what he identified as "the message of the

people's sufferings."

"The climate," wrote Adam Malik, a former member of the National Communist Murba Party, who played a major role in deflating Sukarnoism,[2] "came closer and closer to madness." Yet there was a system in this madness. Sukarno realized that he could survive only by diverting the attention of the politically unsophisticated masses and, as in Alice's Wonderland, by running faster and faster to stand still. His military adventures provide a stunning illustration.

Sukarno campaigned for a decade for the "liberation" of Netherlands New Guinea (West Irian). Finally, in 1962, he sent armed guerrillas into the territory and ignited a brush war to wrest the disputed territory over the gunsight. In a series of accompanying, tactically astute political maneuvers, he simultaneously attracted the diplomatic support of Nikita Khrushchev, John F. Kennedy, Mao Tse-tung, and U Thant— a spectacular feat. He achieved West Irian but, like Napoleon after the Treaty of Amiens, he found himself in a predicament. "What a beautiful fix we are in now," Napoleon is said to have remarked. "Peace has been declared." And so Sukarno swept on and the following year launched a new military-diplomatic drive. This time he would "liberate" the newly established, fragile Commonwealth state of Malaysia, his northern neighbor.

In public, Sukarno was spirited and fun-loving, but beneath the lighthearted manner was the authoritarian personality of a man who had dissolved Indonesia's elected parliament, disbanded the political parties which opposed his arbitrary rule, and suppressed civil liberties throughout the archipelago. He filled his prisons with political opponents and his palaces with wives and mistresses; at one stage he was believed to have five or six wives concurrently, but nobody knew for sure.[3] He liked cheap jokes and cheap people. The massive statuary that he had erected to mark his era was in bad taste, unforgivable in an artistically inclined nation. In sum, he held Indonesia in a trance. "It was a period of collective hypnosis," Malik said. It must have been. As his era came to an end in 1965, National Education Day in Indonesia was being celebrated with book burnings.

In his defense, it is frequently claimed that he, and he alone, held Indonesia together and gave this multitude of islands and peoples a sense of unity. Arnold Toynbee and other academicians have done much to perpetuate this misconception in the West. Superficially, this was true. Before Indonesia achieved her independence, Sukarno was instrumental in uniting the country, particularly in the forties when he had at his disposal the Japanese and then Republican propaganda machines. Nobody could deny his contribution as the "great unifier." But after Indonesia became independent, his role was the opposite. His unquenchable thirst for power promoted disunity and led to disaster. His postindependent rule was punctuated by scattered insurrections in the non-Javanese islands and, finally, by wholesale murder on Java itself.

Like demagogues before him, Sukarno was a poor administrator; he detested economics and was bored by statistics. Still, he could boast to foreigners that the Indonesian people would eat stones if he so ordered.

Even without the order they came close to it. Through his political antics, he systematically wrecked the economy. By 1965, Indonesia was being drowned in an inflationary vortex the like of which Asia had not witnessed since the fall of Chiang Kai-shek in 1948–49. The country's cost-of-living index soared from a base of 100 in 1957 to 36,000 in 1965. The amount of money in circulation rose from 30 billion to almost 1 trillion rupiahs in that same period. By the end of 1965, the budget deficit had grown to an astronomical 1.5 trillion rupiahs and the country began to repudiate its foreign obligations. Quite literally, on the eve of the Gestapu affair, the rupiah was worth less than the paper it was printed on; indeed, the cost of printing the rupiah exceeded the value of the money printed.[4]

For the man in the street, fed on slogans and Pyrrhic victories, the story is best told in a solitary statistic. The price of rice, tantamount to life itself in most of Asia, leaped from 41.25 rupiahs a liter in 1963, at the outset of the "crush Malaysia" campaign, to 1,100 rupiahs two years later when the September 30 affair uncoiled.

This economic disaster was taking place in one of the

world's most richly endowed lands, a country without winter
and without desert, a country of abundant sunshine and rain,
of perennially green landscapes and blue seascapes. Unquestionably, as one agronomist observed, Indonesia's "plight
stemmed from more than a decade of mismanagement." [5]

Sukarno offered a solution to these economic problems.
He exhorted the masses to change their menus from rice to
corn and to "eliminate swindlers." [6] The latter had an Or-
wellian ring. Sukarno was the biggest swindler of all and mis-
appropriated tens of millions of dollars. Mohammed Hatta,
who co-signed the Indonesian proclamation of independence
with Sukarno on August 17, 1945, and later broke with him
over his policies, movingly commented: "Indonesia's fate now
is grimmer than during the Dutch colonial regime." [7]

The brunt of the economic dislocation was borne by the
white- and blue-collar workers of the urban areas. In many
parts of the countryside, the peasants hoarded their grain supply, bartered their produce for small manufactures, and—
where and when they could—paid off their debts with the
worthless currency. But the peasants also paid heavily with
severe shortages of fertilizer and pesticide which curtailed ag-
ricultural output and with a rural atmosphere of mounting
threat and insecurity, a political climate which broke with a
wave of murders.

Throughout this period, as Sukarno gradually consolidated his misrule, he depended increasingly for support on the
mass base of the Indonesian Communist Party. The PKI sup-
plied him with audiences, demonstrators, speech writers,
graffiti specialists, and other "agitprop" personnel as required.
It was a two-way street, however. Not only was Sukarno dependent to a growing degree on the Communists, but they
were equally dependent on him as the "Great Leader of the
Revolution" who commanded the allegiance of the masses.
Only Sukarno could effectively neutralize the power and influence of the solitary organized anti-Communist force left in
Indonesia in the sixties—the Army.

2

The Rise of Indonesian Communism

To APPRECIATE THE NATURE OF THE alliance between Sukarno and the PKI, it is necessary to retrace briefly the turbulent history of the Indonesian Communist movement. This in turn requires an appreciation of the strategic guidelines within which a Communist Party operates.

At a given moment, a Communist Party is said to be pursuing either a "Right" or "Left" strategy.[1] The Right strategy involves the tactical embrace of the bourgeoisie, cooperation with class enemies, and collaboration with imperialists, as necessary. This strategy strikes a posture of compromise, negotiation, and conciliation. Excessively applied, the Right strategy may devolve into what the Communists describe as "revisionism." The Left strategy reverses the field. It adopts a harsh, uncompromising, bellicose, irreconcilable, and recalcitrant stance. This may involve violence on either a major or minor scale; at a minimum, the Left strategy threatens confrontation and violence. When overdrawn, the Left strategy, in Communist terminology, may lead to the pitfalls of "dogmatism" and "adventurism."

The decision whether to pursue a Left or Right strategy at a given time haunts every Communist movement. The crucial decision is rendered through the process of "democratic centralism," a spiral road leading downward from the ruling elite in the Presidium or Politburo to the rank and file in the cell. The Politburo is therefore in a position to turn the Left and Right strategies off and on like a water tap.

Until the Sino-Soviet schism, a reading of Communist history was relatively simple. As a projection of the theory of democratic centralism, the international Communist movement was monolithic in character. It was directed from the Kremlin which, presumably icily, weighed Communist global interests and then applied the advantageous strategy of the moment to the whole movement. This resulted in constant gyrations from the Right to the Left, the zigs and zags which have often confused non-Communists.

Of course, it could be, and was, argued in the days of a monolithic movement that Moscow actually operated in the Soviet national interest, not necessarily in the interest of world communism. This nationalist-oriented motivation, it was said, explained the frequent disasters which befell the Communists —in Germany, in China, and in Indonesia, to cite several prominent examples. After Lenin's death and Stalin's consolidation of power, the latter sought to resolve the conflict of interest between Russia and international communism by formulating a policy of "socialism" (read: communism) in one country, Russia. Henceforth, whatever policy served Soviet interests automatically served the interests of the world movement. One result, unintended, was that communism would spread as an oil stain, expanding from the Eurasian heartland of the Soviet Union. In Asia, it moved first to Mongolia, then to China, then to North Vietnam (and North Korea), each state contiguous to the other.

Stalin's rationalization of the problem, however, gave rise to dissension within the world movement in the twenties. The discord was dramatized by the Stalin-Trotsky feud which rent many Communist parties. In Indonesia, Tan Malakka, a PKI leader and Comintern agent, seized on the Moscow disarray to proclaim an independent brand of national communism. He broke with the PKI, which remained obedient to the concept of democratic centralism, and therefore to the dictates of the Kremlin—and became an implacable foe of the PKI. During the Indonesian war of independence in the forties, he organized a small but influential cadre-type party, the Murba.

The interminable dilemma inherent in the Right and Left strategies, of course, is a significant element in the current

Sino-Soviet "differences of opinion." Peking has denounced Moscow as "opportunistic and revisionist" and the Russians have replied by denouncing Peking as "dogmatic and adventurist." They continue to do so at this writing. At the root of their ideological break is how to advance the cause of world communism in a world of nuclear-tipped missiles. In the twenties, during the Stalin-Trotsky feud, the Communists held power only in the Soviet Union. The consequences of the split at that time were not as damaging to Communist ideology and operations as at present in an era of thirteen in-power Communist parties, each with an outlook colored by national interests. Thus, the Sino-Soviet conflict of today has compounded the dilemma of the Right-Left strategies, destroyed the monolithic character of the international movement, and introduced fragmentation into the Communist world. Many ruling Communist parties have acquired varying degrees of independence by skillfully playing Moscow against Peking. This has given rise to different Communist models—Albanian, Rumanian, Vietnamese, Cuban, and so forth. All Communist states, however, share common political characteristics—totalitarian rule, that is, the suppression of representative government and civil liberties with political control through a single party and its secret police.

Against this background, Indonesia's Communist Party history can be easily sorted out, at least for the years between 1923 and 1962; that is, until the PKI set about to exploit the Moscow-Peking rift to proclaim its own independence.

As for its origins, the PKI—the first Communist Party established in Asia—was founded in 1920 by a group of Dutch radicals. Within six years, following the general Left line of the period, the PKI had organized an armed revolt against Dutch colonialism. The rebellion was badly organized and most of the participants had little or no conception of Marxism-Leninism. They were drawn into the affair by a spirit of nationalism, by a desire to free the country from foreign rule. The so-called "Communists" involved in the rebellion quickly discovered that they had been ill prepared, ill armed, misled, and misused by a small Communist hard core.

The 1926 revolt broke out on November 13 with the early

morning seizure of the telephone and telegraph building in
Jakarta (then Batavia). By dawn, the Dutch Army had easily
retaken the strongpoint and by November 19—in less than a
week—the "revolution" had disintegrated. The masses had
failed to respond to the Communist summons to rise in revolt.
Indonesia's masses proved politically apathetic and disinterested. The Dutch took about 13,000 prisoners and of these
about 90 per cent were either promptly released or given nom-
inal prison terms. The Communists later claimed that the
1926 rebellion marked "the beginning of Indonesia's battle for
independence." Hardly. Dutch rule in the islands from the
seventeenth century onward was punctuated by other similar
short-lived insurrections. By any standard, the revolt was "premature"—an adjective endlessly used in Indonesia to explain
repeated Communist misadventures. Whatever the case, the
1926 revolt ended the first phase of the Indonesian Communist
Party's history.

Then, in the thirties, the Moscow line shifted to the
Right as the Comintern forged "popular fronts" with the
bourgeoisie to oppose the rise of fascism in Central Europe.
The PKI obediently followed suit and this ushered in a period
of cooperation between the PKI and Dutch colonialism in the
interests of the security of the Soviet Union, the primary concern of world communism. Except for a brief leftward lurch
during the period of the Stalin-Hitler pact, the PKI continued
to cooperate with the Dutch into World War II and the immediate postwar period. The latter phase was highlighted by
Communist support for the Linggardjati agreement or negotiated settlement of the Indo-Dutch conflict on less than complete Indonesian terms.

Stalin, however, summoned a return to the Left in 1947 to
forestall, among other things, the recovery of Western Europe
from the devastation of World War II. In Indonesia, this led
to a second Communist attempt to seize power the following
year in what probably was the darkest period of the Indonesian struggle for independence against Holland.

At the time the Dutch had occupied large parts of the
Indonesian Republic, reducing Republican control to overpopulated Central-East Java and isolated parts of Sumatra.

The Dutch applied an air, land, and sea blockade to bring intense pressure on the truncated Republic. In this situation, on September 18, 1948, the PKI staged a coup d'état at Madiun, East Java. The Indonesian Army found itself trapped on two fronts, confronting the Dutch outwardly and the Communists inwardly. It was a "stab-in-the-back" which the Army general staff would never forget.[2]

The Army turned on the Communists and within eleven days had driven them from Madiun and its environs. The Communist revolt was crushed, although the Communists made a halfhearted effort to wage a guerrilla campaign in East Java. Many PKI leaders, including Musso, a verteran Indonesian Communist who had flown from Moscow only a few weeks earlier to take charge of the operation, were shot summarily. Others were captured and then executed before the Dutch, who resumed their offensive against the Republic in December of that year, overran the Communist detention camps.

Why did the Madiun coup fail? The Communists themselves held that "the most important factor causing our defeat was the very deficient support of the population" and that "the most regrettable thing in connection with the Madiun affair was the killing and other atrocities [by 'our People's Army'] which happened in some places."[3] The mass killing by the PKI of its political adversaries in the areas they controlled was a feature of their strategy. Did the failure at Madiun mean that the Communists were wrong? "Of course not," wrote Suripno, a principal figure in the power play. "We are still convinced that our policy and our political platform are right. Our fault was that we did not carry out our political platform properly." This was a Communist theme that would recur following the failure of the plot to purge the Army general staff in 1965.

Hostility between the Army and PKI was largely shaped by the events at Madiun. The Army leadership in 1965, at the hour of the purge, was primarily in the hands of the same group of officers who had helped forge the Indonesian Army during the war of independence and who had survived the Madiun affair. Some had received their military training in the prewar Netherlands East Indies Army (KNIL), others from the Japanese-sponsored army of the occupation period (PETA), still others by osmosis (youth who displayed leadership, courage, and a capacity to organize armed bands during the revolution). To cite a singular example, General Nasution, the minister/coordinator for defense and security and the armed forces chief of staff at the time of the Gestapu affair in 1965, was the Army chief of staff on Java when the Communists struck seventeen years earlier.

But whereas the Army leadership remained the same over the years, a new PKI hierarchy emerged from the Madiun debacle. Their roles had been marginal at Madiun, although they loyally supported Musso and his policies on his arrival from Moscow. The new generation of PKI leaders were prepared to let bygones be bygones; the Army would not. In the last analysis, of course, when the Communists turned on the general staff, they had not forgotten the past either. Indeed, there is a strange symbolism in the Gestapu affair which has attracted Indonesian curiosity. The Madiun revolt collapsed on September 29, 1948. The new PKI adventure opened on September 30, 1965. More than one Indonesian has acidly commented that the one started where the other left off.[4]

After the Madiun affair, the remnant PKI, including its future leadership, continued to cling to the Left strategy to the best of its limited opportunities. The PKI's principal flurry of militancy after Madiun developed in 1951 when the party was linked to isolated acts of terror. Significantly, Indonesia was now independent, but this did not deter the Communists (the Dutch had withdrawn from Indonesia in December, 1949). In mid-1951, Premier Sukiman ordered the Army to curb the rising lawlessness. The Army did so promptly and effectively in what is now known as "Sukiman's Razzia."[5]

Thus, by 1965, the history of the Indonesian Communist Party was pitted by violence: the failure at rebellion in 1926 during the colonial era; the abortive coup and ineffective guerrilla campaign in 1948 during the Indonesian war of independence; and the upended campaign of terror in 1951 in an independent Indonesia. "Left" Communists today look on this bloody record approvingly. In Peking's view, for example, "the PKI has rapidly grown in strength in the fires of protracted revolutionary struggle." [6]

Yet, demonstrably, the evidence conclusively shows that communism in Indonesia always made its most impressive gains, on paper at least, when it pursued a Right strategy. This was re-emphasized after 1952 when, shortly before his death, Stalin ordered a switch from the Left to the Right strategy involving collaboration with bourgeois nationalism. At first, the PKI compromised, then cooperated, and finally collaborated with the symbol of Indonesia's narrowest form of bourgeois nationalism in the person of Sukarno. The results were astonishing.

The new party line was unpacked at a national conference at the outset of 1952 when Aidit proposed the creation of a "united national front" which included the President, whom the PKI had railed against as a "fascist" during the 1948–51 "Left" period. In the event that the message was lost, on May 23, 1952, on the occasion of the thirty-second anniversary of the party's founding, the Communists raised a fresh slogan, "Long Live Sukarno! Long Live the PKI!" It was a catch-cry that would rise to the level of a crescendo by 1965.

The Irian issue, however, proved to be a perfect binder for effecting a Sukarno-PKI reconciliation. Holland had excluded West Irian (Netherlands New Guinea or West New Guinea) from the transfer of sovereignty to Indonesia in 1949, against the recommendation of the Dutch High Commissioner and his cabinet in Batavia (Jakarta). The Netherlands had omitted West Irian from the transfer as a sop to appease right-wing nationalist opinion in Holland. A dispute between Holland and Indonesia immediately erupted over the Irian question, however, and dissipated the good will the Dutch had gained by withdrawing from Indonesia. Sukarno demanded Irian's return and the Communists outdid everyone else in supporting his demand, which soon turned into an obsession. Gradually, the Irian issue dominated Indonesian politics. It was a pity that Western intransigence gave Sukarno and the PKI their big opportunity.

By riding herd with Sukarno in 1952, the PKI sought to transform its traditional cadre-style party into a mass movement. All the previous failures of the Communists in Indonesia could be ascribed to a failure to organize a mass movement—and arm it. Accordingly, the "agitation, organization and mobilization of the masses" became the PKI's basic program.[7] This road to power was openly promulgated at the most important Indonesian Communist Party congress since independence, the Fifth Congress, at which Dipa Nusantara Aidit, then thirty years old, the architect of the PKI's new Right strategy, formally emerged as secretary general of the party. M. H. Lukman, thirty-four, was named first deputy secretary general and Njoto, twenty-eight, emerged as second deputy secretary general. Under the leadership of this trio, the PKI would attain its highest plateau of power and influence— and then plunge over the edge into the chasm below.

The youthful triumvirate was anxious to embark on a new road in its relations with the Army. Accordingly, they began to work, as they did for the next decade, to try to remove the stigma of Madiun, but they never quite succeeded. The Army could not forget the war of independence against the Dutch and, for that matter, the Communist treachery in the rear. It was as simple as that. After the failure of the September 30 affair, Nasution confirmed this analysis. The Dutch aggression against the Republic at the end of 1948, he said, "prevented a proper settlement of the treachery and coup d'état by the PKI under Musso at Madiun." [8]

Within a decade—between 1952, when the PKI joined Sukarno in pressing the Irian question, until 1962, when the Irian campaign ended triumphantly—the PKI expanded its membership rolls from 7,910 cardholders to a phenomenal two million.[9] By 1965, in the midst of the confrontation against Malaysia, the PKI claimed a party membership of "more than three million"; a youth organization, Pemuda Rakjat, of three million; a federation of trade unions, SOBSI, of 3.5 million; a peasant organization, BTI, of nine million; a woman's organization, Gerwani, of three million; a cultural association, Lekra, of a half million; and a student movement, CGMI, of more than 70,000 members.[10]

Although Aidit himself once remarked offhandedly, "you know that in Indonesia figures mean nothing," these were the

golden years of Indonesian communism.[11] They were bur-
nished ever more brightly—only fleetingly, as it turned out—
between 1963 and 1965, when Aidit moved boldly to establish
the PKI as a third force in the Communist world and to
hasten a Communist takeover in Indonesia before the passing
of the "Great Leader of the Revolution."

For years, the PKI had straddled the dispute between
Moscow and Peking as both sides strained for Indonesian
Communist support. In 1963, as relations worsened between
Russia and China, Aidit led a PKI mission into the Communist blocs for a firsthand look as a potential arbiter. The mission touched all the bases—from Moscow to Peking, from
Havana to Hanoi. Wherever Aidit appeared, he was accorded
unprecedented treatment. In China, he was honored for his
"contributions" to Marxism-Leninism, putting him in a
pantheon presided over by none other than Mao, and he became the first foreigner named to the Chinese Academy of
Sciences.* In the Soviet Union, Aidit became one of a select
handful of foreigners who ever witnessed a tactical nuclear
exercise by the Red Army.

Shrewdly, Aidit realized that his posture of nonalignment
and neutralism in the Sino-Soviet dispute was producing ex-
traordinarily handsome dividends for himself, for the party,
and for Indonesia. By straddling the Moscow-Peking fissure,
he was enjoying the best of two Communist worlds. Thus,
when he returned to Jakarta later that year, he was convinced
more than ever that the PKI must reject "the baton of any
other Communist Party."[12] He likewise admonished the
party hierarchy that he would not tolerate a Moscow-Peking
schism within the party, a reminder of how the party was
weakened during the Stalin-Trotsky split by the defection of
Tan Malakka and his emergence as a National Communist
rival.

Aidit opted for the independence of the PKI. In home
affairs, he continued the Right strategy and maintained the
party's intimate relationship with the narrow strain of bourgeois nationalism exemplified by Sukarno. In foreign affairs,
he pursued a Left strategy in collaboration with Peking which

* See page 145.

considered the United States the primary adversary and called for its encirclement by a series of "wars of national liberation." For Aidit, the Left strategy abroad served ideally to strengthen his association with Sukarno since Sukarno pursued a militant foreign policy which threw him into confrontation with *all* of Indonesia's neighbors.

The foregoing was acknowledged by Aidit two years later, after he consolidated the PKI's independence. He explained quite freely that he had gone to Moscow and Peking in 1963 "to stop controversial discussions and to restore unity between those two parties." He said he found that hopeless. It then occurred to him that "Communists who do not use their own judgment are not good Communists." As a result of his analysis, he said, "Indonesian Communists are now enjoying the results of the open discussions (between Moscow and Peking) and consider it a pity if it would stop" (thereby endangering the PKI's newly acquired freedom of maneuver?). Therefore, Aidit confided, when he revisited Moscow and Peking in 1965, "I did not suggest stopping the public discussion of controversies." He said: "I felt it to be unnecessary and useless. Public discussion is not harmful and it is even very useful if a Communist Party approaches it in the right manner. This is what the PKI found out." [13]

Thus, by 1964, the PKI had usurped the National Communist label which Tan Malakka and his supporters had coveted for two generations.

Few Indonesians recognized the significance of the change in the PKI's position, but Sukarno was acutely aware of it and, as a result, threw political caution to the winds. Sukarno tilted sharply toward the PKI as his logical successor. Sukarno turned to the Communists in 1952 in quest of support in Irian because he thought he could use them. Now Sukarno turned to the PKI for other reasons: ideological affinity; a respect for Communist discipline and organization; admiration for the party's ability to command a mass following; a belief that the Communists represented the wave of the future in Asia, if not the world (the Communist victories in Vietnam and Laos gilded the lily); and a conviction that only the PKI could marshal Indonesia's manpower, exploit her natural wealth, insure national unity, and lead the archipelago into her rightful place as a first-class power.

The long Sukarno-PKI courtship was over.

They married their forces publicly on May 23, 1965, at the forty-fifth anniversary of the birth of the PKI. Sukarno and Aidit were the principal speakers at a rally and, in a burst of enthusiasm, Sukarno embraced Aidit before the cheering multitude and shouted to nearby newsmen: "See, I, Sukarno, embrace the PKI!" He repeated this several times, hugging Aidit ever more tightly.[14] Sukarno's tactical alliance with the Communists was now replaced by a strategic alliance.

Sukarno intuitively felt he could entrust Indonesia's future to Aidit and the PKI. Sukarno, of course, thought he was using the Communists at the outset of their relationship; for their part, the PKI thought they were using him. In a sense, in the beginning of their alliance, the Communists were Sukarno's captives. In the end, if he was not their captive, then neither was he their master as clearly as he had been.[15] This is how smoothly their positions meshed by 1965.

The handwriting was on Indonesia's wall.

3

List to Port

THE SIGNS OF INDONESIA'S LIST TO port became so pronounced by mid-1964 that they were unmistakable. In Jakarta, the impression was that Sukarno had ʾgun "a slide to the extreme Left that may be irreversible." [1] Six months later, the consensus was that the PKI seems "increasingly confident and cocky" and is "steam-rollering the opposition." [2] By mid-1965, barely a year later, the Communists themselves concluded, first, that "the pace of events is increasing and, second, the meaning of events is increasingly clear and the pitch is increasingly high." [3]

Sukarno himself made similar observations. Having acquired the habit of employing Communist terminology, he spoke incessantly about a two-stage revolution, the classic Communist model in which first feudalism and imperialism are liquidated, leading to the promised land of the second stage, "socialism." In 1965, Sukarno and the PKI talked freely about approaching the second stage. Sukarno observed that the first stage, "the national democratic stage is now almost concluded." He claimed that "we have stopped imperialism, colonialism, neocolonialism and feudalism in order to establish a national and democratic order (and) now we take a step forward: Our revolution is beginning to enter the second stage; namely, the stage of Indonesian socialism." [4] In Marxism-Leninism, the word "socialism" is a euphemism for communism, which in turn is a euphemism for a form of totalitarianism.

In this atmosphere, the PKI became outspoken. Lukman, for example, was convinced of the "ultimate victory" of communism in Indonesia. Citing the growing participation of the

PKI in the Sukarno regime, he said that anyone who disapproved of the trend of events was "not a true follower of President Sukarno, not democratic, progressive or revolutionary." [5] There was no doubt, however, that the PKI fitted the definition. Subandrio, Sukarno's combination first deputy premier, foreign minister, chief of the secret police (BPI), and commodore in the Air Force, described the Communist Party as "Leftist, progressive and revolutionary" and noted that the Communists had always implemented "Bung Karno's (Sukarno's) teachings militantly." [6]

In this period, there were numerous examples of Sukarno's slide into the capacious embrace of the PKI. Sukarno twice reshuffled his cabinet and each time the Communists acquired new strength. In 1965, Njoto was elevated to the post of minister attached to the cabinet's Presidium. The Presidium was charged with drawing the broad lines of government policy. In the same cabinet, Aidit held the post of an official with the rank of coordinator-minister and Lukman was an official with the rank of minister. Thus, the PKI's ruling Presidium held positions in Sukarno's cabinet. If nothing else, they had easy official access to the President. In addition, the cabinet was laced with a sampling of crypto-Communists and fellow travelers. Njoto, incidentally, who concurrently was editor of *People's Daily*, the PKI's official daily newspaper, also served as a principal speech-writer for Sukarno and largely wrote his 1965 Independence Day speech.[7] This was about six weeks before the purge of the general staff.

It is axiomatic that control of mass media is crucial in creating a "progressive, revolutionary" atmosphere. Indonesia was no exception to the rule. Systematically, the regime tightened its control over public opinion and gradually the Indonesian press came under the strict sway of either the Communists or "Left progressives." Antara, the country's only news agency, which had been founded by the National Communists before World War II—among them Adam Malik—became a PKI stronghold.[8] On television, Chinese and East European propaganda films were standard fare. Admittedly, television in Indonesia (like the newspapers) was limited to the relatively small, affluent, and educated community. But this is the community which ran and runs Indonesia. And, in 1964–65, this community was subject to "mental terror," the popular phrase used by articulate Indonesians to describe the period.[9] (It is clinically interesting that in the Soviet-Czech crisis in 1968, the first Moscow demand on Prague was that the Czech Communist Party reapply censorship.)

For the Indonesian opposition to Sukarno, life became increasingly intolerable. They were approaching a dead end. Sukarno's policy of favoring the Communists in domestic and foreign policy put the opposition in the impossible position of betraying Indonesia's "great revolution" every time they raised their voices against the Communists.[10] But, in the summer of 1964, the opposition struck on a novel idea. Convinced that the PKI was exploiting Sukarno's vanity to its own end and subverting the nation in the process, the opponents of the PKI banded together and formed the Body for the Promotion of Sukarnoism (BPS). Every hue of the political spectrum was reflected in this maneuver, including Islamic and Christian parties, the Murba, the outlawed democratic socialists, the academic community, and the Army and Navy—but not the Air Force, whose chief of staff was committed to the Sukarno-PKI alliance.

General Nasution, warmly endorsing the formation of the BPS, called on the nation to "spread the teachings of Bung Karno" in order to meet the challenges of neocolonialism in a progressive and revolutionary manner.[11] The minister-Navy commander, Vice Admiral R. E. Martadinata, declared that the "crush Malaysia campaign and the spread of Sukarnoism could not be separated from each other." [12] The generals and admirals were not only using the correct vocabulary, but were even bribing Sukarno with the prospect of a military victory over Malaysia. Until then, the Indonesian military campaign had not been especially distinguished and in the Sukarno-PKI inner circle there was a suspicion that the general staff did not have its heart in the war.

However, if any additional evidence was needed to point to the direction in which helmsman Sukarno was steering, the President's angry reaction to the setting up of the BPS should have stopped his most ardent apologist. Sukarno turned on the

BPS, dissolved it on December 17, 1964, accused its founders of promoting disunity among the "progressive revolutionary national forces," and charged that it was endangering the revolution. The regime closed twenty-one newspapers which backed the BPS editorially, including *Merdeka,* which had loyally supported Sukarno since 1945, and temporarily suspended the *Murba,* which had been instrumental in creating the BPS. The decision to suspend the Murba was perhaps the single most important event of the pre-September 30 period because it provided irrefutable evidence that Sukarno had accepted the orthodox PKI as a *"national* Communist" party, obviating the need for a rival Marxist-Leninist grouping. By acquiring independence from Moscow and Peking, the PKI had secured the credentials for leading the revolution after Sukarno's departure from the scene.

Why, then, hadn't Sukarno put the future of Indonesia in the hands of the Murba itself?

For one thing, the Murba was a cadre-type party of infinitesimal size. For another, it was implacably hostile to Peking and Sukarno was gambling that Indonesia could take a short cut to international power status through an alliance with the Chinese Communists. Indeed, the collaboration with China was the centerpiece of Sukarno's foreign policy in the late sixties. As a measure of Indonesia's list to port, Sukarno himself, on August 17, 1965, described Indonesia's relationship with China as the beginning of an "Axis"—with its awful connotation of the Berlin-Tokyo "Axis." [13] Sukarno, who had viewed Japanese fascism as the wave of the future in the thirties and early forties, now thought that wave was probably communism. Envisioning an "inevitable" communization of Southeast Asia, Sukarno worked to contain Peking through a partnership in which Southeast Asia would be divided into respective spheres of Chinese and Malay influence, with Peking and Jakarta as the principal power centers. The Murba, however, considered the spread of Chinese influence in Southeast Asia a long-term threat to Indonesia, especially to underpopulated Sumatra, Borneo, New Guinea, and other islands.[14]

But perhaps underlying Sukarno's reluctance to turn to

the National Communists was a psychological underpinning. Sukarno recognized the Murba as the creation of his only charismatic rival in the revolutionary period, Tan Malakka, who was frequently called "the father of the Republic," a sobriquet which Sukarno had later appropriated for himself. (In 1949, the Army executed Tan Malakka when he moved to assume the leadership of the revolution following Sukarno's voluntary surrender to the Dutch.)

Sukarno, it must be repeatedly stressed, was not a Communist in the accepted sense of the term. He was too independent-minded. His vanity would not permit him to be a cardholder. He was not an organization man, whatever the organization. Moreover, until the PKI acquired an air of independence, Sukarno could never wholly accept the Communists because of their links to the international movement which, he felt, subordinated Indonesia's national interests to the Communist global interest (if not the Soviet interest before the Sino-Soviet schism).

Within a week of the dissolution of the BPS and the Murba, Aidit emerged as a mainspring behind the twin kill. Addressing a youth rally, Aidit warned his listeners to avoid movements such as the BPS which "in fact, are nothing but an effort to eliminate Sukarno's theory and person." [15] As for the suspension of the Murba, the PKI was jubilant. Aidit accused the Murba of preaching "modern revisionism" and "false Marxism" to try to effect the PKI's downfall. Pressing the attack, Aidit called for the "elimination" of the last traces of Trotskyism in Indonesia—the National Communists.

The forty-fifth anniversary of the PKI on May 23, 1965, delineated another watershed of the period. The PKI filled the Senajan sports complex on the edge of Jakarta with more than 105,000 people. All the roads fanning from the capital for a distance of twenty miles were plastered with hammer-and-sickle posters. The throng was entertained by a choir of ten thousand singers, one thousand gymnasts, sword dancers, drum bands, and an eight hundred-woman troupe from Gerwani.[16] The bands and cheerleaders reminded one American on hand of an "Army-Navy football game." Overhead, the Air Force dropped leaflets, one thousand of which were signed by Aidit and brought prizes to those lucky enough to retrieve and return them. The stadium was decked with portraits of Marx, Engels, Lenin, Stalin, Aidit, and Sukarno (no Mao; no Brezhnev). At the start, all their portraits were of the same size, but the police instructed the PKI to use a larger portrait of Sukarno, and the party complied. Like canned applause and laughter on commercial television, the enthusiastic crowd applauded various speakers on cue from polite hand clapping to thunderous roars. It was an awesome display of mass power and nobody was more impressed than Sukarno.[17]

It was on this occasion, as the stadium shook with approval, that Sukarno embraced Aidit, and the PKI, lauding the party as Indonesia's "most revolutionary, progressive group" and describing Aidit himself as "a fortress" of the Republic. Afterward, at a PKI reception which, with a moderate stretch of the imagination, resembled a wedding reception, more than one thousand guests assembled. Fraternal parties sent delegations, including those from the Communist parties of Russia, China, Cuba, Albania, Rumania, North Korea, North Vietnam, and Japan. Hanoi sent no less a personage than Le Duc Tho, the seventh ranking member of the Politburo, who played a critical role in the 1968 exploratory peace talks in Paris. In the presence of his foreign guests, Aidit reasserted the independence of the Indonesian Communists. The PKI, he emphasized, would persist in applying Marxism-Leninism "in accordance with the conditions in Indonesia." [18]

The forty-fifth anniversary was preceded by a party plenum on May 10–13, which provided no major new departures from standard PKI positions. Aidit's report to the plenum required seven hours and twenty-one minutes to read. The United States was slated as the "Enemy No. 1," a position the PKI adopted in February, 1963, a rather interesting selection given the fact that Indonesia was soon engaged in a limited war with Malaysia and Britain which would claim upward of two thousand casualties, most of them Indonesian.

As for the home front, Aidit exuded confidence, appealed to the party "to intensify the revolutionary offensive in all fields," held that "Indonesia is now in a revolutionary situation," and admonished the party to exercise "iron discipline."

In retrospect, this was the heart of his report.[19]

The forty-fifth anniversary celebration provided a display of power which disturbed many thoughtful Indonesians. "It reminded me of Madiun," Hatta, who was vice president and premier in 1948, recalled.[20] "The PKI's Democratic People's Front in those days used the same tactic at mass meetings. It was a form of intimidation." Another Indonesian analyst, however, expected "something to happen" in Jakarta that week as the Communists flooded the capital with their street fighters, drawn from the Pemuda Rakjat.[21] But, when the occasion passed without incident, he concluded that "the PKI had missed its big chance." [22]

One hour after the ceremonies ended on May 23, the Senajan sports complex was buffeted by an unseasonable rainstorm. Within four months, the party would be buffeted by a political storm of even greater intensity.

The Communist power display left an indelible impression on Jakarta and contributed heavily to the growing atmosphere of intrigue and counterintrigue, which moved toward a climax in mid-September when Sukarno conferred a state medal on Aidit for service and loyalty to the Republic.[23] The award was presented at a ceremony in Sukarno's palace with the representatives of the armed forces among the dignitaries invited by Sukarno to attend. Several would be murdered within a fortnight.

By the summer of that year, Indonesia's political scene had eroded to the point where the question which dominated political conversations was: Who would strike first—the Communists or the Army? Aidit openly dismissed rumors that the PKI planned a coup d'état. "It is not true because we support President Sukarno's policy," he demurred.[24] "Whose government should we overthrow? Our slogan is not to overthrow the government because to overthrow the government means to overthrow President Sukarno, whom we support, or to overthrow myself and my friends because we are members of President Sukarno's cabinet." Earlier, Aidit, ever sensitive to the situation, expressed concern that the PKI might be the victim of a provocation manufactured by the PKI's adversaries. He implied that the threat came from the Murba and its sympathizers, especially Chairul Saleh, the second deputy premier, an economic adventurer and known terrorist who was formerly identified with the National Communists. Aidit accused unidentified "contra-revolutionaries" of spreading rumors of a split between Saleh and himself. "This rumor is now spread widely in roadside stands, in restaurants, in the markets, in the jitneys, in offices, and I don't know where," Aidit said.[25] "I understand their aim—to enrage the PKI masses, principally the Communist youth so that in anger they will commit improper actions."

And a political analysis prepared and circulated clandestinely by the democratic socialist underground, which opposed Sukarno and the PKI, theorized at the time:

> The PKI is combat ready. The Nasution groups hope the PKI will be the first to draw the trigger, but this the PKI will not do. The PKI will not allow itself to be provoked as in the Madiun Incident. In the end, however, there will be only two forces left: the PKI and the Nasution group. The middle will have no alternative but to choose and get protection from the stronger force.[26]

In this Byzantine climate of plots and counterplots, an astute assessment appeared in the *Straits Times,* the Singapore daily. "The Indonesian Communist party's show of strength on the 45th anniversary of its founding raises again the possibility of a Communist bid for power in Jakarta," an editorial said.[27] "The Communists are certainly the best organized and disciplined party in Indonesia, and they have always been the obvious beneficiaries of Sukarno's system of misguided democracy. But there is still strong political opposition, even in Central Java, where Communist organization has been most effective, *and since there are no constitutional means of securing power the bid would have to be made, as it was in the Madiun Affair, with the gun.*"

Clearly, at home and abroad, the PKI had failed to shake the stigma of Madiun.

But the most pernicious rumor of the period, which the September 30 movement later employed as the pretext for its purge, was floated in May, during the month of festivities attendant to the PKI's anniversary. According to this *"kabar angin"* (literally: wind news), there existed a Council of Generals composed of forty Army generals—including Generals Nasution and Achmad Yani, the Army chief of staff—which planned a seizure of power.

The Army, of course, had any such number of councils in its table of organization. Such committees dealt routinely with coordination between the chief of staff and his sector commanders, others evaluated the performance of senior officers and so forth.[28] But, according to the rumor, the Council of Generals in question had been set up secretly to plan a coup d'état. The nature of the coup was imprecise. One rumor indicated that the Council of Generals would move against Sukarno and the PKI; another version, against the PKI only; and, still another, that it would seize power in the event of Sukarno's natural death.

The rumor traveled with dispatch at the apex of the Indonesian power pyramid. Only three days after he embraced the PKI at Senajan, Sukarno confronted Yani directly with the report.

"Is it true that there is a Council of Generals which is assigned to evaluate my policy?" asked Sukarno.

"There is, indeed, such a council," Yani replied.[29] "I myself am the head. But the council is not aimed at making an evaluation of the policy of the President."

Yani in turn promptly informed his staff officers that the President had queried him on this point. "Yani told us at a conference of senior Army officers that Sukarno had asked him about these rumors," Major General Alamsjah, then on the general staff, recalled: [30] "Yani said he told Sukarno that such rumors were untrue and that as long as the existing leaders of the army were alive and functioning, Sukarno had no need to worry himself about a Council of Generals. 'We do not think in terms of a Council of Generals [a coup],' he told the President. 'We would not disturb you or the nation. The Army's only concern is how to secure the Pantjasila under your leadership.' " [31]

Sukarno confirmed this later and said Yani had reassured him about the aims of the Council.[32] But the rumor did not rest there. It continued to circulate in ever widening circles. "I first heard of the Council of Generals around July 1 and I asked a friend of mine, General Sukendro, about it," the dean of law at the University of Indonesia, for example, recalled.[33] "Yes, he said he had heard about it, too, and that the rumor was continually being spread by Leftists. Sukendro told me, indeed, there was such a council and that its task was to screen promotions."

Unquestionably, the Communists worked with deliberation to spread the tale. Thus, police Brigadier General Soetarto, chief of staff of Subandrio's BPI, conceded that he first heard about the existence of a Council of Generals from a Communist member of parliament, and that he received a second report on the Council from no less a source than a member of Sukarno's palace honor guard (Tjakrabirawa), who, in turn, said—surprise!—he first learned of it from a member of the PKI.

By the end of September, the alleged existence of such a council had entered the public domain.

4

The Masterplan

COLLUSION BETWEEN PEKING AND THE
Sukarno regime may not have been limited to the field of
foreign affairs. With the political crisis in Indonesia maturing,
the Chinese Communists, inadvertently or not, became en-
twined in Indonesia's internal affairs. There has been considerable speculation over Peking's part in the purge of the
Indonesian general staff. There should be no controversy,
however, over whether or not Peking played a part. The record indicates that the Chinese Communists essayed significant
roles in the two critical issues which provoked the showdown
between the various pro- and anti-Sukarno, PKI, and Army
factions. One issue dealt with the question of the "fifth
force"; the other, with Sukarno's health.

The fifth-force question centered on the PKI's glaring
weakness—the party's failure to develop a paramilitary organization. In Marxist-Leninist parlance, at least as Mao suc-
cinctly described it, "power grows out of the barrel of a gun."
The PKI lacked gun barrels.

The PKI's weakness in paramilitary development was sil-
houetted in 1964–65 amid the scattered, small-scale clashes
between the Communists and Moslem groups on Java—
notably the orthodox, narrow Nahdatual Ulama or so-called
Moslem Scholars Party. The NU, together with the PKI and
PNI, represented the triumvirate of incompatible parties in
Sukarno's philosophy of a tripartite NASAKOM coalition government. The acronym was shaped by the Indonesian words
for nationalism, religion, and communism.

These clashes, mainly in East Java, presumably were over
unsettled land questions. In 1960, Indonesia adopted crop

sharing and land-reform laws.[1] Although many of Indonesia's major islands are sparsely settled, land in Central and East Java is in short supply and the areas are thickly populated. In these regions, both the PKI and NU drew their principal support, the NU essentially from East Java. Rightly or not, for many Indonesians, the problems of scarcity of land, overpopulation, and communism are fundamentally Javanese problems confined to Central and East Java (western Java is inhabited by Sundanese and Bantamese).

Under the land-reform laws, 966,150 hectares of land were to be redistributed, but by the end of 1964 only about 451,068 were actually distributed—less than half. The law was loosely drawn, afforded properties owned by religious (read: Islamic) groups special protection, and required that committees be formed to decide on the division of land. Naturally, each of the NASAKOM groups possessed a right to be represented on the committees. That any land at all was distributed was a singular achievement; in some respects, the whole question of land reform, on Java, short of state ownership of the land, is dubious, given the intricate communal ownership of property and its division and redivision for generations.

To complicate matters, much of the land was in the hands of *santri* or orthodox Moslems. Communist strength in the region—and the PKI was essentially a Javanese party—was based on the *abangan* or landless, animistic, and rural "proletariat." The third social force in Central-East Java was the *prijai* or official class whose roots stretched into Java's Hindu period and who were often identified with the PNI and the governmental bureaucracy. Sukarno's concept of a NASAKOM regime was derived from his Javanese background. He sought to meld the social forces of nationalism (*prijai*), religion (*santri*), and communism (*abangan*). In a sense, Sukarno sought to apply a solution of Java's unique political equation to the whole of Indonesia. Since NASAKOM did not work on Java, it is inconceivable how he felt it could work throughout Indonesia.

In any event, at the end of 1964, Aidit criticized the delay in land reform and told whoever would listen that the PKI had decided to go to "the masses and organize new actions of a legal character." [2] In Aidit's view, the land-reform laws had to be implemented during the first, or national democratic, phase of Indonesia's two-stage revolution.

The PKI launched its aggressive new policy in Central-East Java in a series of "unilateral actions." The Communists occupied land that they felt should be divided under the land-reform bill. In adopting this program, the PKI, of course, bypassed the committees which were supposed to decide the question. The PKI's "unilateral actions" led to clashes in East Java, especially with the NU. The Army sat on the sidelines to see where the true strength lay between the opposing forces. By mid-1965, many towns in East Java, such as Djember, Bondowoso, and Pasuran, were in the midst of a long, hot summer; only on Java the summer is interminable.

Despite its militancy and vaunted organizational ability, the PKI did not fare well in these encounters. The NU displayed surprising vitality, especially since it had never been taken seriously in Jakarta as a political force because of its narrow regional appeal and outlook and the weakness of its leaders, some of whom could be, and were, easily bought by Sukarno.

Aidit conceded that the "unilateral actions" were backfiring.[3] He attributed PKI setbacks to poor planning and other weaknesses in the rural areas. Aidit charged that the BTI, the Communist peasant front, had implemented the program too rapidly, had failed to understand its own limitations, and had failed to await favorable conditions. At the fourth plenum of the party in May, 1965, he emphasized the necessity for "research first" before undertaking "unilateral actions."

The PKI's aggressiveness was variously interpreted. "I felt their move in the rural area as a maneuver to raise the people against the Army," Hatta commented.[4] And, in Surabaya, the capital of East Java, a member of the anti-Sukarno-PKI underground reported back to Jakarta that "the Communist action from below is failing." The report concluded therefore that a PKI assumption of power was not imminent. But Mohammed Natsir, the former premier and chairman of the moderate Masjumi, who was a leader of the abortive 1958 revolt against Sukarno and the PKI, interpreted the Commu-

nist offensive differently. At the time, Natsir was in jail in
Madiun with a number of other well-known leaders of the
opposition to Sukarno and the PKI. "I warned our people that
these clashes, especially from March onwards in East Java, and
to some extent in East Sumatra, were storm signals," he recounted.[5] "I was convinced a bigger clash was yet to come.
The clashes were organized by the BTI over the land question
and some people were of the opinion that only land was involved. Actually, the PKI organized the friction on the land
as probing actions to test their organizational strength."

The PKI also launched "unilateral actions" in East
Sumatra, the big government-owned estate belt which employs
a high percentage of Javanese labor. There the clashes involved the Army. One encounter, the "Bandar Betsy affair,"
became a *cause célèbre* which dragged through the summer.
On May 14, 1965, a group of squatters on the "Betsy" planta-
tion, comprising BTI members backed by the Pemuda Rakjat,
beat an Army officer to death when he ordered the bulldozing
of what they considered their land, not government property.[6]

The situation had an air of unreality. The Communists,
the champions of the collective and commune, were masking
themselves as defenders of the property rights of landless peasants. It was typical PKI hypocrisy. Of course, in the event of a
PKI assumption of power, "agriculture would be reorganized," a euphemism for the state seizure of land.[7] The
"Bandar Betsy affair" had still another sidelight. In 1953, the
Communists created a land incident in the same region, called
the "Tandjong Morawa affair," which toppled the moderate,
responsible, and progressive (in the true meaning of the word)
Wilopo government.

These various clashes "from below" pointed up the PKI's
necessity to acquire a paramilitary force. It was in this situation that the Chinese Communists intervened and proposed a
solution—the fifth force.

To begin with, the Communists for years had sought, by
one means or another, to establish a paramilitary organization. The history of this program dated back to before
Madiun, when the PKI pressed, without success, for the creation of an armed People's Militia. In 1952–53, with the re-

vival of the party's fortunes under Aidit and the Right strategy, the PKI reopened its campaign for arms. It called for the establishment of "public security organizations to render assistance to the state's power instruments" and set up the All-Indonesia Association of Former Strugglers (PERBEPSI) to serve as the principal energumen.[8] But the Army stepped in and brought all veterans' groups under its control and thereby stalled Aidit's plan. In the years that followed, the PKI shifted its emphasis from the development of paramilitary formations to the infiltration of the armed forces and, although the Communists enjoyed a modicum of success, they failed to penetrate the general staff.

On January 14, 1965, the Communists seized on the atmosphere occasioned by Indonesia's withdrawal from the United Nations, the confrontation with Malaysia, the departure of a Subandrio mission to Peking, and the launching of their aggressive "unilateral actions" to reopen the campaign for arms. Aidit proposed to Sukarno that the government arm five million workers and ten million peasants.[9] Although he did not state specifically which workers and peasants he had in mind, it was a foregone conclusion that he meant the "progressive, revolutionary" farm and labor fronts, BTI and SOBSI, respectively, and the Pemuda Rakjat.

Aidit no sooner delivered this suggestion than the usual phalanx of crypto-Communists beat the drums. A member of Sukarno's rubber-stamping parliament, K. Werdojo, for example, expressed full approval for the Aidit proposal and described it as "reasonable and right . . . because our revolution is definitely a people's revolution so that the arming of the workers and peasants would only signify the unity between the people and Bung Karno, our President and the Great Leader of the Revolution." [10]

While the campaign heated up within Indonesia, the Chinese Communists moved to stage center and, apparently coordinating their move with that of the PKI, put pressure on the Sukarno regime to approve Aidit's plan. On January 25, in the course of Subandrio's talks in Peking, the Chinese not only proposed the formation of the "fifth force" but offered to equip it with 100,000 small arms. Chou En-lai said:

President Sukarno is the Supreme Commander of the Army, Navy, Air Force and Police. In the framework of the confrontation against Malaysia, Indonesia has succeeded in mobilizing twenty-one million volunteers. How good it would be if Indonesia has a fifth branch of its armed forces.[11]

Subandrio confirmed the nature of this offer later and disclosed that the Chinese had combined their arms proposal with a program to give the weapons to Indonesia's "progressive, revolutionary people." [12] Subandrio lost little time to exploit the windfall and on his return flight from Peking discussed plans to funnel the weapons into Indonesia without going through normal Defense Ministry channels. Subandrio, a commodore in the Air Force, would use the Air Force as the conveyor belt with the knowledge and consent of Air Marshal Omar Dhani, the chief of staff.[13] Indeed, a fortnight before the purge of the Army general staff on September 30–October 1, Dhani visited Peking to speed up the shipments.

Incidentally, the twenty-one million volunteers mentioned by Chou referred to the recruitment campaign organized by Jakarta in 1964–65 to fight Malaysia. There is no way of verifying that twenty-one million persons were registered, and this is mentioned here only to point up the unreliability of statistics in Indonesia generally, especially given the Malay characteristic of excessive imagination. But the figure is generally considered wild.

Whatever the case, the Chinese proposal introduced a new and ominous element into the PKI's quest for arms, and both Aidit and Sukarno joined forces in pressing the case for a fifth force in speeches at the National Defense Institute, to which Aidit had been appointed as a professor of Marxism. No attempt was made to camouflage the Chinese intervention other than to scrupulously avoid a public disclosure that Peking had offered to arm the paramilitary body. Thus, Suwardi, a member of parliament's defense committee, noted that Sukarno "has proposed a change in the structure or system of our armed forces, while putting forward Chou En-lai's suggestion to add a fifth force," adding, "The suggestion of the Chinese prime minister is actually nothing new; our armed forces, being the core of defense, must consist of people's volunteers and militia." [14]

By mid-July, with the "unilateral actions" sputtering, Aidit pushed the fifth-force proposal vigorously. He cited the party's "revolutionary actions which are increasingly developing" and stressed anew the need for military training. Aidit acknowledged that "there are people who feel afraid of these developments and have the impression that Indonesia is on the road to militarism and all kinds of evil things (massacre? civil war?). But," he said, "on the contrary, the military training *which we are carrying on*" was not intended to be expansionist; rather, it was aimed at serving "the noble task of our revolution to liberate our people from all forms of oppression and exploitation and to help as much as possible the struggle of other peoples in their efforts to liberate themselves." [15]

Without waiting for an official sanction, the PKI admitted that it had begun to train a paramilitary front. Actually, a selected group from Gerwani and the Pemuda Rakjat were already undergoing basic training at Halim Perdanakusuma, the Air Force's main base on the outskirts of Jakarta and the place where the bodies of the slain members of the general staff would be unearthed in October of that year. On the government-controlled plantations in Central Java, too, the Sarbupri, the PKI-controlled estate workers' union, not only insisted on forming a paramilitary unit, but demanded that it be financed by the estate management.[16]

The Communists were playing with fire—and must have realized it. Given their "unilateral actions," the time for requesting arms was hardly propitious. After resisting the PKI on this point for two decades, why should the generals change their position now? Worse, the Chinese endorsement of the proposal was considered an intervention in Indonesia's internal affairs. Given the Army's traditional antipathy toward the Chinese, the general staff was infuriated, especially since some high-ranking officers felt, rightly or wrongly, that in the long term the military threat to Indonesia would come "from the north," meaning Peking, despite Sukarno's deepening alliance with the Chinese and the emergence of a Jakarta-Peking Axis.

"Our feeling at the time was that if the fifth force was set up, the Army—the armed forces—would be separated from the people and we would wind up with a dual command," General Sutopo Juwono, director of Army intelligence, later observed.[17] "We considered the proposal an outside effort, especially by Peking and the PKI, to divide the Army from the people. We already had a sample of what was ahead. There was already trouble in Central and East Java and there was the Bandar Betsy affair in Sumatra." And General Umar Wirahadikusumo recalled,[18] "When the Chinese pressed the concept of a fifth force, we told Yani to tell Sukarno that we strongly disagreed, that such a force was unnecessary because the Army already enjoyed the people's support."

For the record, both Nasution and Yani balked at the creation of such a force, displaying unusual courage in standing up to Sukarno. But if past experience was a guide, neither Nasution nor Yani possessed the mettle to stand indefinitely. Indeed, in July, 1965, Nasution hedged slightly, or so it seemed. He contended that only "in a very critical situation" would the people be armed, which either could be interpreted as a weakening of his resistance or a simple sop to Sukarno. But within the Indonesian general staff, there was a strong current opposed to the arming of the PKI; for, in the final analysis, this is what the Aidit-Chou-Sukarno proposal came down to. The Army considered the fifth force an armed *fifth column*.[19]

In his independence day speech that year, Sukarno addressed himself to the question. He claimed the idea of a fifth force as his own and said he was being falsely accused of "copying others." The audience, especially the generals and would-be commissars, awaited his decision. Sensing the resistance to the plan, Sukarno concluded, "After an even more thorough consideration of this question, I will take a decision on this matter in my capacity as Supreme Commander of the Armed Forces." He then promptly went on to observe that "with islands as many as ours, we cannot maintain the sovereignty of our state without a people who, if necessary, are given arms. . . ."[20] The implication was that Sukarno needed a little more time, but he was determined to push through the proposal. Within a few weeks, the general staff opposing his will would be largely liquidated.

While Sukarno, the PKI, and the Chinese promoted the fifth-force concept, Peking intruded in another delicate issue—the question of Sukarno's health, the issue which triggered the events of September 30–October 1.

For years, it had been patently obvious, except to the most opaque observer, that the death of Sukarno would spell high noon in the confrontation between the Army and the PKI.

Sukarno's "guided democracy," as he euphemistically called his inefficient authoritarian regime, clearly would not outlast him. He had, for example, cultivated no Dauphine. For a time, Chairul Saleh, the former National Communist, was groomed as a potential successor, but Saleh was hotheaded, unpredictable and quarrelsome. He was corrupt and had lost his following and popular base in Bantam, on the tip of West Java. It was unlikely he could carry on the precarious Army-PKI juggling act, assuming, of course, that it was not resolved before the passing of Sukarno.

There was always a possibility that Subandrio would fill the void, or at least make an effort to do so. He was a skilled negotiator—suave, glib, and opportunistic. Like Sukarno, he was adept at speaking with as many tongues as the situation demanded. He already served as liasion between Sukarno and the PKI and, although he himself was not a Communist, he had developed intimate contacts with the PKI leadership. He had also cultivated warm relations with "progressive" officers in the armed forces, specifically, the Army and the Air Force. But, like Chairul Saleh, he had no political base, was relatively unpopular, and commanded neither the respect nor the affection of either the Army or the PKI, nor did he instill fear in them.

Perhaps the blackest mark that history may put against Sukarno's name is that, in his own self-interest, he deliberately fashioned an irresistible force, the PKI, and an immovable object, the Army. The political situation had to end in disaster, not merely for Sukarno and his "guided democracy," but for the impoverished, politically illiterate common people—and it did, in a wave of murders which swept the country after September 30 and took thousands of lives.

The generals and the would-be commissars were sensitive to the slightest impairment of Sukarno's health. A common cold was tantamount to pneumonia in their respective command posts. Both sides were convinced that unless the situation altered dramatically during his lifetime in favor of one or the other, one party would have to pre-empt the other in the event of Sukarno's sudden incapacitation or death.

Aidit doubtlessly would label the above assessment, at least the Communist position, as a "provocative Trotskyite tactic intending to produce a second edition of the Madiun affair." He said so in 1965 and then went on to accuse his adversaries—the imperialists (the West), the bureaucratic capitalists (the Army), and the Trotskyites (the Murba)—of combining forces in an effort to connect the "danger of communism with the impaired health of Sukarno." This, he said, "only demonstrates the lengths to which international imperialism would go in developing a campaign against the people's forces." [21]

Subandrio was equally incensed. He termed rumors that Sukarno was in poor health a "dirty lie" designed to weaken the fighting spirit of the Indonesian people. "The only one who can replace Bung Karno," he said, "is the progressive, revolutionary people of Indonesia." [22] The *PKI?*

To enliven matters, Sukarno passed through several periods of poor health in the sixties, each generating torrid speculation about the future course of events in the country. He was known to have one diseased kidney and had been treated for it in Vienna; the United States, fearful of the responsibility, quietly turned down his request to be treated at Walter Reed Hospital. Functioning on one kidney is not that debilitating, providing the person takes care of himself; for example, Marshall Green, former United States ambassador in Indonesia, lightly commented during a private conversation, "I have only one kidney, too, you know." [23]

Sometime around 1963, Sukarno was cautioned by a mystic that he would die by the knife. In Jakarta, the story made the rounds that doubtless the knife would be wielded by a woman; but Sukarno interpreted the forecast as meaning death on the operating table. He therefore continued Western medical treatment short of surgery and turned increasingly, meanwhile, to Chinese traditional medicine, acupuncture, to alleviate his condition.

Peking provided him with a special medical team, and Sukarno had high praise for their effectiveness.

In terms of Sukarno's physical condition, the year 1965 began auspiciously, with Sukarno in excellent health, or so he claimed. In high spirits, he conferred state medals on the Chinese medical team for their diligent work—among them Professor Doctors Wu Chieh Ping, Fang Chin, Yao Mei Chung, and Doctors Yeng Chia San and Shih Tien Peng. "I am now as fit as ever," he said on the occasion.[24] "This is, among other things, due to the treatment given me by the Chinese doctors."

His mental health may have been another matter, however. It was rarely discussed openly in Indonesia, although as early as 1952, if not earlier, Hatta, Sjahrir, and others were convinced that Sukarno was at times irrational. Whether he was mentally ill or not may be divulged someday because shortly before he was stripped of the last trappings of office in 1967, he was examined by Indonesian psychiatrists and declared to be mentally ill.[25] Their report was not released to the public nor did they specify the nature of his ailment. But there have been striking similarities between Sukarno's endless defense against encirclement by neocolonialism, colonialism, and imperialism and the persecutory delusions manifested in paranoid schizophrenic reaction, a classic form of mental illness.[26]

Interestingly, several of Sukarno's closest advisers were either physicians or had access to medical expertise and, therefore, should have possessed an intimate knowledge of his general health based solely on their day-to-day observations. By illustration, Subandrio and Leimena were physicians. Aidit's wife, Tanti, graduated from a Russian medical school; indeed, she returned to Jakarta on September 26, 1965—four days before the purge of the Army—from a prolonged trip to North Korea where, among other things, she studied Korean acupuncture techniques.

Parenthetically, it should be noted at this writing in 1969, that Sukarno is still alive and presumably well, although there have been periodic reports about his failing health.[27] He is said to be "no longer receiving acupuncture treatments." [28]

But in July, 1965, there was a new round of rumors that Sukarno was not well, and on August 4 all the lights flashed frantically on Jakarta's switchboard. Sukarno was seized by a fit of vomiting and his appointments for the day were canceled. This much is on the record, on the basis of the palace appointment book and the testimony of Rear Air Marshal Muljono Herlambang, who had an appointment with Sukarno at the palace that day and was turned away because of his sudden attack.[29] "He collapsed shortly before August 17," Leimena recalled.[30] "He was sixty-five years old and ran a high blood pressure risk."

Rumors of Sukarno's illness spread rapidly. The nature of his seizure worsened in direct proportion to the distance the news traveled from the palace. Yet General Yani visited him shortly thereafter and found him "OK." [31]

At this time, Subandrio summoned Aidit and Njoto home from abroad. Both had been members of Sukarno's delegation to the abortive Second Afro-Asian Conference which had been scheduled to be held in Algeria. The Indonesian delegation got as far as Cairo when the conference collapsed in the wake of the Algerian coup which unseated the Ben Bella regime. While Sukarno returned home, Aidit and Njoto remained abroad.

Subandrio sent cables to the Indonesian embassies in Moscow and Peking which read: "On orders of the President, both are expected to return home." [32] Neither Sukarno nor Subandrio knew precisely where the pair were other than within the Communist world. It turned out they were in Peking. Subandrio said he sent the cables on July 31 at Sukarno's request, but Sukarno disputes this and said that on August 2 he ordered only Njoto home to help draft his August 17 Independence Day speech. More important, it is also possible that Subandrio or possibly the PKI sent a second cable advising of Sukarno's illness because when Aidit returned on August 7 he brought in tow a Chinese medical team. After examining Sukarno, the Chinese doctors reported that the President was gravely ill. Indonesia's controlled press reported nothing and there is no "hard" evidence of the Chinese diagnosis other than the fact that it quickly became common knowledge inside and outside the palace during this period. Given the past alarms and excursions about Sukarno's health, foreign correspondents ignored the story until after September 30.

It should be constantly borne in mind that this development occurred at a time when the existence of a Council of Generals was also in the air. As can be imagined, the political tension in Indonesia rose indescribably.

Somewhat earlier—in July or possibly toward the end of June—the PKI's Politburo began a series of meetings in Aidit's absence. They may not have been so much formal meetings as simply an effort by the Communist leadership to stay on top of an otherwise rapidly developing political situation. In the past, Aidit had also inexplicably taken leave of the country at moments of crisis.[33] But, after Aidit's return in August, these Politburo meetings acquired significance.

The story of the sessions is pieced together from the testimony of Sudisman, Njono, Peris Pardede, Karel Supit, and other members of the Politburo and/or Central Committee who were apprehended and interrogated after September 30. Such testimony is naturally not above suspicion.[34] The versions are not uniform, however, and they contain a central theme and have a ring of truth. Unlike the Moscow purge trials of the thirties, the Indonesian trials lack the grotesque, insensitive uniformity associated with Pavlov's experiments or Chinese "brain-washing."[35]

Apparently on his return from Peking, Aidit, relying on his own intelligence sources, reported that the Chinese doctors considered Sukarno's illness extremely serious. Indeed, there were only two alternatives, he said. If the President followed the advice of the doctors, there was a chance for his recovery, but, in view of Sukarno's "extraordinary activities" in running the state (and his private life), Aidit concluded that he had little chance of recovery. In effect, Sukarno had two chances: slim and none. Aidit warned the Politburo that the Army was also aware of Sukarno's delicate condition and that, in the event of the President's death, the Council of Generals was poised to strike and, in the process, liquidate the PKI. Aidit, however, not only reported on the critical state of Sukarno's health and the maneuvers of the Council of Generals, but he also disclosed what he termed "the *initiative* of a group of progressive officers to frustrate that coup." [36]

The reference to a group of "progressive officers" within the armed forces was well taken.[37] Although the Communists failed to penetrate the hard-core general staff, the Army, Navy, Air Force, and police were riven by cliques of various strengths and shades. In the Army, for example, there were pro-Sukarno and anti-PKI generals (Adjie and Sabur); anti-Sukarno and anti-PKI generals (Sukendro, Dharsono, Sarwo Edhie); and pro-Sukarno and pro-PKI generals (Supardjo and Sutepu). Special PKI undercover agents worked to cultivate the pro-PKI officers and to establish sub rosa links between them and the Politburo. Sjam, the cover name for Kamaruzzaman, directed this phase of the operations as chief of the PKI's Biro Chusus or Special Bureau.[38] The Bureau was set up in November, 1964; significantly, perhaps, within a month of Peking's first successful test of a nuclear weapon and the rapid coalescing thereafter of Peking-Jakarta policies at the government as well as party level.

Against this background, on August 28, the Politburo unanimously agreed that a pre-emptive strike against the general staff—and thereby the Council of Generals—was warranted and justifiable. The meeting was attended by Aidit, Lukman, Njoto, Sudisman, and Sakirman (the "Big Five"), and Njono and Anwar Sanusi. The decision was made at the top and, given the atmosphere permeating Jakarta at the time, "the decision to launch the military operation was known only to Politburo members to prevent a leak." [39] The rank and file "below" would, of course, follow standard operational procedures in the transmission of the line from "above." For example, each member of a PKI front had standing orders to consider a speech by Aidit as an instructional memo.[40] They were also obliged to study the editorials in every issue of the *People's Daily (Harian Rakjat)* as a guide to the party line.

To heighten the overlay of at least indirect Chinese Communist complicity in the September 30 affair, it should also be put on the record that Foreign Minister Marshal Ch'en Yi arrived in Jakarta at the head of an August 17 Independence Day delegation and, toward the end of the month, prior to his departure for home, conferred privately with Aidit at the latter's residence. Nobody knows what they discussed.[41]

At this point in the narrative, many questions obviously come to mind. Unfortunately, they cannot be answered with any degree of precision—nor is it likely that they will ever be answered.

Did Aidit inform Ch'en Yi of the impending purge of the generals? Would the Chinese doctors have circulated a report on Sukarno's illness without first clearing it with Peking? Were the Chinese Communists trying to provoke their Indonesian counterparts into action? If so, why? Or did the PKI request Peking to sound a false alarm about Sukarno's health to spur Sukarno into taking decisive action against the generals? For that matter, was Sukarno really ill? If so, did the PKI panic? Did the Chinese contrive their report with the knowledge of Sukarno and/or Aidit?

These questions have many variations.

It should be underlined, however, that the role of the Chinese physicians became an issue in Indonesia in the weeks *before* September 30. Sukarno, Aidit, and the Chinese Embassy—if not Peking—had ample opportunity to deny such persistent reports. They did not.

As a case in point, aside from common knowledge and/or gossip in Jakarta, within a week of the coup an analysis of the Indonesian situation appeared on the front page of the Los Angeles *Times*. The dispatch said a Chinese medical doctor had "reported to the PKI that Sukarno's health was again failing and that time had become an imperative factor." [42] The report added that the physician is said to have made his report to Aidit on instructions from Peking and that the PKI was "disturbed (since) Aidit always believed that without Sukarno's protection, the Army would crush the party."

A British author and former long-time Singapore correspondent has written similarly. "Matters came to a head in August, when the President's health—long a cause for anxiety —appeared to take a turn for the worse. . . ." Brian Crozier said.[43] "In September, according to reports reaching Singapore from Jakarta, (his) Chinese doctor—on instructions from Peking—reported to the PKI that in his opinion Sukarno could not live much longer."

But to return directly to the narrative. Sometime between August 28, and September 14, Aidit conferred with Sukarno on the situation and proposed putting aside the general staff. He could say it was not an original thought with him since "progressive, revolutionary" officers had *initiated* the idea. Both Sukarno and Aidit had a vested interest in such an operation. Both had been frustrated by the general staff. In this light, it is not surprising, as far as can be learned in Jakarta, that Sukarno gave his blessing to the plan.

And why not? If Sukarno believed that his health was impaired, given his headlong slide toward the Communists over the past two years, it would have been only natural for him to want to protect the PKI and not leave it at the mercy of a "neocolim-CIA" general staff. Even if the question of his poor health was a hoax, which it might well have been, Sukarno had long recognized the necessity to clean house within the Army if Indonesia was to move into the second phase of its two-stage revolution. Specifically, Sukarno felt that he had to remove those senior officers who suffered from "anti-Communist phobia," his pet phrase for those who opposed the PKI's growing influence within Indonesia. The removal of the general staff and its replacement by "progressive, revolutionary" officers would safeguard the revolution as he defined it.

Only one question remained: how to carry out the housecleaning. Sukarno could not summarily dismiss those general officers whom he felt were challenging his authority as the "Great Leader of the Revolution." The repercussions within the Army might be too severe. Nor could he simply order their wholesale execution. It was neither in Sukarno's style nor in the style of his regime. For all of his regime's oppressiveness, it was largely devoid of the physical brutality and repressive character, say, of such "progressive, revolutionary" states as the Soviet Union or China.

Accordingly, Sukarno drew on his own past experience and proposed a characteristic maneuver.

Before World War II—and Indonesia's independence—Sukarno had been arrested and exiled to Flores by the former Dutch colonial regime.[44] It was a pattern of benevolent despotism which he readily adopted in removing his own political opponents—the Sjahrirs, Prawotos, Natsirs, Agungs, Sjafruddins, Roems, Adjams, Hamzahs, Subadios, Lubises, and countless others. This Dutch-inherited policy blended ideally with a characteristic Indonesian political technique, kidnapping. Abduction in Indonesia has marked the course of political development. Sukarno (and Hatta) were kidnapped by Aidit and Malik, among others, to force the pace of the proclamation of independence in 1945. A year later, Tan Malakka arranged the kidnapping of Sjahrir, who was then the premier. The plan went awry, however; Sukarno got cold feet in midstream when it developed that Tan Malakka may have planned to depose him whereupon Sukarno reversed himself and papered over his rift with Sjahrir. The PKI went on a kidnapping spree on the eve of Madiun, and so forth.

Accordingly, as far as can be determined after scrupulous, independent inquiry in Jakarta in the spring of 1968, it appears that Sukarno returned to this relatively simple stratagem in addressing himself to the problem of the general staff. The obstructionist, obstinate generals would be detained, confronted with trumped-up charges of treason, put on trial, unmasked as "neocolim-CIA" agents, disgraced, convicted, sentenced to prison, and possibly exiled to some remote island. The void on the general staff would be filled with manageable, "progressive, revolutionary" officers loyal to Sukarno, his NASAKOM ideology, and his ultimate objective—the conversion of post-Sukarno Indonesia into a Communist state. If the hard-core general staff officers were thus removed, perhaps a half-dozen or so, other senior officers would get the message and could be expected to toe the line. This was another Indonesian political trait. Decapitate the leadership and the body usually succumbs; change the leadership and the body meekly responds to new directions.[45]

Sometime in the summer of 1965, probably before September 14, Sukarno, the PKI, and the "progressive, revolutionary" dissident officers in the Army and Air Force, with

Subandrio in the role of a midwife, hatched the uncomplicated plan to arrest and prosecute the generals who were subverting the course of the revolution.

On paper, the plan appeared admirable. Neither Sukarno nor the PKI would appear to be implicated. Both the President, with his popular mass support, and the Communist Party, with its mass organizations, would bring their followings into play *after* the detention of the generals. The plan was so deceptively simple that no contingency plans were drawn, another Indonesian political characteristic.

But the Communists committed a fatal mistake at the outset. They assigned a "fifth force" of about two thousand to assist in the military operation, a mixed group drawn from the Pemuda Rakjat, Gerwani, and other PKI auxiliary organizations. They were selected from the 3,700 young Communist men and women undergoing training at Halim air base in collaboration with the Air Force, which fed, clothed, drilled, and armed them ostensibly as volunteers for the "crush Malaysia" campaign. Aidit put Njono in charge of the military phase of the PKI's operation and he, in turn, established liaison with the fifth force through "General" Sukanto, the veteran chairman of the Pemuda Rakjat.

The Communist decision to lend troops to the operation may have reflected a psychological compulsion. The PKI would want a piece of the action to build up its political credit for the future. A PKI role in the purge would compromise the Army and Air Force units involved. For that matter, Sukarno may have wanted to insure the PKI's involvement by a "fifth force" role. Direct Communist military participation, however, would also give the PKI some insurance in dealing with the new general staff.

As for his part, following the arrests of the traitorous generals, Sukarno would proclaim that the revolution, and his person, had been saved. This would spark a mass outpouring onto the streets of the PKI and its mass fronts. The throngs would not only denounce the Council of Generals, but the United States and the CIA in the bargain. In a desire to defend the state from the machinations of the imperialists, the PKI would demand—and receive—arms from a new defense minister and a new Army chief of staff.

In effect, Indonesia would have taken a long, and probably inexorable, stride toward the second phase of the two-stage Sukarno-PKI revolution and the ultimate emergence in the archipelago of a "People's Democracy." In this situation, "world opinion" would batter the United States and link the American disaster in Indonesia with the quagmire in Vietnam. The "Hate America" claque would have a field day. Moreover, the triumph of the "progressive revolutionary" forces in Indonesia would be proclaimed on October 1 as Peking celebrated the Communist assumption of power in China. Clearly, communism would be hailed as the wave of the future—at least of Asia's future. The Asian Communist line would extend from the northern half of the Korean peninsula into the Viet Cong-controlled Ca Mau peninsula at the southern tip of Vietnam and six hundred miles across the South China Sea into Indonesia as far east as New Guinea. Moral in Laos, Cambodia, Thailand, Malaysia, Singapore, Australia, the Philippines and South Korea would be severely shaken; the impact on Japan would be devastating—she would be relatively isolated in her own part of the world.

The masterplan to remove the Indonesian general staff was masterfully conceived.

As summarized by one general, now in an influential position in the Suharto government, "Sukarno knew what would happen, more or less. He knew the plan's general outlines, not the specific details, and he gave it his blessing. His objective was to destroy the Army brain trust whose hard-core was anti-PKI. Sukarno could not handle the Army according to his will. He wanted a TRI, not a TNI.[46] He wanted a fifth force as a counterweight to the Army. So did the PKI. Sukarno, in effect, said: put them aside. The phrase may be interpreted in any way, shape, manner, or form."

Every plot from above requires an executor from below, preferably someone who, if necessary, can also enact the role of "fall guy," if necessary. The candidate selected in this instance was Lieutenant Colonel Untung, thirty-nine, an officer in the palace honor guard, Tjakrabirawa, who had only recently arrived from the Seventh Diponegoro Division and who was a man of intense loyalty to Sukarno, and considered by those who knew him as not especially bright.[47]

Sjam, the PKI agent who served as the principal under-cover liaison man between the Politburo and the "progressive" officers in the Armed Forces established contact with Untung and impressed on him that "it is a public secret that there is collaboration between the Council of Generals and the neocolim," and that Yani was working to subvert Indonesia in league with the United States.

Untung may have played Sjam's record back to Sukarno and, in turn, received the President's approval for the operation to "safeguard the Great Leader of the Revolution." It is inconceivable that Sukarno's personal honor guard, composed of the Army, Navy, Air Force, and police—the four forces—acted on its own initiative without the knowledge and consent of the President, and it is perhaps even more inconceivable that Utung would take it unto himself to singlehandedly save the revolution. General Sabur, the commander of the Tjakrabirawa, who was loyal to Sukarno but hostile to the PKI, was conveniently in Bandung and therefore out of the way, on the night of September 30–October 1. Untung later admitted that it was he who issued the order to "fetch the generals," and he observed that, although he did not have the authority to issue such an order, taking into consideration his purpose—to protect and safeguard the President—he considered that he behaved properly.[48] Loyal to the end, Untung did not publicly implicate Sukarno. Tears welled in his eyes when a special military tribunal sentenced him to death; quite possibly he realized that he had been selected as the "fall guy."

Thus, as Jakarta passed through the climactic month of September, the major forces in the Indonesian drama were on a collision course. Nobody knew precisely what would happen. Sukarno merely gave his approval to "put aside the generals." As it materialized, when the September 30 movement struck, the Army general staff was caught unaware—and so was Sukarno. The generals were not merely kidnapped for a mock trial—they were summarily butchered.

5

Enemies of the People

IN THE LATE SUMMER OF 1965, AS
the stresses and strains within Indonesia reached the breaking
point, the Asian landscape was jarred by a series of tumultu-
ous events, each of which contributed still further to the already foreboding atmosphere in Jakarta.

Malaysia was rent by Singapore's exit from the newly established Commonwealth federation. The Kashmir tinderbox
burst into flame anew, plunging India and Pakistan into another round of warfare. The United States massive intervention in Vietnam was gathering momentum. In Peking, the
Chinese Communists proclaimed the Lin Piao doctrine of
"wars of national liberation."

Thus, the political barometer in and around Indonesia
was plunging rapidly as the end of September approached. On
September 29, viewing the cumulonimbus build-up on the
horizon, the PKI concluded: "The international situation at
present is very favorable for the anti-imperialist struggle." [1]

By mid-September, with preparations for the removal of
the generals at an advanced stage, the Communists and the
Sukarno regime unloosened a massive propaganda campaign
whose purpose was to manufacture the proper political climate for the impending action. That fortnight a basic theme
emerged: the need for the liquidation of "the enemies of the
people," as Aidit himself termed the opposition.[2] The Communists stressed the need to "eradicate" or "exterminate" or
"shoot" their adversaries.

September 14 appeared to be a decisive day as Aidit set
the tone in a violent oratorical outburst. The moment was at
hand, he said, to "operate on the cancer of society"—the capi-

talist bureaucrats, economic adventurers and corruptors.[3]
This terminology was generally reserved for anti-Communists,
especially in the Army and bureaucracy. The PKI had long
ago usurped the label of incorruptibility, although the Communists, no more and no less, contained as many corrupt elements as the Army, the political parties, and the regime itself;
for example, Oetomo Ramelan, the Communist mayor of
Surakarta, in Central Java, was corrupt, and a playboy on the
Sukarno scale.[4]

Yet, attired in the cloak of incorruptibility, Aidit called
on the nation's "uncorrupted leaders" to act. In another
speech, he proposed bringing the revolutionary situation to "a
peak (by) cutting out all the cancers" in Indonesian society.
The generals were clearly one, if not the largest, of these
cancers. Then, on September 27, Aidit declared: "Dare, dare,
again I say, dare! We must act, act, and again I say, act! We
must move, move, and again I say move! Dare, act, and move
against the devils of the cities, that is, the high and mighty,
thieves and corrupters."

The Communist apparatus quickly embellished on the
Aidit themes as September waned. On September 25, a
Pemuda Rakjat rally asked: "What are we waiting for? Weed
out the corruptors."[5] That same day, Communist youth in
Semarang demanded that corruptors be "shot in public."[6]
Two days later, Sadjarwo, the BTI leader and minister of
agriculture, declared that the time was ripe for the liquidation
of subversives. "If necessary," he said, "the big calibre manip-
ulators and their ringleaders must be shot." Finally, two days
before September 30, Aidit told a Communist student conclave: "Children should join in crushing the 'devils of the
city'—the corruptors and the capitalists, who are the enemies
of the people."[7]

By far the most ominous overtone of all was the announcement by the Pemuda Rakjat that their doors would be
open twenty-four hours daily to "receive *new* lists from people
for persons for trial and sentencing equal to their sins."[8] And,
during a PKI-organized march on September 29, the demonstrators demanded that the enemies of the people be "dragged
before court and given death penalties."[9]

September 14 also marked the opening salvo in a similarly heated campaign directed by Subandrio, the most articulate spokesman for the regime other than the President himself. *"The time has now come* to exterminate the capitalist bureaucrats and (those) who manipulate state funds," he declared. Like the PKI, Subandrio also presumed to be above the pale in matters of corruption; later, at his trial, it developed he had been a skillful master manipulator of state funds.[10]

Subandrio contended that there were "only two complete patriots, Sukarno and the workers and peasants of Indonesia"—a direct rebuke to the armed forces. Those, he said, who wish to become full-fledged patriots "should conduct a *banting stir* (a drastic change in policy), that is, do away in a firm manner with all elements who will not follow the course of the revolution." As Subandrio put it, "If we want to be great men or a great nation, we must be able to cope with big problems (the Army?)." [11]

And the *Indonesian Herald,* the country's leading English-language journal, financed and directed by Subandrio's ministry, made a chilling observation in its "off the record" column. It cited approvingly the execution of "enemies of the people" in China and said:

Of course, one main characteristic of our revolution has been that it has caused so little bloodshed. Up to now, we have not heard of any economic saboteur being shot or hanged. . . . Our leniency and human considerations seem to have been taken advantage of by a number of self-seeking swindlers and corruptors. It is about time we act. Otherwise, our leniency and humanity may jeopardize the very interest of the majority of our people.[12]

Without realizing it themselves, the Communists and their sympathizers were digging their own graves by their deliberate creation of a murderous atmosphere of hatred and violence.

During those last two weeks in September, Subandrio and the PKI also suddenly revived the issue of the CIA. At that time, the CIA was not remotely a factor in Indonesian-American relations. As in the case of the Cuban Bay of Pigs episode during the Kennedy Administration, the Eisenhower Administration had been badly burned by the CIA's misreading and miscalculation of the Indonesian situation in 1958 when it clandestinely supported the ill-fated "revolt of the economists" against Sukarno and the PKI. As a former CIA official picturesquely expressed it, "After that mess, they gave us our medals, patted us on the behind and told us to go home." [13]

In mid-September, however, Antara News Agency, now wholly controlled by the Communists, reported that ten CIA agents were arrested in northern Celebes after being smuggled into Indonesia from the Philippines.[14] The story had a contrived air. Then, on September 27, the *Indonesian Herald* devoted several columns to the activities of the American "devil organization" and an editorial proposed "an international campaign to expose and to condemn the CIA." It suggested the issue be taken up by KIAPMA, the International Conference for the Abolition of Foreign Military Bases, a Communist-dominated conclave which was scheduled to open in Jakarta in mid-October, and which would have provided an ideal forum for Sukarno to trumpet that the "revolution had been saved" on October 1 from the CIA Council of Generals.

During September, too, as noted earlier, Sukarno conferred a "Great Son" medal on Aidit and ordered the "total dissolution" of the suspended Murba, another confirmation, if any was still required, that in Sukarno's mind the PKI had become a Nationalist Communist substitute. There was also a new, unpublicized flurry of political arrests, including, for example, the detention of Kasman Singodimedjo, a former Masjumi leader and longtime foe of the PKI. Sukarno also brought new pressure to bear on the Moslems by authorizing Subandrio to "retool" the HMI, the Islamic student front and the only organization thwarting the capture of the Indonesian student movement by the CGMI, a PKI student body.

In this political atmosphere, of course, the economic situation, perilous for more than a year, went to pieces and *Harian Rakjat* summoned the people to take up the law in their own hands to force down soaring prices.

Rumors of an impending climax were commonplace. Who would strike first? The PKI or the Army? And when? General Yani visited the Borneo front and ostensibly talking about the war against Malaysia warned the Army that "we must be ready if anything happens" and, he added, "Indonesia should not hang its fate on any country." [15] The latter reference was to China, given Sukarno's proclamation of a Jakarta-Peking Axis a few weeks earlier. Army intelligence also learned that Air Marshal Dhani had paid an unannounced visit to Peking on September 16 without going through regular defense ministry channels. He had gone to China to accelerate Chinese arms deliveries for the fifth force.[16]

Indeed, Subandrio's own intelligence network, the BPI, was also working overtime and reported back to him on the increasing activities of the PKI, in particular the training of a fifth force at Halim air base. Subandrio pigeonholed their reports.[17] But the BPI's reports multiplied as the month wore on, and even Antara publicly reported on September 26 that the Communist estate workers' union, Sarbupri, had installed a "Maruto Darusman" brigade of one hundred thousand volunteers in Central Java (another example of Malay exaggeration; it is doubtful if the force composed one thousand volunteers). As for its name, Maruto Darusman, a Eurasian, had been a member of the PKI Central Committee and had participated in the Madiun revolt, was subsequently arrested and executed. Later, he was elevated into the PKI's pantheon of party heroes. Among those present at the brigade's installation ceremonies was Munir, the chairman of SOBSI, the Communist labor federation. Munir renewed the demand for a fifth force and went so far as to propose turning government estates into peasant bases from which the fifth force could launch "counterattacks in the event of either subversion within or aggression from without." [18] Never before had the PKI been so explicit about the need for a paramilitary force.

Quite understandably, during these turbulent weeks, Jakarta's rumor mills turned unceasingly. If the PKI was not planning a coup, then the Army must be and, if so, the likely date was October 5, Armed Forces Day. The rumors spread as the Army planned a gargantuan parade to counterbalance the PKI's forty-fifth anniversary celebrations. But if October 5 provided a pretext for bringing 20,000 additional troops into the capital, it also provided an opportunity for dissident officers to bring in disaffected units, particularly from the

Fifth East Java Brawidjaja Division and the Seventh Central Java Diponegoro Division.

These rumors abounded. Subandrio's *Indonesian Herald* on September 22, for example, reported "an air of great expectation" and quoted a spokesman for the Army chief of staff as declaring, again presumably within the context of the Malaysian confrontation, that "we must remain on the alert more than ever before." The newspaper reported a spate of unusual activity in connection "with the coming of October 5, the twentieth anniversary of the founding of the Indonesian armed forces." A naval officer was also quoted as saying: "We are organizing a mammoth thing for this historic day." What was this "thing"? An armed forces coup? In this war of nerves, Sukarno, the PKI, and the "progressive, revolutionary" officers probably concluded that the purge of the general staff must be accomplished before Armed Forces Day, if at all.

The tension is reflected in the recollections of the period. A minister in the present Suharto cabinet recalled, "Ten days or so before September 30 I spoke to General Suprapto, who was Yani's deputy on the general staff. I remember him saying, 'It is high noon.' I asked him what he meant by that. 'Everyone has a pistol in his hand,' he said. 'Everyone is expecting a coup. The question is who will be first?' "

And, on September 28, the Sultan of Jogjakarta, who had held the defense portfolio in the past, recalled meeting Major General Parman, another Yani deputy, and Lieutenant Colonel Suprapto, who was on the staff of the Seventh Division. "They told me the situation was very, very tense," he said.[19] "Jokingly, I said: 'The way it is perhaps it is better not to sleep at home.' "

In another recollection, General Her Tasning, a Sulawesi (Celebes) officer, remembered how Sukarno told Yani the last week in September, on his return from an inspection tour in the Lesser Sundas, "I want a big October 5." This request by the President, he said, dampened rumors that Sukarno himself may have been involved in some impending power play.[20]

The tension also seeped into the cells of Sukarno's political prisons. Sjafruddin Prawiranegara, an economist who headed the Republican emergency government from the jungles of

Sumatra in 1948–49, after Sukarno voluntarily surrendered to
the Dutch, and who was later imprisoned by Sukarno for participating in the abortive 1958 revolt against him, reminisced:
"In our cell block one of the prisoners, who was not one of us,
told us a coup was coming—can you imagine, even in prison
there were people who expected some sort of coup! I also
remember a student friend of our eldest daughter warned her
that something would happen soon. This was September 29.
The children felt the tension. Everyone expected something;
but nobody knew what." [21]

A prominent business executive, who had a distinguished
World War II record as a noncommissioned officer in the
former Netherlands East Indies Army, added another footnote. "Both the military and the Communists were at each
other's throat, one trying to provoke the other," Julius
Tahija recalled.[22] "I remember on September 12 I told General Parman: 'Do not underestimate your adversary. Whatever
you expect, give twelve hours before and twelve hours after.' "

"It was clear a climax was coming," Sudjatmoko, a Sjahrir
aide and presently ambassador to the United States, said.[23]
"There were rumors that Yani would be kidnapped. I heard
such rumors twice. There was a general expectation that something had to give." And General Harjono, a general staff
officer, confided to a friend in late September, "The situation
is extremely serious—I know I am being watched all the
time." Another senior officer, Major General Sugandhi, a
former Sukarno ADC, recalled that he had picked up rumors
on three consecutive days (September 26, 27, and 28) that
"something was going to happen." Disturbed, he went to
Sukarno on September 30 to warn him. "But Sukarno became
angry and snapped at me, 'Mind your own business,' " Sugandhi said.[24] "I was shocked by his outburst—after all I had
come to alert him to possible danger."

Despite the tension, the generals did not reinforce their
guards at home or take any unusual precautions. It might
have been a matter of pride. It might have also been that they
had heard the cry of "wolf" too often. Yani, for example,
rejected the suggestion that week that additional guards be

placed on his house.[25]

Sukarno, meanwhile, like Subandrio and the PKI, also moved to raise the political thermostat in the final weeks of September. In a series of speeches, he confirmed the deepening conviction of many that he had decided to cast his lot with the PKI.

Three days before September 30, he asserted that the first, national democratic phase of the revolution had almost ended and that "we are now about to enter the second stage of the Indonesian Revolution, namely the implementation of socialism." This *banting stir*, he admonished his listeners, should be "greeted with joy." [26] Forty-eight hours before the purge of the general staff, in a biting remark, Sukarno observed that Indonesia's singular achievement since the proclamation of independence in 1945 was the survival of the people, not the armed forces.[27] And, the day before the September 30 movement was launched, he told a conference of railway workers, traditionally in the vanguard of the labor movements, that he had locked his course and set the automatic pilot. "Once on course," he declared,[28] "forever on course." This statement acquired deeper significance later when it was learned that Aidit had informed the Politburo, the day before, on September 28, that the purge of the generals was set for the night of September 30–October 1.[29]

There was also an interesting public dialogue between Sukarno and Aidit at this time—or at least their words could be so construed. In his September 27 statement, Aidit cited Marx's *Manifesto:* "The proletarians have nothing to lose but their chains. They have a world to win." Then, in an aside which may have been intended for the President, Aidit added, "A leader who feels that he can lose something, have something taken from him by revolution, is not a true leader of the labor class." For that matter, he may have been talking to himself, honing his courage. Yet on the fateful day of September 30 both Sukarno and Aidit addressed a Third CGMI Congress and the President appeared to render a reply. It is "theoretically possible," Sukarno said, that the Communists may also deviate from the revolution (as Sukarno saw it). However, he did not expect that to happen. But, Sukarno continued, should the PKI deviate, it would meet the same fate as other "enemies of the state." [30] Was this a warning to his co-conspirators not to double-cross him? We can only speculate.

Then, on the night of September 30, perhaps unintentionally, Sukarno appeared to give the signal for the purge that followed.

In the evening, as the September 30 movement prepared to strike, Sukarno addressed a conference of national technicians at the Senajan sports complex, a speech which was broadcast and telecast. The peroration ended on a strange note in view of the bloody events which unfolded within a few hours. Sukarno recounted to his audience a tale from the Hindu epic poem, *Mahabharata*. [31] The President said:

> It is now almost eleven o'clock. Let us tell a story.
> This is the story of *Mahabharata:* There is a major dissension between two states, the Hastina and the Pandawa. The conflict between them is very great. But the leaders and commanders of Hastina are actually the relatives of the leaders and commanders of Pandawa. Thus, they were all brothers of each other [Army and PKI?].
> Arjuna [Sukarno?] had to defend the state of Pandawa, and had to wage battle against Hastina. Arjuna was heavy-hearted because he saw many brothers-in-law among the Hastina Army, because Arjuna's wife—he has a lot of them—was a Hastina. His teacher Drona, his military teacher Drona [Nasution?] was on the other side.
> How could he kill his own brothers?
> How could he kill his old friends?
> How could he kill his own teachers?
> How could he kill his own brother, Surjoputro [Parman?] who was given birth to by the same mother as he. [32]
> Arjuna felt weak. Krishna [Aidit or Subandrio?] reminded him: Arjuna, Arjuna, Arjuna, you are a warrior. The duty of a warrior is to fight. The duty of a warrior is to wage war, when it is called for. It is the duty of a warrior to safeguard, defend his country. This is the task of a warrior. It is true, they are your own brothers on the other side. Your own teacher. They will destroy the state of Pandawa. Strike back at them.
> This is your task and your duty.
> Carry out your task without regard to the consequences.

The timing of Sukarno's unusual bedtime story, given the spirit of the time, had several curious aspects. The PKI, for example, went to great lengths in advance to disown the conference beforehand. The party's Central Committee complained that Aidit's name was listed among the conference's advisers, although he had never been consulted.[33] The Communist leadership also said it was "impossible for the PKI to support a conference whose beginning and end are not clear" and hinted that the conference "inclined" toward the corruptors—that is, the Army.

Given the almost endless NASAKOM conferences, rallies, and meetings during this tense period, the PKI's disavowal was rare, indeed; unless, of course, the Central Committee's statement was simply meant as a cover in the expectation that Sukarno would, perhaps inadvertently, give the purge signal in the form of a story.

This may all seem far-fetched, but if the PKI was anxious to protect itself, Sukarno apparently was equally anxious to do the same. He was careful to point out to the audience that he was prompted to set the fable straight by someone else.

What happened was this: Senajan was decorated with the usual myriad of banners and posters. By far the most prominent banner, dwarfing all the others, was a legend fifty feet in length which bore the admonition in Sanskrit: "Krishna says carry out your tasks without regard to the consequences." Interestingly, every word on the banner, save one, was misspelled. Anyone knowing of Sukarno's delight in talking down to and lecturing his audience in the manner of a guru, must have realized that such a gross misprint would almost automatically excite him into displaying his erudition by correcting the spelling on the banner and, in the bargain, telling the story.[34] This is precisely what happened.

As it developed that evening, Eddi Elison, a Menadonese television reporter and member of the PNI, was pressed into service as the announcer at the conference. When he entered the hall, he was aghast to discover the misprinted legend. "It was the biggest banner in the hall," he recounted.[35] "It was hanging right in front of the podium where the President was scheduled to speak." He was troubled, and when Sukarno entered the auditorium, "I could no longer hide my heart." As the guests took their seats on the platform, Elison apologized to the President for the signboard's error. "Sukarno asked me how I knew it was wrong and I said I had read it in a book,"

Elison said. "Then he asked me my name and I told him, whereupon he said: 'What is your real name?' and I explained that was my father's name." This kind of banter is typical Sukarno; as for his doubting Elison's name, Menadonese entertainers frequently adopt a westernized name for their popular music ensembles, and this is what prompted Sukarno's question.

Sukarno was the last to speak that night and, before putting the Mahabharata legend straight, he specifically told the audience that Elison had singled it out to him and had asked for the audience's forgiveness. Did anyone prompt Elison to make this point to the President? "No," he said. Did he know who put up the incorrectly spelled banner? The reply was the same: "No." [36]

As he ended his story, Sukarno repeatedly recited Krishna's message: Carry out your tasks without regard to the consequences. And, in what became the last sentence he would ever utter publicly while possessing the undiluted, tangible, and intangible powers of the presidency, the "Great Leader of the Revolution" declared, "Carry out my command!" [37]

As he spoke, the September 30 movement emerged from its chrysalis phase. Indonesia's night of the generals was to begin.

6

Night of the Generals

FOR THE TASK AT HAND, THE ARMED force assembled in Jakarta on the night of September 30 to decapitate the Army was formidable by any measure. The September 30 movement mustered one company from the First Honorary Guard Battalion of the Tjakrabirawa Palace Regiment; the First Infantry Brigade; the 454th Paratroop Battalion; and the 530th Paratroop Battalion. Except for the Tjakrabirawa, each unit was specially designated to partake in the capital's Armed Forces Day exercise. All were crack troops. This mixed force was supplemented by a two thousand-man Communist fifth force—"volunteers"—composed largely of Pemuda Rakjat, the recruiting ground for the PKI's street brawlers. The movement had at its disposal the country's principal air base, including access to its weapons arsenal, quartermaster supplies, motor pool, radio-telecommunications center, and its fleet of Soviet-built fighters and bombers.

Politically, the movement also enjoyed the support of the President and the country's most powerful political organization, the PKI. To this impressive list, China may be added as a source of diplomatic support for the adventure at hand.

At a briefing on the night of September 30–October 1, the purge forces were told of their mission: A CIA-inspired Council of Generals planned to overthrow Sukarno and the revolution. The generals who made up the Council were to be arrested. These traitors were to be brought back to Halim "dead or alive." [1] As a ruse to gain entry into the generals' homes, the purge forces were to tell the generals they were urgently wanted at the palace by the President. On returning to Halim, the captives were to be taken to a small plot on the outskirts of the base, Lubang Buaja—the Crocodile's Hole, a well site.

Seven generals were on the list and the force was divided into seven units. At 3:30 A.M., the trucks rolled through the gates at Halim. The September 30 movement had reached the point of no return.

At the home of the Army chief of staff, the raiders found Yani's young son awake and told him to summon his father. When Yani appeared, he was told that he was wanted at the palace. Yani was agreeable and said he would take a quick *mandi* (cold water dip). A soldier, however, motioned to him with his rifle, indicating the general leave immediately. Aghast at the soldier's effrontery, Yani slapped his face, turned, and walked back into his living room. An automatic rifle opened fire and Yani slumped to the floor. His body was dragged into a waiting vehicle.

At about the same time, a purge unit descended on the home of Major General Suprapto, the second deputy Army chief of staff, who—unlike Yani—had a reputation for incorruptibility. Like Yani, however, he was adamantly anti-PKI. As in the case of most of the generals, Suprapto's home was unguarded. Barking dogs awoke him and, attired in a T-shirt and sarong, he went to the front door. As he opened the door, he was overpowered and marched at gunpoint to a truck. His wife viewed the scene from a window. She thought he had been arrested, and tried to use the telephone. Much to her astonishment, she discovered that the wires had been cut. Suprapto had been taken without firing a shot.

Major General M. T. Harjono, the third deputy Army chief of staff, enjoyed the same reputation as Suprapto— untainted by corruption and a foe of the PKI. He was in charge of the Army's special bureau, which dealt with political affairs. The kidnappers surrounded his home and knocked on the door. Harjono intuitively whispered to his wife, "They have come to shoot me."

The armed detail announced that he was summoned to the palace. Harjono, who was unarmed and never kept a weapon at home, refused to unlock his bedroom door. The purge force shot the door open and, when Harjono sought to disarm one of them, he was knocked down and dragged into the garden. There he made another desperate attempt to either seize a weapon or elude his captors. He was shot dead on the spot for resisting arrest, and his body was dumped into a vehicle. A small son who trailed behind the action was knocked to the ground with a rifle butt.

Harjono's house was opposite that of the Sultan of Jogjakarta, who recalled that he rose early that morning to send his daughter off to Jogjakarta. "It was about 4:00 A.M. when I heard a truck and saw some strange people. I thought of robbers since we had had a robbery nearby the other day. So I went out to check the gate. I saw a number of uniformed men but it was too dark to make out their insignia. Then I heard shots and a voice cried out. Then there were screams. After six or seven minutes I heard a truck drive away and everything was quiet again."

In this manner, the Army chief of staff and three of his four deputies were either killed or abducted. The purge forces ignored his first deputy, Major General Mursjid, whose intense loyalty to Sukarno effectively neutralized him; he would present no problem to the movement in the aftermath of the affair.

Now the housecleaning at the second command level of the general staff commenced, and moved just as smoothly. Of the seven posts of assistant to the Army chief of staff, three were relatively unimportant and were filled either with apolitical officers or men who lacked political influence within the high command. A fourth, Major General Djamin Gintings, the second assistant, was touring Sumatra. A fifth, Major General Pranoto Reksosamodra, the third assistant, was destined that morning to be appointed by Sukarno to fill the post of chief of staff, left vacant by Yani's murder. This left two important figures, both of whom were in the anti-PKI faction within the general staff. Major General S. Parman, the first assistant, was the chief of Army intelligence and, interestingly, a brother of Sakirman, a member of the Politburo who participated in the PKI's purge decision. Brigadier General D. I. Pandjaitan, the fourth assistant, was outspokenly anti-Communist and was in charge of logistics.

Accustomed to being roused at odd hours and being summoned to the palace or headquarters, Parman answered the door when the kidnappers knocked and nodded approvingly when he was told the President urgently wished to see him. As Parman dressed, however, his wife had the presence of mind to ask the soldiers if they carried written orders. When they skirted the question, Parman became suspicious and he asked his wife to telephone Yani. It was too late. The abductors seized the general and, as he was being led outside, she overheard him say, "So, I have been slandered!" At that point, a policeman peddled by on a bicycle. As a precautionary measure, he, too, was bundled off to Lubang Buaja where, in the excitement, he was forgotten. Later, he led the Army to the well where the generals were buried.

Pandjaitan was the only general on the list who lived in Jakarta's satellite city of Kebajoran Baru. The purge force sealed his street, broke into his house, shot his two nephews on the first floor (one of whom died later), and demanded that the general come down from his bedroom. Pandjaitan balked and, armed with a sten gun, decided to fight it out. But when the abductors threatened to butcher his family, he relented, put on his full dress uniform, emerged from the bedroom, and descended. A scuffle developed in the courtyard and he was struck with a rifle butt. As he fell, a soldier opened fire with a submachine gun. Pandjaitan's body was thrown into a truck and whisked away to Lubang Buaja.

Wilopo, a former premier and PNI leader who is now chairman of the Supreme Advisory Council, lived down the street. He was awakened by the shooting. "I had anticipated a rough time," he said,[2] "but neither that day—nor in that manner."

The next victim was Brigadier General Sutojo Siswomihardjo, the Army inspector of justice (or attorney general) who was, in the table of command, directly responsible to the chief of staff, as was Major General Suharto, the commander of the Strategic Reserve (KOSTRAD). Sutojo was a Sukarno loyalist but he was intensely anti-PKI. In part, his job was sub rosa intelligence and he had kept Yani informed about the disposition of pro-PKI officers within the Army. Acting on this information, Yani had rotated these officers to neutralize their influence (by the same token, it can be argued, he also provided them with new opportunities for subversion).

Pretending to bear a letter from the President, the killer squad gained easy access to Sutojo's home. When the general appeared in pajamas, he was promptly overpowered and dragged off. During this brief encounter, the abductors cut his telephone and proceeded to smash his household effects, including Mrs. Sutojo's china. For her, it was an especially difficult experience. At Madiun seventeen years earlier, her first husband, also an Army officer, had been slain by the Communists. It was Sutojo's misfortune to arrive at Lubang Buaja battered, but alive.

Thus far the military operation, although sloppy, was imminently successful. Clearly, there was no operational pattern. Some generals were killed outright, others wounded, and some taken alive, unharmed. They were, to employ that vague Indonesian Army expression, "put aside"—a phrase which is open to any interpretation.

But now the plotters stumbled.

"At about 3:30 A.M. I heard shooting in our garden," Johannes Leimena, who warranted three guards as a second deputy premier, recalled.[3] His house was a door away from Nasution's usual well-guarded residence. "I peeked out the window and saw strange figures. One of them directed a rifle at me and I dove to the floor like a fish. I tried to telephone but there was no service. Then, after a few minutes, we heard more shooting, but nobody tried to enter our house."

Leimena's house had either been attacked by mistake or as a flanking maneuver to neutralize his guards, one of whom was killed.

Apparently the household of the defense minister was roused by the shooting outside and when Mrs. Nasution opened their bedroom door, she saw a soldier with a rifle in the central hall. She slammed the door, but Nasution could not believe it and reopened the door whereupon the soldier fired as Nasution ducked. Displaying remarkable coolness, Mrs. Nasution engaged in a pushing match with two soldiers on the other side of the door and succeeded in closing it. She then thrust her husband into a side room with a backdoor. The general slipped into the courtyard, scaled the wall of his neighbor, the Iraqi ambassador, slipped, fell, broke his ankle, and limped off in the darkness.

Meanwhile, the raiders ransacked his house and when Nasution's sister carried the general's five-year-old daughter outside, a soldier shot them both (the sister was lightly wounded; the child later died in a hospital). During the melee, one of the general's aides, Lieutenant Pierre Tendean, awoke, grabbed a rifle, and rushed into the garden where, apparently mistaken for Nasution, he was overpowered and rushed to Lubang Buaja.

As the tropical sun rose over the air base that morning, the vehicles returned with their prizes. The bodies of the dead generals were then mutilated and the live captives brutally maltreated. Eyes were gouged, genital organs severed. The victims were set on as if by a mob. The orgy was carried out by the fifth force in which members of Gerwani, the Communist woman's front, took part.

Later, a team of five medical doctors—two of them from the armed services and three from the staff of the University of Indonesia—prepared a coroner's report.[4]

The medical examination showed that Yani's body was riddled with fourteen different bullet wounds; that Harjono was felled by bayonet thrusts and rifle butt blows; and that Pandjaitan's body had five bullet wounds and a bayonet thrust. These three were believed to have either died at home or en route to Lubang Buaja.

As for those who had been seized alive, General Suprapto's body bore thirty wounds, including broken bones, bullet wounds, and knife thrusts; Parman's jaw and legs were broken and his body punctured by five bullet holes; Sutojo's body bore wounds which were made by a blunt object in addition to five bullet wounds; and Tendean's head had been split open.

The bodies were dumped into the Crocodile's Hole and covered with refuse and leaves. It was only on October 3 that the well was discovered and not until the following day that the bodies were brought to the surface by a team of frogmen from the Marines (KKO).

As the murder and mayhem unfolded early that morning, additional armed units in the September 30 movement seized Jakarta's radio station, telephone exchange, and other vital installations. They also took up positions in the large *padang* or square in the center of the capital, which is rimmed by the presidential palace, the defense ministry, KOSTRAD headquarters, and other strategic buildings.

With the radio station under their control, the September 30 movement began to broadcast a series of pronouncements and decrees. The action was portrayed solely as "an internal affair of the Army." [5] This was of such thin veneer that it wore through in the initial broadcast. Indeed, as the day lengthened, it was clear that the movement intended to carry out not only a purge of the general staff, but a wholesale purge of "counterrevolutionary elements" throughout the country, down to the village level. If the events at Lubang Buaja were a harbinger of what was to come, Indonesia was destined to undergo a bloodbath of unprecedented dimensions in Indonesian political history.

The movement's first broadcast at 7:20 A.M. over Radio Jakarta announced that "a number of generals have been arrested and important communications media and other vital installations have been placed under the control of the September 30 movement." [6] It said, "President Sukarno is safe under (our) protection." The generals, the radio said, were members of a Council of Generals, which was "sponsored by the CIA and has been very active lately, especially since President Sukarno was seriously ill in the first week of August." The Council hoped Sukarno would die, but when he did not they "planned to carry out a counterrevolutionary coup prior to October 5, 1965." Accordingly, the September 30 movement acted to prevent the coup and "to protect the President and the Republic of Indonesia."

The statement said the action in Jakarta was only a forerunner of "actions throughout Indonesia against agents and sympathizers of the Council of Generals in the regions." To this end, it announced the formation of an Indonesian Revolutionary Council backed in the regions by provincial, district, subdistrict, and village revolutionary councils.[7] The announcement also tipped its hand by declaring that the Revolutionary Council "will not change Indonesia's foreign policy." that is, the Jakarta-Peking Axis. As for the action that morning, the announcement declared that the move against the generals had been "a great success."

At 2:00 P.M. the Revolutionary Council issued Decree No. 1. The decree described the day's work as "a purge," reported again that "a number of generals have been arrested" —giving the false impression that they were simply in custody —and restated the earlier claim that the movement was "confined entirely within the Army." The decree also provided details of the plan to establish revolutionary councils down to the village level composed of "civilian and military personnel who unreservedly support the September 30 Movement." Then it added another political twist: "With the fall of the entire authority of the state into the hands of the Indonesian Revolutionary Council, the Dwikora (Sukarno) Cabinet automatically assumes a decommissioned status." In effect, the cabinet would remain in suspended animation, pending the formation of a new government.

About five minutes later, the movement broadcast Decision No. 1, the composition of a forty-five-member Revolutionary Council. In addition to the senior officers who handled the military operation (Untung, Supardjo, and so on), the Council embraced a politically incoherent hodgepodge of civilian and military personalities. Most of them, however, were either pro-Sukarno and/or pro-PKI. Two prominent names were missing: Sukarno's and Aidit's. They, presumably, were to be swept along by the tide of events.

Then came Decision No. 2, which bore the marks of Untung's personal touch. It stated that "all ranks and equivalent grades in the Armed Forces of the Republic of Indonesia above that of Lieutenant Colonel are herewith declared invalid." Thus Untung's rank, lieutenant colonel, became the highest rank. "It is a measure of the man's pettiness that one of the first things that entered his mind was the question of rank," the Singapore *Straits Times* later cuttingly observed.[8]

It was also a fair indication, if any was required, that Untung was not the architect of the purge. The initiators of the plot had more important questions on their minds.

At 3:30 P.M., the radio broadcast the first support for the movement. It quoted an order of the day issued by Air Vice Marshal Dhani at Halim that morning in which he held that the purpose of the purge was "to secure and safeguard the Revolution and the Great Leader of the Revolution against CIA subversion." He said that the Army has "purged those elements who are manipulated by foreign subversives and who endanger the Indonesian Revolution," and he added that the Air Force, as an instrument of the revolution, "will always and continuously support and uphold any progressive revolutionary movement." He also ordered the Air Force to "prepare for all eventualities."

This was to be the last statement issued by the movement over the radio since it would soon lose control of the transmitter. However, that afternoon, *Harian Rakjat,* the official Communist daily, went to bed with an editorial which appeared on Jakarta's streets the following morning, October 2, expressing "sympathy and support" for the purge.[9] The editorial signed the Communist Party's death warrant.

The Communist organ described the September 30 movement's actions as "patriotic and revolutionary." It condemned the Council of Generals and accused it of plotting a "counterrevolutionary" coup. It set the official PKI line: The event was "an internal Army affair." Presuming to speak for "we, the people," *Harian Rakjat* characterized the elimination of the general staff as "correct." The paper had cast the PKI's support behind the murders.

Significantly, the issue also contained a cartoon in support of the putsch, and an analysis of Anwar Sanusi, the deputy head of the PKI and alternate member of the Politburo. Blending candor with self-confidence, Sanusi described Indonesia's political situation as being in an "advanced stage of pregnancy." He said, "The midwife is ready with her instruments to safeguard the long-awaited (birth of the) new baby." Within the context of the editorial and cartoon, Sanusi's meaning was plain.

Elsewhere in Indonesia, the PKI's regional branches cast their support behind the movement. At Surabaya, the capital of East Java, for example, the Pemuda Rakjat regional branch proclaimed that "in the name of 750,000 members of the Pemuda Rakjat for all of East Java, we declare our full support for, and stand behind, the September 30 movement." And so it went.

The commentary of various personalities on hearing Untung's initial announcement provides an interesting historical footnote and reflects the temper of the hour. At Madiun, for example, former Foreign Minister Anak Agung Gde Agung and his co-political prisoners, were heartened by Untung's announcement. "After learning that something had happened in Jakarta, our first impression was, 'This is good,'" Anak Agung said." [10] "But later, when we read the names of those appointed to the Revolutionary Council, we sensed that something was very wrong. It began to look like a united front with Aidit behind it."

On the campus of the University of Indonesia, Arif Budiman, who later emerged as one of the leaders of the student revolt against the Sukarno regime, felt similarly.[11] "I thought, as did many of the students, that any change was welcome." And when Untung's initial announcement came over the radio, Hatta is said to have surmised that the PKI was involved. He amended his view later when he heard the names on the Revolutionary Council and concluded: "Sukarno instigated the whole affair." [12] The Untung broadcasts also reminded many of the former outlawed Socialist Party leaders such as Hamid Alegadrie, Zainul Abidin, Idham, and others of Sukarno's role in the kidnapping of Sjahrir in 1946.

As for the diplomatic community, it was in turmoil.[13] "We had been out in the cold so long by then that we were almost frozen stiff," a senior American official said. "Nobody knew anything." And a Commonwealth diplomat confessed, "We rushed to the American Embassy to find out what was happening only to discover that they, in turn, had sent out their people to find out what was happening."

Abroad, an Indonesian professor, teaching in Australia, promptly commented after the first Untung announcement,

"Sukarno's finished." In Peking, Chairul Saleh felt differently. His name was not on the list, but Subandrio's was, and he concluded: "This is the work of Subandrio—either he goes down or I go down." [14] As it developed, both went down.

In Singapore, the defense minister of the two-month-old island Republic, Goh Keng Swee, remarked, "My first thought: what a horrible thing can happen to us." [15] To many other Asians, too, the subsequent discovery that the generals were slaughtered in one fell swoop was reminiscent of the wholesale murder of General Aung San and the Burmese cabinet in January, 1948, shortly after Burma acquired independence—and just twenty years later to the month, the Korean Communist attempt to liquidate President Pak Chung Hee and members of the South Korean cabinet, a development which was generally forgotten in the West—and Asia—in the aftermath of the Pueblo Incident.

But, on the morning of October 1 in Jakarta, as the sun rose higher, the question which increasingly came to the fore and soon dominated Indonesian politics was: Where is Sukarno?

7

Sukarno Miscalculates

MISCALCULATIONS, MISJUDGMENTS, and errors of chance began to take their collective toll of the September 30 Movement. Aidit had erred in committing a fifth force to the operation, the direct link between the Communists and the purge of the general staff. By chance, Nasution had slipped his assassins. Now it was Sukarno's turn to falter. Instead of establishing himself at the palace on the morning of October 1, from where he could exercise a semblance of control, Sukarno voluntarily proceeded to Halim. He originally intended to go to the palace. His decision to go to Halim may have reflected momentary panic. Whatever the case, the decision proved politically fatal.

Until the Army and the general public learned the President's whereabouts, his safety was a paramount concern. Some thought he had been kidnapped, possibly slain; others, that he was a prisoner at the palace; and still others that perhaps "it is the game of Sukarno to work with the PKI and let stupid people do the job," as one senior Army officer privately said he thought that morning. Sukarno's adversaries were more charitable. "My first thought was that Sukarno had been taken by the PKI to be used by them as a tool," the then jailed Natsir said, sarcastically adding, "In many ways he had long been a captive President." [1]

When it developed, however, that Sukarno was at the nerve center of the conspiracy and that he had gone to Gestapu headquarters "at my own will," the nation was thunderstruck.[2] Suddenly, in a blinding flash of light, the Emperor stood without clothes. Sukarno's mastery of Indonesia ended at this moment on this inglorious note.

A premier resident journalist in Indonesia, O. G. Roeder, the correspondent for the Düsseldorf *Handelsblatt* and other periodicals, is convinced that this is where Sukarno committed an irreparable error, although Sukarno later sought to paper over his presence at Halim as "the best place for me" in the event that he required a plane "if something which is not expected takes place." [3] Later, he also claimed the decision to go to Halim was made by his bodyguard, elements of the Tjakrabirawa, who reported that the palace was surrounded. [4] "If Sukarno had gone to the palace he would have been in a position to side with either Untung or Suharto or play one against the other," Roeder said. [5] "Instead, he went to Halim, the camp of one side in the conflict." Roeder, incidentally, believes that Sukarno had begun to lose his charm as early as 1963 when "he began to grow fat and piggish, and began to overplay his role like an overaged actor." By 1965, he is convinced, the famed Sukarno charisma had waned appreciably. If this assessment is fair, it may have provided Aidit with another incentive to make his move when he did—before Dorian Gray became unrecognizable. [6]

After his appearance at Senajan on the night of September 30, Sukarno drove to the palace and from there to the Hotel Indonesia, where, by surprise and in an agitated state, he picked up Dewi, one of his wives, a young Japanese, who was attending a diplomatic party. They arrived at Dewi's richly appointed residence, which was enclosed by a wall, shortly after midnight. Significantly, perhaps, Dewi's house was located along the main road linking Jakarta with Halim. Did Sukarno confer at her house with any courier or member of the conspiracy who was en route to Halim that early morning? We do not know—yet. Dewi, given to half truths, claimed that "the bloody attack started while we were still sound asleep." [7]

At 6:00 A.M., his customary hour, the President rose and promptly received information of the kidnappings and shootings of two hours earlier. The report of shooting may have disturbed him. Again, we do not know. During the next three hours, before opting to go to Halim, he received a steady flow of detailed situation reports by courier and radio-telephone.

In this manner, Sukarno learned that Nasution had escaped and that Yani had been murdered. Intuitively, he probably felt that the plan had been botched. In an anxious state, he left Dewi and drove to the home of another wife, Harijati, and from there proceeded to the palace. En route, however, on the receipt of additional information, he abruptly changed direction and headed for Halim, the headquarters of the September 30 movement.[8] He had been expected at the palace. General Supardjo, for example, was waiting there to give him a first-hand account.[9] When Sukarno inexplicably went to Halim, the Air Force provided Supardjo with a helicopter and flew him there, too.[10]

Why did Sukarno go to Halim? Did he fear that the troops guarding the palace were unfriendly? Did the Untung pronouncement indicate a possible coup? Did he fear that he was on the purge list? This is doubtful since the success of the movement depended on a presidential endorsement—and all concerned knew it, the Communist leadership, the "progressive, revolutionary" officers, and Sukarno himself. Or did Sukarno, like Macbeth, have a vision of the bloodied generals waiting for him on the palace steps? It is doubtful if we shall every truly know because it is unlikely that Sukarno can ever tell the story without compromising himself. He has another reason for maintaining his silence: he still dreams of returning to power.

At Halim, Sukarno joined Aidit, Sjam, Supardjo, Dhani, Untung, and other figures in the conspiracy. After additional reports from those present, the President offhandedly remarked that such "incidents" are natural in a revolution. Then, for the first time, he openly displayed uncertainty about the outcome of the affair by suggesting that "the escape of General Nasution would have effects and consequences." [11] Sukarno, according to Dhani, also patted Supardjo approvingly on the back and said, "Good. Very good. . . . Now . . . I do not want any more bloodshed." Supardjo, however, put the gesture in a different light and said that when the President slapped his back it was because he had promised to prevent further bloodshed, an indication that he, not Untung, was in overall military command. "Mind you," Supardjo said

Sukarno jokingly added, "if you cannot stop the movement, I will kill you." Untung, incidentally, was dismissed lightly at Halim as a bit player, which he was.

In the accounts of what transpired at Halim that morning, there is no evidence that Sukarno ever expressed anger or remorse over the fate of his generals. Nor did he issue an order for the arrest of those who had participated in the kidnappings and murders.[12]

Nasution's escape clearly troubled him. Indeed, it may well have been the single most fatal flaw in the plot which, as an Australian commentator put it, "came within a hairsbreadth of success."[13] Sukarno must have realized that Nasution could muster the support of the remaining generals. Moreover, the murders must have also troubled him. Why the murders? Did the affair simply develop an irresistible momentum as it progressed? Or was the killing a maneuver on the part of the PKI and the "progressive, revolutionary" officers to compromise him? Whatever the case, Sukarno moved to extract himself from the situation, at the expense of his erstwhile allies, if necessary. It was characteristic of him. In the thirties, he had betrayed the nationalist movement to the Dutch and was rewarded with exile to Flores instead of to inhospitable West Irian, like Sjahrir and Hatta. He collaborated with the Japanese with a certain amount of relish. After the Japanese surrendered in 1945, he had to be kidnapped by a band of youths, including Aidit and Adam Malik, and pressed to proclaim Indonesia's independence; he had wavered for fear of being branded a Japanese war criminal by the Allies. In 1948, after declaring that "if the Dutch attack us, I will lead a total guerrilla war against them," he flew the white flag and voluntarily surrendered to them. In the fifties, he promised rebel leaders, like Andi Aziz of South Sulawesi, safe-conduct passes and negotiations and had them arrested on their arrival in Jakarta. As Sukarno once put it, "Cold, cold power is all I care about."[14]

Sukarno was determined to survive on October 1. He stopped midstream and did not issue any statement in support of the movement, although the conspirators had control of the radio network for the whole day. Aidit must have sensed that the plan had misfired somewhere and Sjam protested that Sukarno's issuance of a standfast order to Supardjo's forces was not in conformity with the plot.[15]

Without Sukarno, however, Aidit could not order the Communist rank and file into the streets, so fragile, undependable, and unreliable was the party's mass base, or, to phrase it more accurately, so closely identified with Sukarno was the PKI membership. Aidit had mobilized a mass movement by defining communism as a form of excessive nationalism and by identifying himself with Sukarno, the epitome of narrow nationalism. The PKI had built a mass-based party through Sukarno and, in the process, lost control over that base to him. A question which will be endlessly debated is whether, by the late sixties, the PKI was Sukarno's captive or whether it was the other way around. The point is rather academic, however: The political reality was that they worked together harmoniously to their mutual advantage.

From Aidit's standpoint, a unilateral outpouring of the PKI rank-and-file masses in support of the purge of the CIA generals, as planned, would isolate the PKI from Sukarno, unify the Army under the elusive Nasution, and bring about the delayed showdown between the Army and the PKI which Aidit had hoped to circumvent by the pre-emptive strike against the general staff.

In sum, the plan had gone to pieces.

When the conspirators at Halim learned that the Army was regrouping under the command of General Suharto, the KOSTRAD commander, who was threatening to attack the air base, they abandoned the field. Untung, Supardjo, and Sjam slipped off in various disguises. Aidit commandeered an Air Force plane and flew to Jogjakarta after failing to induce Sukarno to join him. Sukarno, at the urging of Leimena, who had been summoned to Halim by the President, departed by road for Bogor, a hill station south of Jakarta.[16] The principals in the affair departed and left behind the bodies of the generals and abandoned the military units and Communist volunteers who had carried out the murders.

Sukarno's retreat sounded the collapse of the conspiracy since its ultimate success was wholly contingent on his open support. Sjam, for example, later conceded as much. "If the movement meets with success," he told Untung as early as September 9 in the presence of Colonel Latief, another principal in the plot, "the President will surely agree to it." [17] In any event, during the drive between Halim and Bogor, Sukarno apparently decided to downplay the affair as a *"small incident"* and to dissociate himself from the movement.[18]

In his first public statement following the demise of the plot, Sukarno issued an order of the day in which he reported himself "safe and well," announced that he had temporarily assumed the command of the armed forces, and assigned General Pranoto "to carry out day-to-day tasks within the Army." Then he called on the armed forces to stand fast and "move only on orders." [19] The standfast was a clever stratagem. By this maneuver, he hoped to freeze the situation and terminate what was then beginning to develop into Suharto's counterattack, a thrust which he probably felt was directed behind the scenes by Nasution. A standfast offered Sukarno, and the Communists, the only possible chance of surviving the crisis intact and of possibly still salvaging their plan. There is circumstantial evidence, cited in the following chapter, to suggest that the President and Aidit jointly developed the strategy before their flight from Halim.

By the time Sukarno broadcast directly to the nation, at 1:33 A.M., October 3, the radio was in Suharto's hands and the September 30 movement had dissipated. In this broadcast, Sukarno called for the "creation of a calm and orderly atmosphere," but he revealed that he was already bowing to Suharto's pressure. Sukarno announced that the Army would now be ruled by a triumvirate, not the Sukarno-Pranoto diumvirate he had authorized earlier. The trio would comprise himself, with the "leadership of the Army directly in my hands"; Pranoto, who would "discharge the day-to-day tasks within the Army"; and the new addition—Suharto, who would "carry out the restoration of security and order." [20] This was also a clever stratagem since it provided Sukarno with room for maneuver, playing Pranoto and Suharto against each other—assuming, of course, that Suharto was prepared to play the old Sukarno game. Which he was not.

The acknowledgment that de facto operational control of the Army would be exercised by Suharto changed the complexion of the whole situation. "We waited for Sukarno to speak; it was like a second Madiun," Ali Budiardjo, the former secretary general of the Defense Ministry, recalled.[21] "First he referred to Pranoto's appointment and we all thought: Sukarno has won after all. But then he named Suharto as the operational commander and we all thought: Now we've won!" This was the universal reaction of virtually all the opponents of Sukarno and the PKI—the intellectuals, the students, and the members of the outlawed Masjumi and Socialist parties.

It was not until October 8 that Sukarno finally condemned "the atrocious murder of the Army officers" and said he "did not justify the formation of the Revolutionary Council." Nevertheless, he sought to camouflage his role and that of the PKI by equating the purged with the purgers. He said he would take measures against "all sides" and would search for "a political solution." We should not let ourselves be driven by our emotions lest the revolution is jeopardized, he warned.

As he spoke, the tensions of the Sukarno-PKI era exploded and there was an unprecedented mass outpouring against the Communists. During the first week of October, the PKI headquarters in Jakarta was burned, the homes of Aidit and other Politburo members were ransacked, *Harian Rakjat's* offices were smashed, and demands were raised for the dissolution of the PKI and its front organizations. Soon Sukarno found himself engulfed by demands for his impeachment. The whole flimsy structure of "guided democracy" was buckling.

Sukarno was determined to ride the crest of the public outburst. Although he conceded that the September 30 movement was a "condemnable affair which has seriously harmed our revolution,"[22] he made it patently clear on October 16 that he planned to close his eyes to the purge. "Frankly speaking," he said, "what has happened in our revolution . . . is merely, to say it in Dutch, *een rimpel in een geweldige oceaan* (a ripple in a vast ocean)." And he added that the "key to our future does not depend on *small incidents*." Indeed, several days earlier, he had the audacity to assert, "We must regard events like those of last Friday as training in our revolution."

Although Sukarno was prepared to debunk the transparent Communist line that it was an "internal affair of the Army," he was circumspect in involving the PKI other than to concede that in addition to the involvement of the Army, Air Force, and Tjakrabirawa, "something [also] happened in our political life." [23] Shortly thereafter, with the country in the throes of a massive purge of the PKI, in which thousands of Communists were slain, Sukarno insisted that communism must retain an integral role in Indonesian life. He claimed, too, that the PKI made greater sacrifices in the struggle for Indonesian independence than any other group.[24] He admitted, however, that the Communists did commit "excesses" (Madiun? September 30?) and said such "excesses" must be removed. Later, with the incontrovertible evidence of the PKI's involvement in the affair in the public domain, Sukarno held that three currents were responsible for the September 30 affair; namely, the stupidity of the PKI's Politburo, the cunning of the neocolims, and "the fact, indeed, that there were persons who were irrational." [25] He has never elaborated on the last remark.

The reason for Sukarno's deep desire to protect the PKI was obvious. Without the Communists at his side, he and his regime would be prisoners of the Army.

The President's steadfast refusal to outlaw the PKI focused increasing attention on his own role in the affair. A student working party from the University of Indonesia, for example, framed a series of questions and demanded answers: Why did he leave for Halim? Why was Pranoto appointed "caretaker" when the fate of Yani was still unknown? Why did he order all forces confined to their barracks when Suharto was counterattacking? Why did he remain silent for two days while the fate of Yani was still in doubt? Why did he pat Supardjo on the back? Why did he fail to denounce the Gestapu-PKI? Why did he hesitate to give an account of his responsibility in the affair? [26]

Evidence that Sukarno was implicated in the affair, or at least that the Army thought so, continued to grow in the months thereafter. On January 23, 1967, for example, twelve days after the capture of Supardjo, the Armed Forces Information Center officially disclosed that Sukarno maintained "a direct relationship" with Supardjo and other prominent figures in the conspiracy. Nasution also raised questions publicly about Sukarno's behavior. Sukarno's appointment of Pranoto, he said, had been made with the consent of Aidit.[27] And he asked: Why did Sukarno go to Halim instead of KOSTRAD headquarters? Why didn't he appoint Suharto "caretaker" of the Army in accordance with the Army's standing order. Why did he order the Army to "move only on order," which meant forestalling Suharto's counteroperations? [28] And Lieutenant General M. Panggabean, whom Suharto later appointed Army chief of staff, observed: "Time and again General Suharto has asked the President to take a firm stand against Gestapu–PKI. But until this moment the President has not. . . . Why?" [29]

The burgeoning student-teacher movement, composed of KASI, KAPPI, and KAMI, demanded that Sukarno be placed on trial.[30] The Indonesian Supreme Court, in a 120-page decision, also demanded that he be tried for treason, and for the misappropriation of state funds.[31] The court held that Sukarno has an obligation "to account for everything he knows." Sukarno's own opportunistic, rubber-stamping parliament joined the parade, turned against him, and demanded his trial before a special tribunal.[32]

For his part, Sukarno adamantly denied any complicity in the purge. He claimed it was a "complete surprise" and denied possessing foreknowledge of the affair. Cindy Adams, who wrote a favorable, if not distorted, official biography of him when he was in power and an unfavorable account of him and Indonesia after he was dismissed from power, put the issue directly to him during a television interview. "One question that remains unanswered, Mr. President, is did you know about the attempted coup of September 30 in advance?" she asked.[33] Sukarno, with a feigned surprise in the best traditions of the theatre, replied, "Hmmmm?" When she repeated the question, he said, "No. No. And why should you put this question to me? . . . I did not know, not before."

Yet Suharto and the new general staff have incontrovertible evidence that Sukarno was implicated. "There is no evidence that Sukarno wanted them killed," confided one general. "But we possess evidence that he was involved." Later, General Sutopo Juwono, the Army's new intelligence chief, categorically declared on the record that the government had evidence of Sukarno's role and that it was "impossible to dissociate him" from the purge of the general staff.[34] This "incontrovertible proof" has been known abroad as early as October 13, 1965, yet it has never been made public.[35] Why? Some prominent Indonesians, such as Mashuri, a member of the Indonesian Lawyer's Association and a minister in Suharto's cabinet, has accused "some groups of trying to cover up" Sukarno's complicity.[36] Why the cover-up? Why doesn't Jakarta disclose the evidence? Why isn't Sukarno brought to trial? Why was Sukarno's involvement gingerly skirted at the trials of some of the conspirators and others, causing one observer to describe the cover-up effort as "ludicrous," although the public trials were really trials of his very own regime.[37]

The answers are not difficult to fathom. For almost twenty years, Sukarno played the role of "father" of his country. He was the "infallible Great Leader of the Revolution." Many of the generals in power today—if not all—bore him unquestioned allegiance in the past. Like the leaders of the existing political parties, notably the PNI and NU, they are largely responsible for the spiritual, political, and economic decline which marked the Sukarno era. It is difficult, of course, to wipe out the past when you happen to have been a part of it. Whether these men inwardly approved or disapproved of Sukarno's policies is immaterial. They stood with the crowd and applauded his every move and utterance. Neither Suharto nor any other Indonesian leader wishes to assume the responsibility for destroying Sukarno. Future historians will never be able to say that the generals stabbed him in the back. And perhaps this is a good thing. As Prawoto Mangkusasmito, the former Masjumi leader, observed, "Sukarno's involvement has been brought out by the trials—even though they only give an outline, not the full picture."[38] The most damaging testimony concerned Sukarno's voluntary presence at Halim and his pat on Supardjo's back. In this connection, it is significant to note that Dhani fled abroad after the coup, but that he voluntarily returned to stand trial. Like all the principals placed in the dock, Dhani was found guilty and sentenced to death. Unlike most of them, he is still alive. And prepared to talk publicly.

Four days before Sukarno's formal dismissal from the presidency on March 11, 1967, Suharto delivered a lengthy report on the role of Sukarno in the September 30 affair which has gone a long way to answer the question of why he is not placed in the dock. Since then, Sukarno has become an "unperson."

The Suharto report was worthy of a Mark Antony; for Sukarno was an honorable man. Suharto did not indict Sukarno, although he could have easily done so. As Arthur Koestler once said, "People don't mind if you betray humanity, but if you betray your club, you are considered a renegade." Suharto's position on Sukarno is contained in a single, simple, and straightforward sentence. "Do not let the present generation be blamed by the coming generation," he told parliament,[39] "for the improper treatment of the patriotic leader of the people." As a result, Sukarno has even been robbed of martyrdom.

In this fashion, then, the Sukarno era in the history of Southeast Asia closed. We have dealt at length with Sukarno's role because his very involvement in the affair confirms the involvement of the PKI. In the atmosphere of the period, Sukarno would not undertake the removal of the general staff without the knowledge of his most powerful political ally, Aidit. For that matter, so dependent was one on the other, Aidit would not have become involved without Sukarno's approval. This explains Aidit's farewell statement that "if you shoot me, you must also shoot the President." [40]

8

Gestapu or Gestok?

WE MUST DIGRESS BRIEFLY IN STILL another direction before gathering up the threads of the Communist denouement in Indonesia.

As observed earlier, one of the demands made on Sukarno was that he explain his preference for the term Gestok to the popular and propagandistic Gestapu, with its obvious connotation in the literate world to Hitler's terror organization, the Gestapo.[1] Sukarno labored to popularize Gestok as the name for the affair. In a speech before a group of naval officers, for example, he asserted, "I condemn Gestok, which is but a ripple in the ocean of the Indonesian revolution." And he appealed to his audience "for understanding" and proposed that the Navy and other services join him in denouncing Gestok. Clearly, he equated Gestok with Gestapu.

One possible reason why Sukarno may have sought to replace the acronym Gestapu was to remove the odious comparison between Nazi and Communist terror. But this was hardly as important as to create the impression of coup (Gestapu) and countercoup (Gestok), with himself the innocent bystander. Thus, Sukarno glibly argued that since the affair occurred on October 1 it should rightly be known as the October 1 movement (*Gerakan Satu Oktober*—Gestok). Technically, he was correct except that, as Untung revealed in his first pronouncement, the conspiracy had self-styled itself the September 30 movement.

Sukarno's great hope was that Gestapu would refer to the kidnapping and murder of the generals, a "small incident." Gestok, from his viewpoint, would refer to the Army's, specifically Suharto's, seizure of power on October 1—the countercoup.

The distinction between Gestapu and Gestok is important in historical terms since a future PKI may conceivably resurrect the term as a counterweight or equation to Gestapu. Accordingly, it is necessary to explore the question of whether or not the Army and/or Suharto seized power on October 1, as the term Gestok implies.

For Suharto, the day started at around 5:30 A.M. when a neighbor who served on his staff informed him that there had been some kidnappings and shootings. Thereafter, he received reports from others, including Army colleagues. "None of them, in giving their reports, had any idea of what, at that moment, was the fate of the kidnapped generals," he said.[2] On the basis of the sketchy information at hand, however, he concluded that "the Army leadership could be said to be paralyzed."

In terms of seniority, Suharto was the officer next in line after Yani. Although, at first glance, it would seem normal that Yani's first deputy (Mursjid) should have assumed temporary command of the Army in his absence, Yani had long ago issued a standing order that in the event of his inavailability, Suharto should assume temporary command of the Army. This Suharto did whenever Yani went abroad. Yani may have selected Suharto because of his seniority or out of respect since Suharto formerly had been his commanding officer. Yani may have also named him because of his wide experience. Like Yani, who came into prominence as the field commander against the anti-Sukarno–PKI rebels in 1958, Suharto was a seasoned field officer.

Born at Kemusu, Jogjakarta, Central Java, on June 8, 1921,* Suharto served in the Netherlands East Indies Army (KNIL), the wartime Japanese-sponsored Army (PETA), and held various commands during the Indonesian war of independence. It was he, for example, who led the spectacular attack on Dutch-occupied Jogjakarta in 1949. A year later, he suppressed the South Sulawesi (Celebes) insurrection and in 1962, after holding various posts on Java, he was appointed

---

* Sukarno's birthdate is June 6, 1901. Both, therefore, were born under the sign of Gemini.

commander-in-chief of the Theatre for the Liberation of West
Irian.

During this period, he fell from Sukarno's grace. Sukarno
was angered when Suharto bluntly told him that the Army
was unprepared for a major assault against the Dutch in Irian
"even for propaganda reasons." [3] After the Irian triumph,
which Sukarno engineered diplomatically, Suharto was
"kicked upstairs" and shunted to the command of the strategic
reserve, KOSTRAD. An Army analysis, prepared in 1964, described KOSTRAD's units as "providing a manifold striking
element against any enemy which tries to disrupt the security
and well-being of the Indonesian state and nation." [4] KO-
STRAD boasted of its mobility and declared itself capable of
"moving anywhere in a relatively short time." [5]

Suharto then, as now, in the best Javanese tradition, was
modest, perceptive, and unassuming. He lived unostenta-
tiously with his wife and family—in sharp contrast to the more
polished Yani who had two wives and enjoyed the glitter of
Jakarta's bright lights. By 1965, Suharto was deep in the background. He spent much of the time either fishing (he is an
ardent salt-water sport fisherman) or playing golf.

Suharto arrived at KOSTRAD shortly before 7:00 A.M. on
October 1 and discovered that "among all of my staff officers,
there was not one who knew anything about the affair." [6]
Then he was stunned to learn that the President was not at
the palace and that Supardjo had been seen there. Supardjo's
presence in the capital troubled him especially since the General was the commander of the Fourth Combat Command of
KOSTRAD and should have been at his post in western
Borneo (Kalimantan) within the framework of the confrontation against Malaysia.

At this critical moment, Suharto decided to assume command of the Army. "When I learned the names of my kidnapped colleagues, including that of General Yani," he said
later,[7] "I realized that the Army was in danger and I decided
to assume the leadership of the Army.

"I acted with a sense of responsibility in accordance with
a standing order, what you would call, SOP [standard operational procedure]," he continued. "When the Army com-

mander was not present, I was the acting commander."

In their military planning, the September 30 forces seized Jakarta's telecommunications center, but did not interfere with the Army's internal communications system. Through this system, and the use of couriers, Suharto conveyed his decision first to General Umar Wirahadikusumo, the commander of the Jakarta garrison, who would be named that afternoon to Untung's Revolutionary Council without his knowledge, and whichever senior officers he could contact in the Army, Navy, and police. He met "difficulty" only in establishing contact with the Air Force.

The rest is history.

After a brief skirmish, the radio station and other Gestapu-occupied installations were swiftly retaken. The commanders of the dissident paratroop battalions holding the main square to protect Sukarno and the Republic were informed of the true situation whereupon they withdrew without firing a shot. Suharto in late afternoon dispatched a courier to Halim to inform those at the air base that it would be attacked, the report which sent Sukarno, Aidit, Untung, and the others scurrying in different directions. The air base was easily reoccupied. All told, these military operations did not claim more than fourteen killed. The Gestapu collapsed as speedily as the Communist-led insurrection in 1926 and the Communist coup d'état in 1948.

That evening, Suharto and Nasution were reunited and, in an emotional scene, embraced each other. Suharto promptly offered command of the Army to Nasution, but the latter declined to accept it. Nasution was injured, depressed by the events which had occurred at his home that morning. He also doubtless felt that if he assumed command of the Army it would confirm the Untung-PKI thesis that he plotted an Army seizure of power through a CIA Council of Generals.

A recital of these developments raises an inevitable question: Why did the September 30 movement fail to place Suharto's name on the purge list? His home was unguarded. He could have been abducted effortlessly.

They did put him under surveillance. Doubtless, they discussed his removal, too, but apparently considered him pliable, capable of being handled by the President, outside the "inner circle" of the general staff and effectively neutralized by a tragedy within his family.

"Two days before September 30," Suharto recalled,[8] "our three year old son had an accident at home. He poured hot soup on himself and we had to rush him to the hospital. Many friends visited my son there and on the night of September 30 I was there, too. It is interesting to look back. I remember Colonel Latief dropped into the hospital that evening to inquire about my son's health. I was touched by his thoughtfulness. Of course, later Latief turned out to be an important figure in the events that followed.[9] Today I realize that he did not go to the hospital that evening to check on my son but, rather, to check on me. He must have verified the genuine seriousness of my son's accident and confirmed my preoccupation with his condition. I remained at the hospital until about midnight and then returned home." Another factor which may have spared Suharto's life was sentimentalism, another Indonesian political characteristic. Untung had served under Suharto and the previous April Suharto had attended Untung's wedding.[10]

While Suharto was taking command of the Army and organizing a counterattack, Sukarno was at Halim. There the President decided to assume command of the Army; appointed Pranoto, in effect, acting chief of staff; and called on the armed forces to stand fast. Sukarno's apppointment of Pranoto was a major blunder, for it constituted another challenge to the Army leadership. The President knew of Yani's standing order—as did everyone else. One of the most intriguing aspects of the Gestapu affair is that Untung was present at Halim when Sukarno announced the appointment of Pranoto and that the President clearly did not believe there had been a coup d'état. Certainly there was no coup in the generally accepted sense of the word.[11] Sukarno himself claimed that he was "continuously carrying out the leadership of the state" throughout his stay at Halim. Thus, when Suharto rejected Sukarno's order to come to Halim—Leimena, Navy chief of staff Admiral Martadinata, and others obeyed similar orders— Supardjo considered Suharto's behavior an "act of disobedience." [12] When Suharto announced that he would assault Halim, Supardjo, in obvious military command of the Gestapu forces, ordered Dhani to use the Air Force to blunt the Suharto attack. But Dhani, like Sukarno, realized the game was over and refused to do so. In his defense, the air marshal pointed to the President's cease-fire and standfast order. Sukarno had painted Supardjo into a corner; he certainly could not exclude the Air Force from his order of the day to the armed forces.

Viewed from Sukarno's perspective, Suharto's behavior on October 1, in defiance of the President, constituted insubordination, if not a coup. His term Gestok, therefore, would appear to have some validity. Interestingly, in this connection, in the world at large the events surrounding September 30–October 1 in Indonesia are often thought of as simply a coup and countercoup. But this ignores the established history of the Indonesian Army which has found itself before in situations where the chief of state has been behind the enemy lines.

"You must consider the traditions of the Indonesian Army," Lieutenant General Simatupang, the former chairman of the joint chiefs of staff, explained.[13] "At a time when the President is in enemy hands, for example when he surrendered to the Dutch in 1948, his orders no longer have authority. From Suharto's point of view, Sukarno was in the hands of the enemy—in the area controlled by Untung's forces. Therefore, his orders had no validity. From Sukarno's standpoint, Yani was not exercising his command so it was Sukarno's duty to appoint a new Army commander. Of course, in terms of power politics, Sukarno favored the rebels by naming Pranoto. From Suharto's position, this was an act of treason on Sukarno's part."

Suharto's first speech on the night of October 1 pointedly noted that Sukarno had been in the hands of the enemy, the self-styled September 30 movement. Therefore, Suharto said, it was "necessary" for him to report to the nation that the President was now "in safe and sound condition" and that "for the time being the leadership of the Army is in our hands." He said the Army, Navy, and police had arrived at a common understanding aimed at "liquidating" the September 30 movement. He omitted any mention of the Air Force. As for the movement, Suharto said, "they had taken over the state authority, which is usually called a coup, from the hands of His Excellency the President, Supreme Commander of the Republic of Indonesia," declared the cabinet demissionary, and "kidnapped a number of high-ranking Army officers." These acts, he continued, are "clearly counterrevolutionary and must be erased to the end." On October 2, Suharto announced to the nation that "as of this moment" the Army leadership was back in Sukarno's hands and confirmed that Sukarno had entrusted him "to restore security." By now, of course, Sukarno was so severely compromised that he had little choice in the matter. Although Sukarno insisted that he had gone to Halim voluntarily, the fact was that he was in the territory of the enemy when Suharto acted; indeed, in 1948 he had acted voluntarily, too, when he went against the decision of the Hatta government and then colonels Simatupang and Nasution, and handed himself over to the Dutch rather than join the guerrillas.

When Pranoto and Suharto met for the first time after Pranoto's "appointment," Suharto, in front of a group of staff officers, snapped, "You must be kidding." Pranoto made no move to enforce Sukarno's appointment. Although not a Communist, Pranoto was widely held responsible for the PKI infiltration into the Diponegoro Division during his period of command. He was amenable to both Sukarno and Aidit and, had the movement succeeded, would have served admirably as Army chief of staff, presiding over the reorganization of the general staff in congruity with the conceptions of Sukarno and Aidit. There is no evidence that Pranoto was a member of the movement or had any inkling about it. Like Untung, he was picked as another "fall guy"—this time for the staff, not operational, level. Given Supardjo's growing role, it is likely that he would have ultimately emerged as the real Army chief of staff.

In the early days of October, there was considerable public confusion over the status of Suharto and Pranoto. General Ibnu Subroto, the Army Information Department chief, was moved to issue a clarifying statement to "dispel any mistake or misunderstanding which might exist as to the task assigned to Pranoto by Sukarno." [14]

"Pranoto was not appointed acting minister and chief of staff of the Army," he said. "Sukarno has assumed the leadership of the Army, named Pranoto as officer in charge of Daily Affairs, and placed Suharto in charge of Operations to Restore Security and Order."

But this did not dispel the doubts until mid-October. "Sometime ago, I announced that . . . as a temporary caretaker for day-to-day administration, a caretaker for daily affairs of the leadership of the Army, I appointed General Pranoto," Sukarno declared.[15] "Now I have reached a decision to appoint permanently a minister and Army commander." He named Suharto.

Nonetheless, Supardjo went to his execution convinced that Suharto and Nasution were guilty of "indisciplinary action" on October 1 for not obeying Sukarno's orders. As for the controversy over terminology, parliament and the extraordinary military tribunal which tried the conspirators (Mahmillub) officially declared the events surrounding September 30 "the Gestapu affair." Gestok became a footnote.

9

Debacle on Java

WHILE DISASTER WAS IN THE MAKING
in Jakarta, everything appeared to move effortlessly in Central
Java, the main base of the Indonesian Communist movement.
Radio stations in the three principal cities of Semarang, Jogjakarta, and Surakarta broadcast the Untung pronouncements.
Local revolutionary councils were set up. In Surakarta the
mayor, a Communist, issued a proclamation enthusiastically
endorsing the September 30 movement. In Jogjakarta, the
Communists were soon on the streets in a demonstration of
support for the purge in Jakarta.[1] To facilitate matters, the
governor of Central Java was absent in Peking celebrating the
sixteenth anniversary of the founding of the Chinese People's
Republic that very day, October 1. The acting governor was
his deputy, Sujono Atmo, a crypto-Communist. Better still,
the command of the Seventh Diponegoro Division, the most
heavily Communist-infiltrated division in the Army, was
usurped. The action had a familiar ring. Two key divisional
officers were kidnapped and slain (beaten and strangled with
wire). But the Seventh's commander, Brigadier General Sur-
josumpeno, escaped. The new divisional commander was his
chief of intelligence, Colonel Suherman (the Communists, it
later developed, had concentrated on infiltrating the division's
intelligence and civic action programs).

With the division behind them, with "popular" support,
and with the backing of the civilian administration, what
could possibly go wrong in Central Java?

Lukman and other Communist functionaries in the province must have asked themselves that very same question that
morning. While Aidit was at the President's right elbow at

Halim, he had assigned Lukman, his first deputy, to Central Java.[2] Lukman had reason for satisfaction and, indeed, celebrated at breakfast in the company of Sakirman, the fifth member of the Politburo's inner five, as they both listened intently to their radio transistors.

Later in the day, however, Lukman must have become troubled when Sukarno failed to broadcast, as programmed, his message endorsing the movement and the liquidation of the CIA's Council of Generals. Then the news reached them that the movement had failed in Jakarta.

At 2:00 A.M. on October 2, Aidit landed at Jogjakarta and established contact with Lukman, Sakirman, Sujono Atmo, and Colonel Suherman. Aidit provided an account of what went wrong—Nasution's escape, Sukarno's vacillation, and Suharto's regrouping of the Army. On the flight from Halim, Aidit apparently developed his strategy. His best hope was to "muddle through." Everything depended on Sukarno, as it had since 1952; but now, more than ever. The safety and security, the fate and future, of the Indonesian Communist Party was in Sukarno's hands.

Aidit had to mark time in Central Java until Sukarno could restore a balance of power between the Army and the PKI. He also had to buy time to develop Central Java into a counterweight which would provide Sukarno with leverage against the Army by warning Suharto that without the President's balancing act, the country would be plunged into civil war. The dual strategy probably made sense to Aidit and the hierarchy, but it sowed confusion in the rank and file. The party's mass base turned into a quagmire from which the Aidit leadership could not extract itself.

Aidit tried desperately to do so. Thus, on the day after the unearthing of the bodies of the generals, the Politburo released a statement calling on "all members and sympathizers of the PKI" to fully support Sukarno's appeal for unity and calm as the President set about to resolve the affair politically. The statement characterized the September 30 movement as "an internal problem of the Army" and denied Communist complicity.[3]

The PKI's regional committees promptly transmitted the

line. The Jogjakarta regional committee declared that "the affair is an internal problem of the Army and, therefore, the Party had no part in it." [4] The North Sumatra regional committee said it was "inappropriate to issue a hasty opinion" on the September 30 movement "especially for us here, in an area so distant from the scene." The acting governor in Central Java ordered the dissolution of any Revolutionary Councils set up in the province and called on local officials to assist "the efforts being undertaken by the *armed forces of Central Java* to restore security and order." Clearly, he hoped to restore the status quo ante.

As a further testimony of the PKI's good faith, Aidit dispatched Lukman to Bogor by automobile after Radio Jakarta announced that Sukarno had summoned a cabinet meeting for October 6. Sukarno had summoned the session to undercut the Army, which had held an unofficial cabinet meeting on October 4 in Jakarta at which it presented preliminary evidence of the role of the PKI's fifth force in the purge.

Njoto, who returned from North Sumatra with Subandrio, also attended the first formal meeting of the cabinet. According to Roeslan Abdul Gani—a former foreign minister and aide to Sukarno before the rise of Subandrio—who was present, "Lukman and Njoto acted as if nothing had happened." [5]

Aidit also maintained direct contact with Sukarno through letters delivered by Lukman and other couriers. One of these letters, which Subandrio had ordered the BPI to burn "because it involved the President" in the affair, was introduced at the deputy premier's trial. [6] In the letter, Aidit prescribed a remedy for overcoming the situation. He advised the President to equate the September 30 movement with the Council of Generals (Gestapu-Gestok?), entrust the restoration of security to the police and the Sukarno-PKI-dominated National Front, and authorize "all political organizations, mass organizations, the press and radio to resume operations as prior to the September 30 Movement." Aidit must have been deluding himself. All of Sukarno's horses and all of Sukarno's men could never put the *status quo ante* back together again.

It was far too late. Following the discovery of the generals' bodies, crowds of enraged youth burned PKI headquarters to the ground, swarmed over the buildings housing Pemuda Rakjat, Gerwani, and SOBSI, first looting and then putting the torch to them, and reduced the homes of Aidit and other PKI leaders to rubble. The Army seized more than 1,000 Communist functionaries in the capital, including Njono. The Hotel Indonesia was raided and four persons arrested; a fifth fell to his death from a third-floor parapet while trying to elude his pursuers.

By then, too, the PKI and its affiliates were being denounced, banned, and suspended in piecemeal fashion. In Jakarta, the military command "temporarily prohibited the activities of political and mass organizations involved in the counterrevolutionary September 30 movement." [7] In Central Java, the Army "temporarily prohibited all activities of the PKI and its affiliated organizations." [8] In North Celebes, the regional military commander authorized "the temporary suspension of all activities of the PKI." In Jakarta and Bandung, the provincial capital of West Java, tens of thousands of youth demonstrated and demanded the nationwide dissolution of the PKI in its entirety. Fourteen "universities" were closed, including the notorious Aliarcham Academy of Social Sciences, which trained PKI cadres.

If Aidit was daydreaming, so was Sukarno. In mid-October, KIAPMA opened as scheduled, attended by Communist and pro-Communist delegations from twenty-seven countries, including North Vietnam, North Korea, China, and representatives from the North Borneo National Liberation Front, the Malayan National Liberation League, the South Vietnamese National Liberation Front, and so forth. Bertrand Russell sent a message which declared that the CIA must be "exterminated" the world over.* [9] Ho Chi Minh termed the conference a "great contribution to the victory of the national liberation movement." [10] Sukarno spoke and raked over all the old chestnuts of his glory days—colonialism, imperialism, neocolonialism, and so on. KIAPMA served one function, however. It was a taste of the potion the Communists, their sympathizers, and admirers would brew if the Gestapu affair

* See page 66.

had succeeded.

Nothing could halt the flood of rising anger against the PKI. Yet it was not until March 14, 1966, after Sukarno bowed to Suharto's pressure and stepped aside, that the PKI, from its central board down to its regional chapters, was "banned throughout the territory under the jurisdiction of the Government of the Republic of Indonesia." The order took effect March 12, the day after the collapse of the Sukarno regime.[11]

Early in October, too, massive defections took place within the PKI. Although this breakdown will be discussed later in an analysis of why the mass-based Communist Party collapsed almost overnight, an example of this collapse is inserted here only to show that it occurred *before* the hard-core PKI decided to make a final, armed stand in Central Java. In Bandung, our illustration, thousands of people jammed Madjalengka Square to hear the nine section committee members of the PKI and its affiliates in the city read themselves out of the PKI and announce the dissolution of party branches in the area. The Communist executives who took this action included four sectional committee leaders and five officials from Pemuda Rakjat, Gerwani, and SOBSI. In a desperate attempt to cling to Sukarno while dissociating themselves from the September 30 movement, they renewed their oath of allegiance to Sukarno and expressed their readiness to implement his every command.

These disastrous developments during the first two weeks of October must have made plain to Aidit that his strategy of buying time in Central Java was failing. The stratagem collapsed totally on October 19 with the arrival of two battalions of Indonesian "Red Berets" or shock troops, the Army Paracommandos (RPKAD), under the command of Colonel Sarwo Edhie. The RPKAD, whose companies bear names such as Dracula, was set up in 1959. By 1965, it comprised twelve battalions totaling 50,000 men. Their arrival in Central Java foreshadowed an Army decision to sweep the PKI's strong points in the province.

An unofficial Indonesian White Paper holds that on October 19 the PKI leadership, "informed through their excellent intelligence organs that an operation was being mounted to crush their organization, realized that it was of no further use to maintain the pretense that they were not implicated in the coup . . . [and they] belatedly . . . began to organize for their defense." [12] Other Indonesian sources believe the RPKAD's arrival "generated panic" within the PKI high command.

In any event, the PKI hard core braced itself for the impending onslaught and began arming with stores from disaffected Diponegoro units, setting up regional commands in the villages, initiating strikes, disrupting communications by felling trees across roads and cutting telephone lines. The White Paper makes the interesting point that the RPKAD arrived in Central Java not to suppress an armed rebellion but to prevent a large-scale insurgency. In effect, then, the RPKAD was engaged in a pre-emptive strike in much the same fashion that the PKI had struck pre-emptively at the general staff eighteen days earlier.

On October 23, the PKI reverted to a policy which was a playback of its behavior at Madiun in 1948—the wholesale liquidation of the party's political enemies in PKI-controlled areas.[13] A wave of mass murders swept the Central Javanese strongpoints of the party. In the Klatan-Bojolali area, upward of two hundred fifty political leaders, largely from the PNI and NU, were executed. About fifteen thousand persons fled the region. Arthur J. Dommen of the Los Angeles *Times* was one of the first foreign correspondents on the scene and told of "a savage reign of terror by the PKI which culminated two weeks ago in a barbarous night of murder and kidnapping throughout this region." [14] In one village he visited, Djambul Kidul, the "mental terror" of the PKI in the preceding years was so extensive that "only five of some 600 families still dared to voice any opposition to Communist orders." The five were affiliated with the PNI.

The Communist rank and file in Central Java, however, were so stunned and repelled by the link between "their" PKI and the murder of the generals that the party's base in the area began to erode. The local PKI leadership sought to hold the organization together by claiming that Sukarno had been killed by the generals and that Radio Jakarta's news broadcasts were fabrications. When the RPKAD arrived in Central Java, they claimed it was the advance guard of a Malaysian invasion. But the PKI's mass base continued to dissipate. In this situation, the Communist leadership resorted to "naked terror." [15] In Djambul Kidul, for example, eighteen members of the five families which had refused to join the PKI were rounded up and publicly harangued and lectured on the errors of their ways. Then they were bound, gagged, and butchered. One was hanged by his feet and burned to death. The villagers were told that this is "what happens to those who do not accept Communist direction without question." [16]

In the third week of October, fighting developed between the RPKAD and the PKI. It was short-lived and bloody. As in 1926, 1948, and 1951, Communist resistance buckled. By the end of November, the "Red Berets" completed their formal military operations and the following month they were withdrawn from Central Java. Another correspondent in the area in November, Harald Munthe-Kaas, reported from Surakarta that in mid-November he still saw "truckloads of prisoners being brought in for questioning at military headquarters both in Jogjakarta and Surakarta." He was not, however, permitted to go on Army operations because "however much they would like to let me accompany them on patrol, my white face would only prove to the people that they were really neocolim (Malaysian) forces." [17]

During this period, the hunt for Aidit intensified. Aidit probably realized that the game was lost. His only option was to go underground and try to reorganize the party from below at some future date. For eighteen days, Aidit remained at large in the Surakarta area, traveling by day on a motor scooter to maintain contacts with various underground cells. Gradually, the Army closed in on him. On the night of November 21, which was marked by an unusually heavy rainstorm—comparable to the storm which drenched the forty-fifth anniversary celebrations—Aidit was trapped in the home of a party worker. He was held for a day or two and then summarily shot. Three photographs were taken of him, one standing between two soldiers attired in parkas and another at a writing table putting his signature to a document. No official announcement of his arrest and execution has ever been made. On being apprehended, Aidit is said to have demanded to be taken to Sukarno. "I am a member of the cabinet," he told his captors.[18] "I demand to see the President." When Aidit was to be shot, he declared, "If you shoot me, you must also shoot the President!" This statement is part of the evidence the Army is holding on Sukarno.

The question of whether or not Aidit "confessed" before his execution is speculative. According to Risuke Hayashi, the correspondent of Tokyo's Asahi *Evening News,* Aidit's "confession" covered more than fifty pages. In it, Hayashi said, Aidit never compromised his dedication to communism, answered the questions when he could, refused to say anything when he did not want to give an answer, and at all times maintained "a dignified attitude." [19]

Aidit assumed responsibility for planning and implementing the September 30 movement in the Asahi confession. "The highest responsibility for the September 30 coup lies with myself," Aidit is said to have written. He said the party sought to establish "the government of a national united front" and that "it was our policy to guarantee President Sukarno's status even after the coup, but to criticize and revise his policy gradually." This had a strong ring of authenticity.

He said that he was prepared to move against the Army in May, before the forty-fifth party congress, but that other members of the Politburo—notably Lukman, Njoto, Sakirman, and Njono—opposed the action because of "insufficient preparations." These preparations were purportedly undertaken in June and July. In August, Aidit said he "stopped in Peking and talked with the Chinese Communist Party leaders about President Sukarno's health and other matters." On his return to Jakarta that month, according to the confession, he felt "we had no choice but to carry out the coup ahead of schedule" because the party had obtained intelligence that Yani planned to investigate the PKI's illegal possession of arms.[20] Untung's appointment as chairman of the Revolutionary Council was "a tentative measure." As for the failure of the plan, Aidit termed it premature. "Not a few PKI leaders opposed the coup attempt as untimely," he said. "I myself admitted that the coup was premature." Although he claimed that the Party had infiltrated about 25 per cent of the Army, "these Communist forces did not move as we had expected." Sukarno then balked at endorsing the Revolutionary Council and "seemed not to place any merit in what I told him." If we assume the statement is authentic, Aidit has sought to implicate Sukarno. If we assume the statement was concocted by the Army, then the Army has sought to implicate Sukarno.

When Suharto recaptured Radio Jakarta, Aidit concluded that the movement had "ended unsuccessfully" and he flew to Central Java to "maintain and revive our forces."

After November 5, the situation became hopeless. It became increasingly difficult to maintain contact with PKI leaders in other areas. "To make matters worse, I was in danger," he said. "I was always escorted by about twenty members of the Pemuda Rakjat, changing my residence frequently." [21]

Although the Asahi confession sounds authentic, it will always be a source of conjecture and controversy. Nonetheless, it appears devoid of irresistible propaganda. Aidit's ultimate fate was shared by his two deputies. Lukman attended the October 6 cabinet session and was arrested shortly thereafter. He was executed in December. Njoto was arrested in early December and also disappeared. He, too, is believed to have been executed that month.

On the eve of his arrest, Njoto granted an interview to Asahi.[22] He clung to the contention that the Gestapu "is an internal matter of the Army" and claimed that the PKI "knew nothing." He wrote off the presence of the PKI's fifth force at Halim as volunteers to fight Malaysia. He remained loyal to Aidit's strategy, reiterated the party's loyalty to Sukarno, and said the party strove to "prevent a civil war." If murders and other acts of violence happen, he said, "this is not the responsibility of the PKI," but the responsibility of those who defy the commands (Gestok?) of the President." In the interview, he signed his death warrant. He had avoided arrest until then because he had been in Sumatra with Subandrio at the time of the putsch—and because he was identified with the Moscow wing of the party.[23]

Almost a year later, Dr. Sutanti Aidit, the party leader's wife, was captured on the outskirts of Jakarta. "Who has betrayed me?" she asked, adding, "Shoot me on the spot and be done with it." [24]

By then, however, Indonesia had been engulfed by a tsunami of murder which claimed tens of thousands of lives.

10

A Final Solution?

IN THE MONTHS THAT FOLLOWED THE
Gestapu affair, Indonesia looked and beheld a pale horse: the
name that sat on him was Death, and Hell followed with
him.

There are no figures available on the number of persons
slaughtered in the turbulent wake of the September 30 affair.
The lowest estimate is enormous—seventy thousand. The
PKI's regrouped Politburo holds that "not less than 200,000
Communists, including their principal leaders as well as non-
Communist progressives were brutally murdered." [1] Sukarno
once put the figure at eighty-seven thousand and, curiously,
corrected himself to say he meant seventy-eight thousand.[2]
The London *Times* surmised that the figure may have been
as high as one million—so did a team of 150 investigators
from the University of Indonesia.

An American academic escalated the figure to "one or two
million"—that's a difference of not one, but of one million.[3]
On Taiwan, and perhaps in Peking, it is held that between
one hundred thousand and five hundred thousand were slain,
"most of them presumably Chinese." [4] This is also unreasonable. If anything, most of them were presumably Indonesian.

A figure of about one hundred fifty thousand is today
generally accepted as "reasonable." [5] But who is to say? "According to one story, thousands were buried in the sand under
the over-arching coconut palms and bamboo clusters," a correspondent in East Java reported.[6] "According to another version, only a few hundred found their graves there. And some
people argue there are no bodies in the Kali Wadi at all." An
Australian commentator pointed out that one raft carrying

ten bodies floating down a stream seen by ten different people becomes quite easily one hundred dead.[7]

Yet unquestionably thousands of persons, Communists and non-Communists alike, either disappeared or were killed between October, 1965, and March, 1966.

"I had five cousins in Magelang," an old acquaintance remarked. "Now we don't know where they are. They were not in the PKI, but they were considered 'leftist.' One, for example, was in a PKI-led teachers' organization." And another Javanese said, "A relative of mine is a *wedana* south of Wonogiri. His wife still trembles when she recalls the shooting on the outskirts of the village one night when the PKI were slaughtered like cattle."

A Czech correspondent in Jakarta, a Communist, said 80 per cent of his contacts vanished. "A young Balinese, who had studied in Prague, was held in prison four months and then released," he said.[8] "When he returned to Bali, he discovered that his brother and sister had been killed." The Czech revisited Jogjakarta in 1967 and looked up five friends at old addresses. All were "leftists"; one was a local newspaper editor, another a lecturer at Gadja Mada University, and the others "Far Left" (PKI?). "All had disappeared," he said. "It is very depressing for me to remain in Indonesia." A Yugoslav diplomat, also a Communist, said, "Even assuming the guilt of the Politburo, which I do not, does this justify genocide?" He added: "Kill the Central Committee, but do not kill 100,000 people who did not know and had no part in it."

Sukarno, whose disastrous policies were primarily responsible for turning Indonesia into a charnel house, accused his people of "running amok like monkeys caught in the dark." [9] He addressed himself to the subject of the mass murders for the first time on November 22, the day Aidit was purportedly executed. A situation has arisen, Sukarno said, in which Indonesians are "killing, shooting and slandering each other." About a month later, Sukarno accused the *santri* or Moslem community of perpetrating the massacre. Sukarno charged them with violating the codes of Islam by not burying the dead, and said the bodies of Communists were "mutilated and left decaying in streets, under trees, or floating in rivers." [10]

The murderous orgy immediately raises questions: Why the killings? Who carried them out? The former is the least difficult to answer.

In Indonesia, one repeatedly hears these themes: "We had to do it." "It was them or us." "We killed them before they could kill us." "To understand, you must appreciate the bullying tactics of the Communists." "We were on their liquidation lists." "Either kill or be killed." "The fate of the generals awaited us." "Westerners do not understand the mental terror they inflicted on us." "If we had not done it to them, they would have done it to us."

In many respects, the PKI invited the massacre by raising the spectre of another Madiun. Indonesia's present generation of leaders have not forgotten Madiun and the PKI's wanton slaughter in 1948 of its political opponents. That event marked the introduction into Indonesia of the totalitarian technique of mass political murder. Until then, the turbulent politics of the revolutionary Republic were marked by occasional murders and kidnappings and frequent arrests. Invariably, those detained were released unharmed. The PKI changed all this.

In objective terms, communism's political record is generally a register of almost perpetual state violence—the secret police, the purge, the whole nasty business of totalitarianism. Communism's saving grace in this matter is that, unlike its fascist counterpart, the Communist states murder in the name of peace, freedom, and humanity. Animal farm, indeed. The Soviet Union, after all, bears the distinction of being the first modern state to deliberately set out to "liquidate" (albeit only as a "class") a particular category of its subjects.[11] The Communist record in Southeast Asia and China is equally depressing. In Southeast Asia, the only regime which has consciously murdered tens of thousands of its political opponents is found in the solitary area where the Communists have acquired state power—Vietnam. Knowledgeable Asians are aware of this. Similarly, Westerners. The late Bernard Fall calculated that Ho Chi Minh slew fifty thousand or more political adversaries during his consolidation of power,[12] and Joseph Buttinger has observed that the "Communists prac-

ticed a policy of physical extermination from the very beginning of their revolution" and that Vietnamese whom the
Communists regarded as dangerous competitors "were simply
murdered." [13] As for China, the Mao Tse-tung leadership
once boasted to the first Indonesian ambassador to Peking,
Arnold Mononutu, that the regime had liquidated millions of
its political opponents between 1949 and 1953, and Han Su
Yin, an admirer of the commune, writes easily about the million people who were murdered in "actual, real physical
purges." [14] Perhaps, when all is said and done, the Indonesian
reaction to the murder of the general staff can best be summed
up by a teaching of Mao himself: "If you have learned that
your opponent intends to kill you, never fail to kill him, or he
will kill you."

The mass murders in Indonesia are frequently compared
to the genocide practiced by the Hitler regime. Yet the comparison is artificial. The murders in Germany were coldly calculated and carried out over a considerable period of time.
They were not emotional outbursts, cases of running *amok* in
the literal sense of the Malay word. Moreover, Nazi apologists
have claimed, "Of course, it was terrible to kill all the Jews,
but in a way the Jews had invited it." Hardly. The Jews of
Germany, unlike the Communists in Indonesia, were not organized into a single, disciplined party, whose history was
steeped in violence and who were dedicated to the acquisition
of state power by any means and its retention interminably.
Unlike the Communist minority which terrorizes the majority
in a Communist state, the Jewish minority in Germany was
the victim of the terror, not the perpetrator.

In still another sense, the comparison between Germany
and Indonesia is shallow. What happened in Indonesia, in
some respects, was more akin to civil war than mass murder.
There was a raw struggle for power and survival. It was a
peasant affair, settled in a peasant manner and without for-
malities.[15]

In part, this explains the first question: Why the killings?
It also partly answers the question of who carried out the
murders. As much as can be pieced together of this tale of
utter horror, the Indonesian massacre was more of a sponta-

neous reaction to the PKI involvement in the murder of the generals than an organized affair. The killings fitted no pattern. Some Communists, for example, were summarily executed; others tried and sentenced to death, life imprisonment, or short prison terms; and still others were detained and then released after brief questioning. In Indonesia, the massacre lacked the cold-blooded efficiency and intellectuality which characterized the savage butchery in the principal authoritarian states of the twentieth century—Russia, Germany, and China. Nor is this analysis meant to condone the brutal bloodletting which took place in what was formerly called the Emerald Isles.

Orthodox Islam clearly played an important role in the murders. Natsir, the former chairman of the Masjumi, recalled slipping out notes from his prison cell appealing to his followers to halt the carnage in the name of God. "But they always sent me messages in turn," he recalled,[16] "and their messages always read the same: 'If we do not kill them, they will kill us'." Natsir is convinced that the murders can be characterized as a "psychological explosion" among a repressed people who had suffered grievously from the PKI's "mental terror."

Yet the massacre was not a case of solely Islamic authorship. On Bali, for example, the killing was conducted by a people who were nominally Hindu. And although "deaths from the Army's mopping up operations were relatively few," [17] the secular Army also played an important role in the mass murders. Like the civilian population, the military also wanted to put an end to what it considered the PKI virus in the Indonesian body politic. Unquestionably, the murders had the approval and encouragement of the Army. In some areas, the Army actively participated in the purge. In other areas, the Army protected the Communists.[18]

Nasution, for example, shocked by the murder of his daughter and by the realization that twice within his own lifetime he had been "a target" of the PKI,[19] called for the extirpation of the Communist Party. "All of their followers and sympathizers should be eliminated, otherwise the incident will recur," the General told an Army staff conference as the RPKAD arrived in central Java.[20] Not only must actors be eliminated, he then told a student organization, but also the PKI's "masterminds and supporters." [21] And, during a visit to the Surabaya naval base, Nasution again called for the PKI's total extinction "down to its very roots so that there will be no third Madiun." [22]

In mid-November, as the murders gathered their awful momentum, Suharto signed a formal order authorizing an "absolutely essential cleaning out" of the PKI and its sympathizers from the government. The directive, No. 22/KOTI/ 1965, set up "special teams" to carry out the instruction and authorized the teams to request military assistance, "if necessary." [23]

The Nasution and Suharto orders emboldened Subandrio to demand that Sukarno discharge the two generals, charge them with mass murder, and place them on trial before a special military tribunal.[24] But, with the Army's evidence of Sukarno's involvement in the Gestapu affair, the President was powerless. In the end, it was Subandrio, as Sukarno's alter ego, who stood trial for having helped shape the political conditions which led to the mass murders. Indeed, the President's refusal to take a strong lead against the "Gestapu-PKI" is blamed by some Indonesians for the massacres that began in late October.[25]

Many explanations have been offered to rationalize man's peculiar propensity to kill—and even enjoy killing—on a mass basis when such crimes are sanctioned by his country or society.[26] The Malthusians believe that population and economic pressures impel mass murder. Biologists suggest a person's genetic make-up may affect behavior; chromosomal abnormalities, for example, have appeared sixty times more frequently in men convicted of violent crimes than in the general population.[27] Can this also be true, too, of a whole race, the Malay race? Then on Bali it is said that Hinduism preaches reincarnation and that when Communist Balinese (an odd phrase) were led to their execution, their executors explained that they did not act out of malice, but only out of duty and wished their victims a better incarnation.[28] On nominally Moslem Java, the slaughter was proclaimed as a sort of *jihad* or "holy war." Inexplicably, the Communist prisoners often

offered little or no opposition and let themselves be killed
without a gesture of revolt. The victims even helped the
killers with their work of extermination, a not unfamiliar oc-
currence in the Nazi concentration camps.[29]

Despite the enormity of the massacre, the world took relatively little notice of it. U Thant, empowered with the moral
authority of the United Nations, said nothing. Indeed, nobody at the United Nations said much; on the contrary, Indonesia was warmly welcomed back to the world organization.
Albeit, the Albanians boycotted the session and from the bal-
cony above a Left claque hurled abuse on the delegates below,
shouting, "Murderers! Murderers!"

The nonaligned states were as unconcerned about the
killings as the United Nations. Yugoslavia, India, and the
United Arab Republic welcomed an Indonesian good-will
mission shortly after the murderous wave. So did Indonesia's
immediate neighbors—the Catholic Philippines, Buddhist
Thailand, Moslem Malaysia, Protestant Australia, and Con-
fucianist Singapore. Indeed, Adam Malik, Indonesia's new
foreign minister, reported that his good-will visits brought results "beyond expectation." [30]

Communists the world over, of course, lamented the passing of their comrades in Indonesia. But here again power
politics, the everlasting, primitive tribal interest of every state,
transcended religion and ideology. Russian criticism was
harsh. The Soviet nuclear physicist who helped develop Moscow's hydrogen bomb, Andrei D. Sakharov, described the
"tragic event" as an "extreme case of reaction, racism [?], and
militarism." This commentary appeared in the "underground" essay which he circulated among Soviet intellectuals
in 1968. The essay called for the universal fulfillment of the
Rights of Man. Yet official Soviet party and state criticisms
were relatively subdued as compared to the indignation and
outrage expressed by Peking. Moscow, of course, took grim
satisfaction in the destruction of a party which had strayed
from the Kremlin's authority. For their part, however, the
Chinese were stunned by the loss of a potentially most powerful ally in Asia and the Communist world. Peking termed the

murders "heinous and diabolical crimes . . . unprecedented
in history." [31] Mass murder is, indeed, a matter of perspective.

Vietnam's reaction was another lesson in perspective. In
the north, Hanoi denounced the Suharto government as a
"military fascist regime." The Vietnamese Communists, of
course, were dismayed by the collapse of the second front in
the rear of the Americans. Nevertheless, North Vietnam maintained its diplomatic representation in Jakarta, and when the
Indonesian envoy to the Communist regime, Sukrisno, refused
to return home for consultations and took sanctuary in Peking, Hanoi accepted a new ambassador from Suharto,
Nugroho (also no first name). In the South, meanwhile,
Saigon was elated by the favorable turn of events across the
South China Sea. Yet, in the South, which has been the
world's bloodiest battlefield for a generation, the reaction to
the savagery in Indonesia betrayed man's ability to engage in
honest delusion. "We were not surprised by the murders con-
sidering that it was done by a people who traditionally carry
long knives [the *kris*]," a high South Vietnamese official explained in Saigon.[32] "When something like this happens in
the Malay world, we Vietnamese find it normal. We feel it is
something inherent in the character of the Malay people. We
recognize, of course, that when there are upheavals, there must
be cycles of barbarism."

In the West, the massacres were treated lightly as compared, say, to the widely publicized killings in Biafra in 1968.
In Britain, the *Times* ran a series of articles on Indonesia and
the *Guardian* was mortified. If 150,000 persons were killed in
Indonesia, the *Guardian* said, this was "higher than the
number of deaths (in) the five previous years of the Vietnam
conflict." [33] Bertrand Russell, who once advocated that the
West engage in preventive nuclear war against Soviet Russia
to "save" world civilization, declared: "The massacres in
Indonesia demand an international investigation and I congratulate those who have initiated it." [34] Unfortunately, he
was applauding the wrong people for the right reason. He
referred to the "Youth Against War and Fascism" (YAWF), a

"fascist" group itself which sponsored a "public inquest" at Columbia University in 1966.* But YAWF was not as much interested in Indonesia as in pinning the Gestapu affair and purge on the United States. Two years later, it concluded that Hubert Humphrey and Ellsworth Bunker were the "architects of the massacre[!]." By then, Humphrey had become the prime target in the 1968 presidential campaign of the New Left Fascists who were bent on polarizing politics in the United States and thereby promoting a "revolutionary situation."

As for the United States, neither President Johnson, Secretary of State Rusk, nor Ambassador Green ever commented publicly on the mass killings in Indonesia. The argument against such a course was that nobody knew for sure how many people had been killed and that to have condemned the massacre would have left the United States open again to charges of "interference" in Indonesia's domestic affairs. Moreover, if Moscow viewed the destruction of the PKI with grim satisfaction, one can appreciate the character of the reaction in Washington.

Nonetheless, the United States, out of respect for humanity, should have spoken out publicly against the horror. As an American, I expected it to do so. Unofficially, however, the Administration was appalled. On his return from Indonesia in 1967, Vice President Humphrey privately expressed horror at the slaughter but he, too, maintained public silence. Only one major American political leader referred to the massacre openly, the late Senator Robert F. Kennedy. "The slaughter of thousands in Indonesia," he said, like the jailing of intellectuals in Soviet Russia or racial discrimination in New York or Capetown, are "differing evils [but] are the common works of man [and] call upon common qualities of conscience and of indignation." [35]

This is not to infer that there was no adverse public reaction in the United States or the West generally. Indeed, the strongest adverse reaction on humanitarian grounds came from the West. John Hughes, the British-born correspondent of the *Christian Science Monitor,* won a Pulitzer Prize for his

* See page 187.

coverage of the Indonesian upheaval.[36] The National Broadcasting Company (NBC) devoted a one-hour documentary to the subject whose title accurately reflected the uneasy conscience of the West: "Indonesia: the Troubled Victory." The Overseas Press Club of America presented its Asia reporting award to Horace Sutton of the *Saturday Review,* which devoted almost an entire issue to his cover story, "Indonesia's Night of Terror." [37]

Yet, matched by the enormity of the crime, the Western reaction was relatively mild. Anger over the inadequate attention was reflected in the Western press, however. For example, in letters to the *New York Times.* A reader who said he supported American policy in Vietnam wrote, "I think it is high time the Johnson Administration condemn the Communist purge in Indonesia." [38] Another, the author of *Stalin's Russia,* said, "It will be interesting to see whether the public and moral authorities of America protest against this massacre of Communists, as they have so rightly protested against massacres by Communists in the U.S.S.R., Eastern Europe, China and Southeast Asia." [39] Still another observed that when Castro executed 500 followers of the former Batista dictatorship, "a storm of violent indignation raged in the United States," but he said on Indonesia that "hardly a word of disapproval appeared in the same press." [40]

Why, then, did the world take the mass slayings in Indonesia so relatively lightly? Were there mitigating circumstances—or has the world become jaded by mass murder since the trench warfare of 1914–18 and the subsequent rise of totalitarian police states?

Fantasies, fables, and myths have a deep hold on the Malay world and this was certainly a mitigating factor. Within the compass of that world of endless seascapes, the slightest ripple becomes a tidal wave. The unbounded imagination of the Malays has exercised a deep influence on their politics. Permit an example.

Captain R. P. "Turk" Westerling of the Dutch colonial army is said to have massacred forty thousand persons in the South Celebes during the Indonesian war of independence.[41] Shortly after the bloodletting, the late Quentin Pope of the

Chicago *Tribune* and I traveled through the area. Each night for a week, guided by Republican partisans, we visited the villages scattered on the periphery of Macassar, the capital of the South Celebes. After intensive investigation, we arrived at this conclusion: Westerling had gone from village to village and lined up the men, selecting one or two at random. He had accused them of acts of terrorism and demanded a confession. If they confessed, they were shot. If they did not confess, they were shot. In this criminal and grotesque manner, he murdered as many as 120, perhaps two hundred, individuals. Each village spread the tale that thousands had been slain in neighboring villages. In this fashion, the figure of forty thousand was engraved in the history books. Interestingly, the terror was politically effective; it broke the back of the armed resistance.

In addition to the fertile imagination of the average Malay, it is difficult to assess the depth of the massacre for other reasons. There is, for example, an inexplicable lack of photographic evidence. In an era in which still and motion-picture cameras have been perfected, not one television network in the world has carried even a solitary film clip on the mass murders, nor have the world's news agencies or pictorial magazines.[42] If one assumes, as apparently some do, that "one or two million" persons were slain in a five-month period, the almost total absence of photographs raises doubts as to the ascertainment. Or is the medium the message? Veteran combat photographers and film producers are at a loss to provide an adequate explanation.[43]

Eyewitness accounts by trained observers are also difficult to come by. One can comb the world press, for example, without hardly ever uncovering an eyewitness account.[44] A rare exception appeared in the *Christian Science Monitor.* "In several days of driving we saw perhaps several hundred prisoners escorted down the road guarded casually by one or two soldiers," Charlotte Saikowski, a *Monitor* correspondent, wrote from Jogjakarta.[45] "In one village we came on a man who had been hanged and was just being cut down." Then she added:

"Despite indications of tension, the fact remains that this reporter and an American woman friend were able to drive through the area with absolutely no untoward incident and with every courtesy from these warm Javanese."

There are other incongruities. Bali, it said, was drenched in blood. Yet, within a few months, both Indonesian and foreign travel agencies labored to publicize the opening there of a new ten-story, 300-room hotel, with air conditioning, of course. Later, an Associated Press correspondent visited Bali and concluded that there had been no mass murder in the accepted sense but that perhaps in every other village one or two persons had been slain.[46] His firsthand tour reawakened memories of Macassar two decades earlier.

Another unexplained aspect of these awful killings is that it is widely accepted that the Moslems provided the main thrust for the killing. Yet there was no mass murder reported in deeply Moslem West Java, which was once the stamping ground of the Darul Islam, a movement to replace forcibly the secular Indonesian Republic with a theocratic state. Is it just a coincidence that West Java also happens to be the most accessible part of Indonesia for most foreigners? The capital, Jakarta, as well as the popular hill stations of Bogor and Bandung, are located there.

Furthermore, as the Nuremberg and Eichmann trials demonstrated, the Nazis, employing an up-to-date transportation system, modern gas chambers, and other elaborate devices, found that mass murder was time-consuming and the disposal of bodies the more so. Is it conceivable that in technically primitive Indonesia as many as one million people, or half that figure, could have been disposed of within such a short period in such localized areas as Central-East Java, Bali, and North Sumatra?

Yet there can be no question that thousands were butchered. Even assuming the accuracy of the "reasonable" figure of one hundred fifty thousand killed, this means that almost one thousand persons were shot, hanged, or beheaded daily for five months, a chamber of horrors perhaps unequaled in the history of the Malay world.

Where was the Indonesian press? "The press did not dare to report these events in detail for fear that they might affect public feelings," *Sinar Harapan* said.[47] ". . . It is rather embarrassing for one to try to talk about them now." The daily

made the point, however belated, that many of those killed
were not necessarily Communists, but were the victims of personal rivalries. "The campaign to smash the September 30
Movement," the paper said, "was often manipulated by criminal elements, exploiters and by elements who sought to give
vent to personal spite." In another uncommon Indonesian
press report, *Angkatan Bersendjata,* the armed forces' daily,
acknowledged that some of the Army's political prisoners had
been "set free on the road to eternity." [48]

Again, we must raise the question: Why has the world
taken the mass murders in Indonesia so lightly? Has the world
come to expect unorganized lethal outbursts in politically unsophisticated societies—the Congo, Sudan, India-Pakistan, Biafra, Indonesia? Has it also come to expect organized murder
in the totalitarian states—Germany, Russia, and China? I think
a strong case can be made for this argument. Yet, it too is inadequate. It does not explain why the world still shudders over
Hitler's carnage, but has quite forgotten the organized state
murder of millions in the Soviet Union. In the climate of our
times, obviously, genocide is the ultimate horror, while the
wholesale butchery of political opponents—on however massive a scale—does not trouble us. Why? Are we, indeed, blasé
—if not because of the filmed horrors of trench warfare during
World War I then perhaps subconsciously by The Bomb
which awaits us in the future?

One illuminating answer is offered by Bernard Wolfe,
who served as a secretary to Leon Trotsky in Mexico in 1937.
He thinks the reasoning may be this: A man is born into his
race, without options; he chooses his politics, if indeed, he opts
to have any at all. Thus racial—and, I would add, linguistic,
religious, and cultural—punishments are somehow seen as
visitations; political punishments are somehow invited or "solicited."

In reality, mass murder is a manifestation of a primitive
mentality—the notion of collective guilt. One might have
hoped that the logical fallacy and the moral monstrosity of the
concept of collective responsibility would have been demonstrated by now. But, in Asia, this concept is even stronger than
in the West. As Professor Richard Pipes of Harvard points out,

however, responsibility for any act and guilt for any injustice
can be ascribed only to the individual or the individuals who
commit them. He concludes that if, indeed, all guilt were
collective, then all retribution would have to be collective as
well and, once this principle was accepted, the natural consequence would be mutual collective extermination. It may yet
come to this.

In Indonesia, the thought of retribution is not far from
the surface. The regrouped, underground PKI, on the occasion of the forty-seventh anniversary of the founding of the
PKI in 1967, sounded the call for revenge. Referring to its
slain comrades, the party's newly reconstituted Politburo declared that "we pledge to avenge their death." It added: "The
Indonesian reactionaries must pay [the] blood debt they have
incurred in blood!" [49]

Clearly, the trauma of the post-Gestapu period has left an
indelible scar on the lives and feelings of millions of Indonesians. It would be overly hasty to believe that a recurrence of
violence has been entirely ruled out. Rational solutions to the
economic and social problems of Java are not easy to arrive at,
or painless to implement, if they are found. And, as one pessi-
mistic observer concluded, the irrational solutions of the immediate past do not constitute a hopeful precedent for future
action.[50]

In Indonesia, some apprehensive Indonesians have warned
that a sudden American withdrawal from Vietnam could easily incite another chain of murders. Borderline PKI suspects,
spared in the first round, may be destroyed in the next round.
A Communist triumph in Vietnam, it is said, would renew the
hopes and aspirations of the PKI, indeed steel the Communists
throughout the Malay world, and excite fear among Indonesian non-Communists who would then be anxious to get on
with a "final solution" to the PKI question.[51]

There is no question that Suharto is already struggling
with the dilemma of how to eliminate the rump PKI without
encouraging another lethal outburst. "I ask the people not to
take actions of their own or to be suspicious of one another,"
he pleaded in 1968 following the liquidation of a "liberated
area" which a revitalized PKI Politburo sought to establish in

Blitar, East Java.[52] Suspicions, misunderstandings, and dissension, he said, "will profit only the PKI." Nonetheless, after Blitar a new round of murders was reported on Java.[53]

Clearly, the modern concept of political murder, which the Communists introduced into Indonesia, has been not only turned against them but may have tragically become a feature of Indonesian political life.

11

Why the Communists Failed

WHY DID THE INDONESIAN COMMU-
nist Party collapse overnight? Why did the party fail to take to
the streets? Why did it fail to initiate a general strike?

Communist apologists and/or admirers cite the inaction
of the PKI as "evidence" that the party was not involved in
the September 30 movement, that the movement was an "internal affair of the Army." The PKI was caught off guard, the
victim of some sort of "rightist" plot. The analysis is never
detailed; for example, there is no explanation of why the
"rightists"—Suharto?—would liquidate the "rightist" general
staff and ignore "leftist"-tinted general officers. The most ludicrous suggestion I ever heard came from a European Communist who suggested that Nasution was conceivably behind the
purge since he, alone, eluded the killer squads. One must
suppose, then, that he ordered the gunmen to shoot up his
family and house to provide an air of authenticity.

None of these views stand up in the face of known facts:
the tempo of the Communist agitprop campaign on the eve of
the affair; the participation of the Pemuda Rakjat in the killing of the generals; the endorsement of the purge by *Harian
Rakjat;* and Aidit's presence at Halim with the other principals—Sukarno and such "progressive, revolutionary" officers as
Army General Supardjo and Air Marshal Dhani.

Even accepting the nonsensical view that it was an "internal affair of the Army," this still does not explain the Indonesian Communist Party's docility, its lack of stamina, and its
inability to withstand pressure—political characteristics which
marked the PKI's failures in Indonesia in 1926, 1948, and
1951. Not only did the Communists fail to organize a general

strike and street demonstrations, but the party's mass base dissolved. PKI members burned their party cards, voluntarily dissolved branches, and detained and turned their leaders over to the authorities.[1] Disaffection was not restricted to the party's lower echelons. It spread as high as the PKI's Central Committee; Umar Lesteluhu, the regional party chief of the Moluccas and a member of the PKI's Central Committee, endorsed the dissolution of the party and accused it of "leaving the rails of the revolution [a Sukarno metaphor] and even obstructing the revolution." [2]

In analyzing the collapse of the party, it must be emphasized again that the 1965 adventure was not so much a coup as a purge from the top. Aidit was quite correct when he said the Communists had no intention of overthrowing Sukarno and therefore themselves. Yet had the conspiracy succeeded, Sukarno would have placed the Army general staff in the hands of "progressive, revolutionary" officers—at a minimum, those who were at least not hostile—if not sympathetic—to the PKI. In such a situation, Indonesia would have moved irretrievably to the Left. The second stage of the two-phase revolutionary strategy of Sukarno and Aidit would have been placed in motion. Within a short time, certainly by 1970–71, when the Communists openly boasted they would ascend to power, the Republic of Indonesia would have been transformed into a "Democratic People's Republic" under the dictatorship of a single party, the PKI. Accordingly, it must be reemphasized that the Communists did not plan or participate in a coup d'état. The Untung pronouncements, read by themselves, gave the impression that a coup had occurred, but nobody at Halim took Untung seriously. By all accounts, Sukarno and the others treated him with disdain as a minor character. Untung made no political decisions at Halim and, indeed, was inconspicuous during the deliberations which took place at the center of the conspiratorial web.

Having established that the operation resembled a purge from the top more than a coup d'état, the question remains: Why did the PKI fail to mobilize its mass following and order a general strike in support of the putsch—even assuming it was "an internal affair of the Army"—especially since the purge was directed against a group of generals who had presumably sold out to the CIA, the PKI's *bête noire*. Here we must take three principal factors into account: the party's absolute dependence on Sukarno, the party's lack of internal security, and the character and nature of the party's mass base.

The success of the September 30 affair hinged completely on Sukarno. Sukarno's public support for the liquidation of the "CIA generals" would have most assuredly signaled a mass outpouring of the Communist rank and file—and here we gain some insight—perhaps more out of loyalty to Sukarno and/or the Republic than to Marxism-Leninism.

"When Sukarno decided not to fight at Halim, the PKI collapsed," a professor at the University of Indonesia said, in a capsule summary of the situation. And another Indonesian academic, presently in the Suharto cabinet, added: "After October 1 the PKI did not want to jeopardize Sukarno further since the Communists depended on him for their recovery; therefore they held back—no strikes, no demonstrations."

A Sjahrir aide, who was imprisoned during the Sukarno regime, added another dimension. "As a Marxist," laughed Subadio Sastrasatomo,[3] "I must say I was disappointed in the PKI. After they captured the radio station, Aidit should have launched a general strike. Aidit could have paralyzed the country. But he did not. Why? Because he relied on Sukarno, not on the party itself, not on their mass organizations. He acted at the top as if he was already in power, which he was not."

Manifestly, the PKI depended on Sukarno. A senior Australian diplomat with long experience in Indonesian affairs, dating back to the revolution, who was in Jakarta on October 1, believes that Aidit passed through "a crisis of indecision." Aidit waited for Sukarno to talk the PKI out of the crisis but, he added, "Sukarno turned to jelly as usual." And another Commonwealth observer, Singapore's Goh Keng Swee, independently arrived at a similar conclusion. In his assessment, too, Aidit passed through "a crisis of indecision," but he hastened to point out that in Chinese the radical and phonetic which make up the character "crisis" are *danger* and *opportu-*

nity, an extremely subtle terminology by an extremely sophisticated people.[4] Aidit must have been aware of the danger and opportunity after he fled to Central Java. But, under the circumstances, did Aidit have an alternative? His best opportunity, he probably reasoned, lay in Sukarno's adroit maneuvering in Jakarta. Aidit should have known better than to pin his hopes on Sukarno. But then he should have known better from the start in 1952. Yet without the President's charismatic appeal in a country of impoverished, politically illiterate masses, how else could Aidit hope to develop a mass-based party overnight?

The fear of infiltration and the nature of the Communist mass movement deepened the PKI's dependence on Sukarno. Aidit, Lukman, and Njoto were acutely aware that the party had been seriously infiltrated by the Army and the BPI. Nor was this surprising, given the party's unprecedented growth from less than ten thousand to more than two million members within a decade. Accordingly, it was impossible to transmit confidential orders from the top to the rank and file without their probable interception at some point along the line by the PKI's principal adversaries. This situation was a major factor in the Politburo's decision in August to restrict knowledge of the September 30 plan within the party to the Politburo and certain members of the Central Committee. Of course, Sukarno's open support for the purge would have been simultaneously transmitted to every member of the PKI over Radio Jakarta. So would Aidit's endorsement of Sukarno's endorsement of Untung's action.

At this juncture, it should be noted that the concept of operating from the top is a tactic of the Right strategy, which was discussed earlier.* In proclaiming the PKI's independence in 1963, and opting to continue the Right strategy within Indonesia, Aidit also endorsed the Right tactic of "united front from above." This meant cooperation and collaboration between the Communist and bourgeois leaderships. The tactic of the "united front from above" rationalized, in theoretical terms, the PKI's collaboration with Sukarno at the top. Incidentally, a feature of the opposite Left strategy is the "united

* See page 22.

front from below." In this strategy, the Communists openly attack the leadership of non-Communist parties and seek to turn their base of support against them. This last happened in Indonesia in 1948 during the PKI build-up which led to the abortive Madiun revolt.

Thus, for whatever it is worth, the PKI's participation in the 1965 affair "from above"—as in 1948 "from below"—dovetailed with Marxist-Leninist theory. Further, the decision to work "from above" with Sukarno and the "revolutionary, progressive" officers in the armed forces was rendered through the process of democratic centralism and this feature of Marxism-Leninism worked against the PKI. The Army officer who interrogated Njono throws light on this process.

"I interrogated Njono informally for about two weeks," Colonel August Marpaung said.[5] "He was blindly obedient to Aidit. Aidit told him, and the others, that Sukarno was sick and the time was ripe for a move. Nobody within the Politburo challenged Aidit's analysis. There was no debate, no demand for evidence—just obedience. Aidit had a brilliant record, a record of triumphs. He was infallible. Why should they doubt him now? Njono never considered that the plot could fail. It simply did not enter his mind and he made no contingency plan.

"Njono was their principal trade union organizer and the district leader in Jakarta, yet he made no plans for a general strike. Firstly, he felt that such actions were unnecessary. Then, he considered the September 30 movement as a military operation run by Aidit and Sjam and therefore outside his province. Finally, he lacked confidence in his own district organization which, he feared, had been infiltrated. He sat at home waiting October 1 and 2, and only on the second, when a courier reported that Aidit and Sukarno had left Halim, did he abandon his house."

Sumitro Djojohadikusumo, an economist and a prominent participant in the 1958 rebellion against Sukarno and the PKI, who lived in exile for about ten years and was the author of numerous underground economic papers on the Sukarno regime, drew the same conclusion from other sources. "The PKI was very sure of itself," he said.[6] "They never planned for a reversal."

This brings us to the third factor in the PKI's collapse, the composition of the party's mass movement.

An East European Communist offered this insight. "Everyone in Eastern Europe asks: How is it possible for the PKI, once the strongest party in the country, to collapse without a fight?" he said. "But they do not understand the structure of Indonesian society and the structure of the PKI.

"There is no proletariat in Jakarta, only a weak working class. There are no big factories, a source of party strength. The members of the PKI in Jakarta are small clerks. There are no blue collar workers. Intellectuals, yes, but without a working class the intellectuals are useless. Moreover, the PKI mass organizations were dispersed, made up from a *lumpen* proletariat consisting of *betjak* (tricycle) drivers and the like. It was not the fault of the party that the party failed, but it was the fault of the society."

He, too, touched on the inescapable relationship between Sukarno and the PKI. "The party was disorientated," he said. "The rank and file waited for an order from above which did not come. In turn, the party leadership waited for Sukarno. They waited—and were killed."

This evaluation of the party's structure has a familiar ring. Eight years earlier, Khrushchev, no less, had implied as much. During a tour of Java, the Soviet party chairman reminded Aidit of Lenin's admonition that the strength of a Communist movement is not judged by numbers but by militancy. "The Communist Party is not a grocery store where the more customers you attracted, the more soap, rotten herring, or other spoiled goods you sell, the more you gain," he said.[7] In fairness to Aidit, however, it should be noted that Khrushchev himself was pursuing a Right strategy at the time and, indeed, endorsed the PKI's strategy and tactics by citing the Indonesian maxim, "a peaceful buffalo is much stronger than a predatory tiger."

Retreating further into history, we find that before Khrushchev a founder of the PKI and its first vice chairman made a similar assessment. Darsono observed in 1957 that the PKI's leaders at the branch level were "still dominated by superstition [and] traditional mysticism" and felt the party had attracted a mass following not because the masses had endorsed its Marxist-Leninist program, but because the PKI had promised "land to the tiller" and made other promises which it could not—nay, would not—redeem even if it could.[8] And, receding still further back in time, Sutan Sjahrir, in exile in west Irian in the thirties, concluded similarly. The Indonesian humanist and philosopher, three-time Premier of the Republic during the war for independence, and the principal democratic socialist leader of the Malay world, described his "Communist" prison mates as politically unsophisticated villagers who would have followed "any prince, or venal quack or lunatic," termed their brand of communism an irrational blend of Hinduistic, Islamic, and animistic influences, and concluded that the Communists had exploited their credulity, their natural grievances, and their deep desire for independence and a new life.[9]

In the spring of 1968, Hatta, who shared exile in West Irian with Sjahrir, echoed this view. "The PKI has always misjudged its strength," he said.[10] "This time it developed a great mass following which, except at the top, lacked spirit. Further, the party leadership miscalculated and depended on Sukarno to protect them." Sukarno's former confidant, Roselan Abdul Gani, offered a similar analysis. The PKI overestimated the strength of the masses and underestimated their lack of a critical faculty, "something which cannot grow overnight," he said.[11]

The PKI strength lay in numbers and yet it failed to appreciate that the more illiterate the mass, the more unstable and unreliable it is politically. He continued, "The Indonesian masses, because of their lack of critical faculty and their low interest factor in politics, were prepared to accept everything." In the West, Gani said, "a political party meeting attracts members of the party, but who attends in Indonesia?" Mochtar Lubis, the journalist and author who became a symbol of defiance to the Sukarno regime, put it differently. "The mass following of the PKI was artificial," he said.[12] "Basically, the party membership was more Indonesian than Communist. The PKI paid children to attend their rallies—

everyone knew this. Moreover, the old PKI leadership was trained in Berlin, Moscow, and Yenan. They were tough and inspired, but this was not true of the contemporary leadership of the PKI."

By far the most encompassing analysis of the collapse of the PKI came from Elkana Tobing, an admirer of Tan Malakka and the principal political adviser of Adam Malik, Suharto's foreign minister.

"The PKI's growth was too rapid," Tobing said.[13] "They did not have the time in which to develop convictions among their rank and file. It takes years to develop political convictions. The PKI's mass base was superficially contrived. Their mass educational program resulted in lectures on ideology and strategy to groups ranging from two hundred to eight hundred in number. The PKI engaged more in a psychological exercise than in education. But a psychological advantage can evaporate in minutes. A political atmosphere can change suddenly. At best, the real strength of the PKI lay somewhere between fifty thousand and one hundred thousand. They were dispersed, spread thin. How could they fight? They had no firm foundation. Their backers melted away and the party tumbled like a house of cards."

Tobing added, "The PKI also overexaggerated its own power—and that's another critical factor in explaining their failure."

This "other factor" is frequently cited by Indonesians as a basic cause for Aidit's misadventure. The PKI, it must be understood, exercised de facto control of Indonesia's press, radio, and television in the years 1964–65. The daily diet of PKI propaganda (interlaced with the regime's own propaganda) robbed many Indonesians of their courage and determination to resist the Communists. Most Indonesians, by mid-1965, considered a Communist triumph "inevitable." [14] In point of fact, as events after October 1 lucidly demonstrated, the PKI's real power was not as great as it appeared, but for years it had been a bluff that was working.[15] A failure of the PKI leadership was that it came to believe its own propaganda. Tobing, with customary directness, said, "If you tell a lie to yourself a hundred times you may come to believe it."

Leimena held that "essentially the PKI was show business." [16] And Prawoto said: "The PKI resembled a goat herd more than a group of truly conscientious revolutionary fighters. Many of them were either not convinced of the party's goals or were convinced that the goals were not worth fighting for. Often the PKI recruited its membership by intimidation. When the organization at the top broke down, the bottom scattered like a goat herd. Through their own propaganda, the PKI leadership deceived themselves." [17] As John P. Roche, a former White House adviser, once observed, "When you start believing your own press releases, you've had it."

Two former Indonesian premiers confessed that they had misjudged the PKI's leadership, strength, and wisdom. "We overestimated their wisdom," Natsir, the former Masjumi leader, said.[18] "We thought they were wise enough to avoid a physical showdown." And Wilopo, the PNI leader, candidly confessed, "I valued Aidit the higher." [19] As General Simatupang put it, "The logic of history demanded that we go Communist—Thank God we did not." [20]

There are a myriad of other explanations for the sudden demise of what was vaunted in the mid-sixties as the largest Communist movement in the non-Communist world. Deception was clearly another element. "Many persons," wrote Burhan and Subekti, two Indonesian journalists,[21] "feeling that they had been deceived by PKI propaganda, surrendered to the local government authorities while everywhere, branches of the PKI itself and of its mass organizations disbanded themselves." The murder of the generals jarred not only the nation, but the party's camp followers, too. "Some rank-and-file members were shaken by the murders," Gani felt.[22] "The murders jolted them back to reality."

What gradually emerges from this portrayal is that there were "two PKIs," not one. One Communist Party, at the top, was composed of dedicated, devoted, and disciplined Marxist-Leninists. The other Communist Party, at the bottom, was comprised of uneducated, politically unsophisticated workers and peasants who were attracted to the PKI by its identification with Sukarno, its lavish promises, and its narrow, jingoistic nationalist appeals. The upper echelons of the party were positive in their outlook. They had a program for power. The lower echelons had a negative outlook and executed the destructive aspects of the program. The apex of the party's power pyramid was composed of tough-minded, politically astute, hardened totalitarians; the base was composed of sympathizers and fellow travelers whose allegiance to narrow nationalism was deeper than to the Marxist-Leninist leadership. This explains why the PKI role in the September 30 movement must be viewed as a tactic of the "united front from above" and why the bottom was mistrusted by the PKI hierarchy and was therefore caught unaware when Sukarno failed to follow through on October 1.

Most significant of all, perhaps, is that Aidit himself, in an obscure reference, distinguished between two PKIs and thereby confirmed their existence. Aidit pointed out that the Indonesian Communist Party "is at the same time a party of leaders and [a party] of mass membership." In retrospect, this is the most illuminating evaluation he had ever made about the true nature of the Communist movement in Indonesia. It may also be applicable to in-power and out-of-power Communist parties elsewhere in developing Asia.

Another element in the PKI debacle, of course, was the poor technical execution of the master plan on October 1. Nasution, for example, should never have escaped and, after seizing control of the telephone exchange, the conspirators should have silenced the Army's communications center. Moreover, all the soldiers involved in the affair were drawn from central Java (other than the palace honor guard) and therefore they had no direct contact with the people in Jakarta. Then, too, when the Communist leadership finally decided to make a stand in central Java, they retreated to their old strategic line of Semarang, Salatiga, Surakarta, and Wonogiri. This was the same complex they employed during the Madiun affair. An unimpeachable Javanese source suggested that if the PKI had changed its strategic line to Semarang, Magelang, and Jogjakarta, "the outcome might have been otherwise." He did not elaborate. However, an Army colonel, from Sumatra, thought it was "inconceivable that the PKI believed it could get away with it." With Armed Forces Day in the offing, he said, Jakarta was "an armed camp with troops garrisoned in every *kampong*." Then he wistfully added, "But, of course, Sukarno was their turnkey."

Still another failure in the technical implementation of the plan was to take Suharto for granted. The PKI was not alone in this assessment; obviously, Sukarno and the "progressive, revolutionary" officers in the armed forces felt similarly. They probably considered Suharto politically ineffectual, perhaps apolitical, someone who could be used. "They underestimated him," Anak Agung said.[23] And another political figure recalled, "I remember him from Jogja days as a calm man, always in the background, never flamboyant, but apparently he had one great capacity—the capacity to seize the moment."

If the PKI misread Suharto's political capabilities, it also misread the situation within the armed forces, especially the Army. The Army appeared split. It was split over support of Sukarno, over his foreign policy of collaboration with the Chinese, over the Malaysian war, over questions of corruption within the military, and so forth.[24] But the Communists forgot that the leadership of the Army was drawn from the revolutionary period, 1945–49, and despite internecine quarrels considered themselves part of the same family. The PKI's neglect in this matter is the more surprising since Aidit himself once observed that "there is much foolish talk about the character of our armed forces, but it should not be forgotten that our Army is new . . . that Sukarno exercises great influence on the ranks and has rejected military dictatorship." [25] Indeed, he continued, the Army could not destroy either Sukarno or the PKI, and, he prophesied, "if we are destroyed, what follows will be worse." Both evaluations were faulty, although what followed was worse in a way that Aidit did not suspect.

Aidit knew, like everyone else, that the economic and social conditions for the average foot soldier in the Army were deplorable and that there was great dissatisfaction in the ranks. Apparently Aidit reasoned that if the top generals, who were adamantinely anti-Communist, were removed, there would be no resistance from below. Indeed, perhaps the purge would be met with satisfaction. Aidit apparently distinguished between two armies—just as there were two PKIs. His assumption, of course, was based on the reasonable conclusion that resistance in the Army would collapse once Sukarno exercised his "great influence on the ranks" in support of the purge.[26] But Sukarno did not, and nothing untoward occurred within the Army. Indeed, as we have seen, the battalions unknowingly drawn into the power play to "protect" Sukarno put down their guns after Suharto's emissaries explained the nature of the situation—and after Sukarno failed to openly endorse the September 30 movement.

Then, too, as at Madiun, in Suripno's words, the PKI learned that "the people did not support us." As the Sultan of Jogjakarta explained, discussing the events surrounding the Gestapu affair, "There was no popular uprising of the people."[27] The Communists, he said, misjudged the temper of the people. "Here was a mass party which lacked the support of the masses," is the way Umar Seno Adjie characterized it.[28]

As early as 1953, when the PKI embarked on the high road to "organize, agitate, and mobilize the masses," the inner council of the party debated the question of whether or not to develop a broad, mass-based party and whether or not to pursue a policy of unqualified identification with and dependence on Sukarno. Aidit triumphed. Tan Ling Djie, an advocate of a small, cadre-styled party, was expelled from the Central Committee that year and, three years later, another old-line member, Alimin Prawirodirdjo, a former party chairman, "resigned" from the party in a dispute with Aidit over strategy and tactics which also masked a struggle for power.[29] Both Tan and Alimin considered the unsophisticated masses unreliable and scoffed at Aidit's prescription for power, the "organization, agitation, and mobilization of the masses." Tan in particular preferred a return to the strategy of 1935–47 based on developing a small cadre party, a massive popular front, and the concealment tactic of "bloc within" during which Communists infiltrated non-Communist parties and thereby sought to influence or control them.[30] During this debate, the PKI leaders also argued the question of how far to go in the alliance with bourgeois nationalism—that is, Sukarno. Aidit and other Moscow-oriented party leaders considered Sukarno another Sun Yat-sen—in effect, a pathfinder for the Communist Party. Lukman, who was identified with the Peking faction, is believed to have considered Sukarno potentially another Chiang Kai-shek—that is, an authoritarian nationalist who might betray the Communist movement at a critical moment as the Generalissimo did in 1927.[31] In this instance, Aidit's assessment of Sukarno was correct; Sukarno did not turn on the PKI (he was far too compromised) but, as demonstrated later, Peking accused Sukarno for his failing to act decisively during the crunch.

By 1964–65, too, following Aidit's proclamation of the PKI's independence after his visits to Moscow and Peking, there was evidence that the Sino-Soviet schism was exercising a baleful influence within the party hierarchy. In 1964, for example, Aidit—now independent of Moscow—accused the Kremlin of trying to develop a "pro-Moscow" faction within the PKI by encouraging the creation of a "new Marxist-Leninist Party" as a PKI rival.[32] But at no time in this later debate was there a hint that the conflict turned on such basic questions as the alliance with Sukarno or the development of a cadre as opposed to a mass-based party. After the collapse of the PKI in 1965, however, the aging Semaun, a founder of the PKI, suggested that he might undertake the establishment of a new Marxist-Leninist Party.[33] But the reaction against the Communists was so severe, and on such a massive scale, that he promptly abandoned the notion.*

In assembling the various Indonesian explanations for the collapse of the PKI, it should be noted, too, that the PKI was also partly victimized by the rapid growth of its influence at home and abroad. The PKI, especially during 1963–65, exercised a deepening influence on higher councils of both the Communist and non-Communist worlds. Consequently, almost inexorable pressure developed on Aidit and the PKI to act decisively in any given situation. Surjotjondro, chief of the office of the Foreign Ministry during Subandrio's reign, made the point strikingly. "The pressures on the PKI were tremen-

* See page 165.

dous—from Sukarno, from the Army, from Moscow, and from Peking," he said.[34] "The PKI was in the center."

From this catalog of explanations emerges the varied causes for the fall of the Indonesian Communist Party. Interestingly, a thesis which has gripped the imagination of many Western academicians attracts little support in Indonesia. This is the view that Sukarno deliberately "domesticized" the PKI, that is, brought it into the government apparatus, tamed it, Indonesianized it, and gave it a vested interest in Indonesian nationalism.[35] Perhaps; most Indonesians consider this a rationalization for what they consider to have been a deliberate Sukarno policy to gradually prepare the PKI for the assumption of power on his death. In the light of events, the Indonesians were right. The "domesticization" of the PKI appears to have been little more than a successful penetration and infiltration of the government on the Czechoslovak model, 1945–48.

In reciting these different views on why the Communist mass movement buckled so swiftly, it appears that in many respects they constitute a replay of the reasons for previous PKI debacles in Indonesia. Despite these failures, however—or because of them—it is unlikely that Indonesia will avoid another challenge from the PKI. The Communists have invested too much in time, funds, and human resources to give up the ghost. If the Indonesian Communists operated in a vacuum— for example, as the Nazis did in Germany—the Communist threat to Indonesia would have dissipated long ago. But since the PKI is part of a global movement, however shattered from within, it maintains sanctuaries aboard. It can, and does, incubate in hospitable political environments overseas. Although the monolithic international Communist movement of the Lenin, Stalin, and Malenkov models has passed into history and is not likely to return, individual Communist parties know they can find havens and secure diplomatic, propaganda, financial and military support from one or another group in the Communist world. There is also the possibility, of course, that the PKI may one day learn from its past failures and adopt a new approach to Indonesia in its unremitting drive for absolute, interminable power. Non-Communists must not be overconfident that the very nature of Marxist-Leninist dogma precludes such a development. Perhaps you cannot teach an old dog new tricks; but, then, it is also said that it is never too late to learn.

12

Impact on Peking

HOW DID THE COMMUNIST ENTER-
prise outside Indonesia react to the PKI debacle? As can be
expected, the schism within the Communist world led to a
variety of reactions and put a new strain on relations between
Moscow and Peking.

For China, the Communist disaster was a setback of the
first magnitude. In a single blow, Peking's grand strategy in
Southeast Asia was reduced to a shambles. The maturing
Jakarta-Peking alliance was shattered. The within-reach objective of dishonorably liquidating the Anglo-American presence in the region dissolved. The opportunity to divide the
area into respective Sino-Malay spheres of influence under the
direction of Jakarta and Peking—and, in the process, destroying the non-Communist Asian states between them—was lost.
To paraphrase Heine, Peking sowed dragon-seeds and reaped
fleas.

Clearly, then, the downfall of the PKI was a particularly
cruel blow for Peking. It snatched from the Communists a
splendid base from which they could have supported campaigns of "national liberation" in Malaysia (Malaya and
northern Borneo), Singapore, Brunei, and the Philippines.[1]
To this list could be added the Isthmus of Kra or southern
Thailand. It removed, for the immediate future, the threat of
a Communist presence overlooking the main sea route linking
Japan and Western Europe, and the threat of Communist
control of the 600-mile Strait of Malacca between Sumatra and
Malaya through which two hundred ships steam on an average
day. Given the closure of the Suez Canal two years later, the
combined effect on world trade would have been incalcula-
ble.

To appreciate the dimensions of the setback, we must briefly trace the sinuous relationship between Jakarta and Peking since 1949 when, within a hundred days of each other, the Communists ascended to power on the mainland and the Indonesians assumed control of the archipelago. Their relationship has alternately waxed and waned since then, as it did in the precolonial or premodern period. One feature of this relationship has been the widespread hostility toward the Chinese which is deeply ingrained in the Malay world and is an outgrowth of conflicting racial, linguistic, cultural, economic, and religious factors. The consolidation of Sukarno's authoritarian regime after 1958, however, coupled with the emergence of the PKI as a major political factor within Indonesia, marked a period of unprecedented collaboration between China and Indonesia which gave rise in 1965 to the formation of the so-called Jakarta-Peking Axis.

Peking's understanding with Indonesia was with both the PKI and Sukarno, and it was reached in 1963. That year, with Mao Tse-tung in eclipse, Peking, under the leadership of Chairman Liu Shao-chi, tossed caution to the winds, banked on the eventual emergence of a Communist state in Indonesia, and irrevocably committed itself to Aidit and the Sukarno regime.

In 1963, Aidit was named an honorary member of the Chinese Academy of Sciences,* and thereby earned the Chinese salutation of not simply "Comrade Aidit" but "Respected Comrade Aidit," a distinction of political significance among Chinese Communists. Aidit was lionized in Peking and was placed on a footing with Mao and Stalin as a "contributor to Marxist-Leninist theory." Ku Mo Jo, the president of the Academy, held that "we will learn from Respected Comrade Aidit," and he described the Sumatran leader as a revolutionary activist, distinguished fighter in the international Communist movement, and close friend of China who "expounded revolution." Amid deafening applause, Ku declared that the brilliant achievements of the PKI had inspired the Chinese people.

* See page 30.

Aidit, perhaps fearful of losing to Peking his newly acquired independence from Moscow, "hesitated for a long while" before deciding, with an assist from Sudisman, to "accept such a high honor." [2] In his acceptance speech, he modestly and pointedly noted that the PKI had "Indonesianized" Marxism-Leninism only to a certain extent and that "we still do not know what the outcome of our struggle will be in this direction, and *we are still awaiting our final test,* that is, the fulfillment of the Indonesian people's revolution." But Aidit had cause for confidence. In 1963, the first exchange of visits took place between the Chinese and Indonesian chiefs of state in a same year.[3] Sukarno visited Peking; Liu visited Jakarta. Thus, the Chinese had established rapport with Indonesia at both the party and government levels.

In 1964, these relationships deepened and in 1965, for all practical purposes, both sides were allies. Subandrio, for example, headed a special mission to Peking in January; Sukarno conferred in Jakarta with Premier Chou En-lai and Vice Premier–Foreign Minister Chen Yi in April; Peng Chen, a member of the Politburo, conferred with Aidit and Sukarno in May; that same month, Subandrio and Njoto revisited Peking; in August, Aidit and Njoto were in Peking conferring with Liu and Mao; that month, Chen Yi returned to Jakarta and conferred with Aidit, Lukman, Njoto, Sudisman, Sakirman (the PKI quintumvirate), and Sukarno. September was an especially hectic month, ranging from Dhani's unannounced trip to Peking to the arrival of six hundred Indonesians in China—including deputy premiers, generals, governors, and former premiers—to celebrate the sixteenth anniversary of the founding of the People's Republic of China on October 1.

In 1965, the Chinese also began to exercise increasing influence in Indonesia's internal affairs. They did so not only by proposing the formation of a fifth force, by offering to arm that force, and by suggesting that Sukarno may have been seriously ill, but through such indirect methods as molding Indonesian public opinion. Antara News Agency, the sole distributor of news to all mass media in Indonesia, came under complete PKI domination in this period. As a consequence, Antara's use of New China News Agency (NCNA) reports trebled. Most startling of all is that Antara began to use NCNA stories on Indonesian developments. *Duta Masjarakat*, still under NU control, complained editorially that Antara's reliance on reports from NCNA on Indonesian Domestic events was "not a healthy trend." Hardly. NCNA in 1957 described journalism as a tool for class struggle, a weapon for overthrowing capitalism and building "socialism," which in this context means communism.

If 1963 marked the beginning of substantive Sino-Indonesian collaboration, then 1965 was a bench mark. Non-Communist fortunes in Southeast Asia were ebbing. As the year opened, Indonesia had withdrawn from the United Nations and had intensified its pinprick raids against Malaysia (and Singapore). South Vietnam was on the edge of collapse. Against this backdrop, Subandrio visited Peking and concluded what may be interpreted as a military alliance with China, a compact which Sukarno dubbed later in the year the basis for a Jakarta–Pnom-Penh–Hanoi–Peking–Pyongyang Axis (the Cambodians were upset by Sukarno's inclusion of them in his grandiose scheme). Aside from Cambodia, each of these states was outside the United Nations, was authoritarian and expansionist, and was either Communist or, as in Indonesia's case, Communist-oriented. Interestingly, the Axis covered the extent of the former Japanese Empire at its apogee in 1942—from Korea to New Guinea.

Subandrio's forty-four-man delegation included Njoto and senior military advisers. It arrived in Peking on January 23, only twenty-three days after Sukarno announced Indonesia's withdrawal from the United Nations. Subandrio was greeted at Peking by a galaxy of Chinese Communist leaders, including Chou En-lai, Ku Mo Jo, Peng Chen, and Lo Jui Ching, the Red Army chief of the general staff and former head of the secret police (Minister of Public Security). Subandrio was received by chairmen Liu and Mao.[4] Peking's newspapers repeatedly declared that Indonesia and China were linked in a common, militant struggle.

Subandrio did not disappoint his Chinese associates. At a formal banquet, he put on an awesome performance. "I never saw anything like it," Baron Sastradinata, the head of the

Indonesian Embassy's economic section at that time, said: [5] "Bandrio put emphasis on the growing alliance between China and ourselves and loosely employed the word 'axis.' His theme was direct: our withdrawal from the U.N. and the 'axis' with China would drive the imperialists into the sea. At the end of each sentence, the Chinese roared their approval. Each sentence, mind you; as if it were a ritual. The noise was deafening."

A Sino-Indonesian joint statement at the conclusion of Subandrio's negotiations reaffirmed their opposition to Malaysia and South Vietnam, and announced a mutual desire to "strengthen friendly contacts in the *military* field." [6] Both sides, explained Ganis Harsono, Subandrio's spokesman, "unanimously decided to oppose imperialism, colonialism, and neocolonialism with all means." [7] By the end of the month, the Chinese-Indonesian alliance was being rapidly solidified. It may be of historical significance, as discussed in Chapter 15, that the following month the United States opted to intervene massively in Vietnam.

By September, 1965, with the purge of the Indonesian general staff at hand, the relationship between China and "progressive, revolutionary" officers in the Indonesian armed forces also acquired intimacy. Lo Jui Ching described Indonesia as a "comrade-in-arms." [8] An Indonesian military mission to Peking was greeted with a banner which proclaimed, "Long live friendship between the Chinese and Indonesian people and *armed forces.*" [9]

On D-day, September 30, 1965, seven documents—including economic, trade, and "technical" cooperation agreements between China and Indonesia—were signed at Peking; chairmen Liu and Mao received the official Indonesian delegation to the October 1 festivities; and Chu Teh, a member of the Politburo and the chairman of the National People's Congress, gave a banquet in honor of the Indonesian delegation. The delegation was led by Chairul Saleh, former Premier Ali Sastroamidjojo, and the late Major General Wilujo Puspojudo, the president of the Indonesian Defense Institute. Unknown to the trio, only a few days earlier Air Marshal Dhani had paid an unannounced visit to Peking to discuss the clandestine shipment of Chinese arms to Indonesia. Dhani reported on his mission directly to Sukarno.

When hundreds of Indonesians began pouring into Peking for the October 1 anniversary, they received "fantastic hospitality." [10] "Indonesia was accorded VIP treatment and received privileges extended only to Albania," Baron Sastradinata said. "The PKI members and sympathizers within our delegation received special courtesies. Every PKI front was represented; so was every ministry in the government. We had more delegates than any other country." Indicative of the attention the leaders of the Indonesian delegation received, Ali Sastroamidjojo, a former premier and chairman of the Afro-Asian Conference at Bandung in 1955, was provided a foreign guest house which was equipped with a short-wave radio. He first learned of the October 1 putsch over the BBC "so that when Chou En-lai gave us the radio report it came as no surprise to me." [11]

There is controversy over what transpired in Peking on October 1. According to one of the Indonesians present in Peking, Brig. General Achmed Sukendro, the Chinese were in possession of a complete list of the assassinated generals by 11:00 A.M., that is, approximately five hours before the event. Sukendro said their list included Nasution's name.[12] There is also a general impression that the Chinese assembled the Indonesian delegation and told them of the putsch shortly before it was officially announced over Radio Jakarta. As for the latter, there is no evidence to support this, however. "This is not true," Sastroamidjojo flatly states.[13] "When Chou gave us the radio report I already knew about it. Nor did he give us any additional details other than what had already been broadcast by BBC."

H. R. Trevor-Roper, the British historian, was among the foreign guests invited to Peking for the October 1 celebration. He recalled:

My own visit to China happened to coincide with the Indonesian fiasco and it was clear to me, at the time, that the effect of that failure might be serious. The Chinese may or may not have provoked the attempted Communist coup in Indonesia (on this the evidence is unclear), but they certainly took credit for it as soon as it had happened, and until it was known to have failed. I well remember how solemnly the coup was reported to us. It was the only piece of news which we visitors were ever told, and we were told it in circumstances which clearly indicated a deliberate policy, determined on high; for the news of the coup was not released to the Chinese people. That same night, we learned by chance—from the Voice of America, just audible through the jamming—that the coup had failed. Thereafter, every day I would ceremoniously ask our Chinese sponsors if they had any further news from Indonesia, and maliciously enjoy their blank response.[14]

The Indonesian delegation was also receiving blank responses. "Our situation was serious," Sastroamidjojo said. "We were cut off and did not know what was happening." Everybody wanted to know the whereabouts and position of Sukarno. Saleh took charge of the delegation and through an Indonesian Embassy official arranged with the Cambodian delegation to take refuge, if necessary, in Pnom-Penh. Saleh apparently had plans to establish an emergency government there pending the outcome of the affair in Jakarta. But, with the swift collapse of the September 30 movement, Saleh and most of the delegation stopped over in Cambodia only briefly and proceeded directly to Jakarta. They were home within a week.

Before leaving China, however, the delegation's top functionaries headed for Canton, where they got a plane for Pnom-Penh but from where they could also take refuge in Hong Kong, if necessary. In Canton, the delegation divided. M. Zaelini, the representative of the Central Committee of the PKI, and the various members of SOBSI, Lekra, BTI, Pemuda Rakjat, and other Communist fronts opted to remain in China. Several PKI members of parliament also remained behind.[15]

Peking's first formal acknowledgment of the Gestapu affair was contained in a two-paragraph message which Liu and Chou sent to Sukarno on October 3, the day before the unearthing of the generals' bodies. "From radio broadcasts," they said, they learned that Sukarno was in good health and they expressed the hope that under his leadership Indonesia would continue to develop "still further the spirit of opposing imperialism." [16] The following day, NCNA informed the

Chinese people, in two sentences, that "a sudden domestic incident" had occurred in Indonesia and that Sukarno was in good health. Nothing more.

For fifteen days thereafter, the Chinese public was in the dark, not simply the masses (who could not have cared less, in any case), but the comparative few who, by their very positions in the party, army, and government were automatically bound to know and, as Jacques Marcuse, the Agence France Press correspondent in Peking, has suggested, "bound to wonder, and perhaps to criticize." [17] By now, the Indonesian debacle had capped a series of devastating setbacks which had thrown Chinese foreign policy into disarray—the overthrow of Ben Bella in Algeria, the collapse of the Second Afro-Asian Conference, the ineffectual aggressive posturing during the India-Pakistan war, the loss of Cuba to Moscow in the Sino-Soviet polemic, and the United States intervention, at the last moment, in Vietnam.

On October 19, Peking broke its silence. NCNA carried a lengthy roundup on Indonesian affairs containing seven thousand characters and divided into ten sections. The following day, the roundup and other material on Indonesia filled four pages in *People's Daily*. The rigidly controlled press in China attributed the delay in reportage to the failure of NCNA to receive a single story from its own correspondent in Jakarta between October 1 and October 16. The roundup contained familiar themes: CIA plot, "internal affair of the Army," and so forth. Of significance, perhaps, was that the Chinese reported that the generals had been "executed" (an interesting word given the circumstances in which they were slain). The roundup, however, related for the first time that the failure of the September 30 movement had unleashed an anti-Communist and anti-Chinese campaign in Indonesia, that the United States was "jubilant," and that the Soviet Union had reported the event with "an air of satisfaction." [18]

In studying the impact of the Indonesian Communist collapse on the policies of the Chinese Communists, the question of the Great Proletarian Cultural Revolution necessarily arises. The evidence suggests that the total failure of Chinese policy in Indonesia may have been the straw that broke, in this instance, the dragon's back. By the end of 1965, a purge in China was "inevitable," to quote Marcuse again: things had to be explained away, mistakes acknowledged, scapegoats found, and at such a high administrative and party level that the mistakes would take on the appearance of criminal negligence bordering on deliberate treason. In the aftermath of the Cultural Revolution, Liu, Peng Chen, Lo Jui Ching, and many other Chinese luminaries associated with Chinese foreign policy generally, and Indonesian policy in particular, were swept from the scene. It may be worth recording, within this framework, that the opening shot in the Cultural Revolution was fired on November 10, a few weeks after the Indonesian debacle.[19] In any event, during the upheaval which racked China for more than three years, Liu was attacked as a revisionist, as "China's Khrushchev," and, among other things, was accused of supporting collaboration with radical nationalist leaders such as Sukarno. Liu's wife, Wang Kuang-mei, was fiercely assailed for wearing a sumptuous gown when she visited Indonesia in 1963, of walking arm-in-arm with Sukarno, and of indulging in a "bourgeoise life" in Indonesia.[20] Mao's wife, Chiang Ching, ordered the film on the Indonesian visit of Liu and his wife to be shown privately so that the Red Guards, in the vanguard of the Cultural Revolution, could "criticize" it. Within China, the ensuing virulent anti-Indonesia campaign was directed by Red Guards.[21]

While the defeat in Indonesia obviously could not have triggered so titanic an upheaval in China as the Cultural Revolution, it appears to have been a factor in the Cultural Revolution's development. Moreover, the PKI is identified with the most important document in the history of contemporary Chinese communism. This is the thesis promulgated by Field Marshal Lin Piao, who replaced Liu as Mao's heir apparent. Entitled "Long Live the Victory of the People's War," it developed the theme that underdeveloped Asia, Africa, and Latin America constituted the rural areas of the world taken as a whole, while Europe (both West and East), Japan, and North America were its cities.[22] To achieve victory in the world revolution, the rural areas must become the bases for the encirclement and capture of the cities. Vietnam was singled out as the "most convincing example" of this thesis.

Essentially, the Lin Piao thesis applied the strategy Mao developed during the Chinese civil war to the world situation, i.e., encircling the cities from the countryside accompanied by the armed seizure of political power. Fascinatingly, the evidence suggests that the idea of such an application may have been Indonesian in origin. Indeed, this is probably Aidit's most important "contribution" to Marxism-Leninism and explains his election into the Chinese Academy of Sciences. On May 23, 1965, more than three months before Lin Piao published the celebrated doctrine, the Chinese Communists publicly acknowledged that Aidit was the source for this variation on a Maoist theme.[23] The recognition was made at the level of the Chinese Politburo by Peng Chen, who was subsequently purged during the Cultural Revolution. Lin Piao, of course, was not. This debt to Aidit might partly explain—other than direct Chinese complicity in the Gestapu affair—Peking's fidelity to Aidit. Following the PKI debacle, *People's Daily* termed Aidit the "outstanding helmsman" of the Indonesian Communist Party, although, with Aidit's hand on the tiller, the PKI foundered.[24] The fidelity weakened in 1967.[25]

In any case, relations between Indonesia and China deteriorated rapidly in the aftermath of the September 30 movement. The reverse, of course, would have been true had the putsch succeeded.

Indonesian mobs repeatedly attacked the Chinese Embassy and finally put a torch to it. Chinese diplomats were maltreated. Anti-Chinese riots erupted on Java and Sumatra. A Chinese detained for questioning as an alleged spy was reported to have committed suicide by "pouring hot water on his own body." [26] Anti-Chinese graffiti appeared: "Hang Chinamen!", "China Engineered the September 30 Movement!" and so on. The initials CIA acquired a new definition: Chinese Intelligence Agency. Some of the anti-Chinese eruptions were Army-inspired; as in the case of the mass murders, however, the incidents were largely spontaneous and civilian-oriented.

Indonesia's three-million-odd "Overseas Chinese"—there is no exact figure—have long played the role of hapless minority, exposed to, and accustomed to, pogroms. The Peking-PKI-Sukarno collaboration placed them under additional pressure since most Indonesians mistrusted at least two of the three legs—Peking and the PKI. However, Chinese identification with Sukarno provided them with an aura of protection. Despite their own misgivings, many "Overseas Chinese" had little choice but to join the bandwagon. In so far as Sukarno served as their shield in implementing foreign policy, he was their "protector."

Suharto, Adam Malik, and other responsible Indonesian leaders sought to blunt the post-Gestapu anti-Chinese outbursts with mixed results. Suharto appealed to the people "not to get trapped into activities inclining to racialism." [27] Sukarno lent his hand to this effort but, as usual, in terms of power politics. Anti-Chinese disorders, he warned, would adversely affect relations with Peking and might endanger the Jakarta-Peking Axis which, he said, "is an absolute necessity for crushing neocolim." [28] But his appeals backfired and they served to reinforce the popular sentiment that Sukarno was trying to protect the Chinese and the PKI. His admonitions incited further anti-Chinese violence.

The deterioration in Sino-Indonesian relations resulted in a lengthy exchange of diplomatic notes and public statements between the two countries and finally in a suspension in relations. Peking repeatedly warned Jakarta that one day it must repay the "blood debts incurred by the Indonesian reactionaries." [29] In turn, Indonesia accused Peking of intervention in Indonesia's domestic affairs.[30]

A nadir in relations was reached on October 9, 1967, when Indonesia took the initiative and announced a suspension of diplomatic relations with Peking, a move short of a formal rupture. The policy of avoiding an outright break was skillfully managed by Malik, who astutely realized that a suspension left open future options in treating with Peking. By then, Malik had also succeeded in breaking the Jakarta-Peking Axis without breaking relations—no mean feat.[31] The Axis was formally dissolved by Suharto two months earlier. "We have abandoned the 'Axis' policy of the Old Order era which is clearly in contradiction with our independent and active foreign policy [of nonalignment]," he said.[32] Accordingly, Indonesia returned to the United Nations, abandoned the policy of "confrontation" against Malaysia and Singapore, restored friendly relations with all her neighbors, and renewed close contacts with her former trading partners, notably Britain, Holland, Singapore, Japan, and the United States.

Of special historical signficance, perhaps, is the Suharto government's repudiation of the Sino-Indonesia treaty on dual nationality which was not due for reconsideration, if at all, until 1980.[33] This action threw open again the whole messy question of the Overseas Chinese, an issue which has plagued Sino-Indonesian relations since 1949. A Special Staff for Chinese Affairs was also established and a fixed policy toward Chinese enunciated. The gist was that alien Chinese (Communist) and stateless Chinese persons (Nationalists) who "behaved well" would be protected by the government. Those who did not would be "exiled or isolated." [34]

China retaliated to the best of its ability, although opportunities for inflicting physical punishment on Indonesians were limited. There is no Indonesian community in China other than the PKI community or the tens of thousands of Overseas Chinese refugees from Indonesia who have taken refuge on the mainland since 1949—others have found sanctuary in Taiwan, still others in Singapore.[35] The Chinese, however, were in a position to harass the Indonesian diplomatic mission in Peking and proved themselves past masters at the technique. For example, Sastradinata, chargé d'affaires at the time of the suspension in relations, his wife, and four children were forced to run a gauntlet of jeering Red Guard demonstrators to reach the plane that flew them out of Peking. "They acted like robots," he recalled.[36] "I think their hatred of us was artificial. They never looked in our eyes. One cannot believe it. There is no place in the world like Peking. It is very frightening. It is a city of robots."

In the political arena, however, the Chinese maintained a distinct advantage. They could, and did, bring pressure against Indonesia and doubtless would have done so for ideological reasons whether or not the Indonesians embarked on an anti-Chinese campaign at home.

Peking became a base of operations for the shattered, now underground, PKI.[37] Peking afforded fugitives from Indonesia financial, diplomatic, and propaganda assistance, and incited them to take up political activities against Jakarta. China's massive propaganda apparatus, including its powerful radio transmitters and its plethora of international publications, also unleashed a campaign to discredit the Suharto government at home and abroad as "a fascist military regime." Peking brought pressure to bear on its associates abroad to do likewise. Albania, its only ally west of Lop Nor, the Chinese nuclear test site, joined the campaign, as did Peking's ideological brethren—notably the Burmese, Malayan, Thai, and New Zealand Communist parties.[38]

Since 1965, the Chinese Communist Party position on Indonesia has remained unchanged. In Peking's view, the Indonesian Communist setback was a severe blow to the hopes and aspirations of the international Communist movement. But the Chinese Communists contend the defeat is of a temporary nature and "the crimes of persecution perpetrated by the Indonesian reactionaries against the Indonesian people will surely bring about a more widespread and violent revolution of the Indonesian people and quicken the approach of a hightide in this revolution." [39] As for the lesson the PKI learned, in Peking's estimation it was this: develop a fifth force and seize power forcibly. A blunt summary of the Chinese Communist assessment of events in Indonesia was contained in an editorial by *People's Daily*. "From the lesson they [the PKI] paid in blood," it said,[40] "they have learned with profound understanding the incontrovertible truth of the great leader Chairman Mao that 'political power grows out of the barrel of a gun' and are determined to follow the road of the Chinese revolution. We are convinced that whatever difficulties and twists and turns the Indonesian people may meet on their road of advance, the tide of revolution is irresistible."

This analysis appeared as early as August 12, 1966, at the eleventh plenary session of the Eighth Central Committee of the Chinese Communist Party. The session held that "the bloody massacre and barbarous suppression" of the Indonesian Communist movement by a right-wing military clique has

aroused "the revolutionary consciousness of the broad masses."
It is doubtful, however, whether this is the case: in Indonesia,
the Communists were not merely rejected by the "right wing"
(whatever that means) but by a whole people—and a whole
generation—very much as they were, in a different context, in
Tibet, Hungary, and elsewhere, only there the lesson is that in-
power Communists cannot be turned out of power because
their power rests on the barrel of a gun in the hands of a secret
police. In this sense, the Brezhnev Doctrine, as promulgated in
1968 and applied to Czechoslovakia, may be considered a
variation on a Maoist theme.

When Sukarno meekly submitted to his removal from
power, albeit after a stubborn struggle to retain power, Peking
reappraised its opinion of the man whom they once hailed
as a "comrade-in-arms and heroic revolutionary, progressive
fighter." Peking treated him with contempt. "The myth that
President Sukarno of Indonesia was 'helpless' to stop these vi-
cious attacks against Indonesian progressives, especially Communists, and against Chinese diplomatic and trade personnel,
ought to be blown sky-high," the Chinese Communist financed
and edited *Malayan Monitor* declared.[41] "From being a pas-
sive 'prisoner' of the right-wing, President Sukarno himself
was instrumental in suppressing the progressive elements of
the brutal massacre of many individuals," the journal said.
The monthly accused Sukarno's cabinet of rejecting Aidit's
call for a fifth force and said this rejection was a signal to "all
reactionary elements to start driving a wedge between the PKI
and other progressives, on the one hand, and the rest of the
country, on the other." The analysis contained a hint of where
Sukarno may stand in a future rewriting of PKI history. "The
PKI, headed by D. N. Aidit, has not been destroyed, despite
the brutal massacre of many individuals," the journal said.
"The general situation in Indonesia is now in a state of stern
reappraisal; and the position of those who have betrayed their
trust is far from secure."

As a political sanctuary, Peking has provided protection
for a number of Indonesian Communists.[42] These include at
least the former Ambassadors to China, North Vietnam, and
Cuba (Djawoto, Sukrisno, Hanafiah); Sobron Aidit, the

younger brother of Aidit; former PKI front officials such as Suroso of the Pemuda Rakjat; journalists like Anwar Dharma, the *Harian Rakjat* correspondent who was expelled from Moscow; and at least two members of the PKI Central Committee, M. Zaelini and Jusuf Adjitorop. Of all these, and other figures, by rank Adjitorop, an old-line Communist, is easily the most important. He is the sole survivor of Aidit's Politburo and was deputy head of the secretariat of the PKI Central Committee at the time of the Gestapu affair. In 1954, he was elected to the Central Committee by the historic Fifth Party Congress at which Aidit's leadership was consolidated. Two years later, he was elevated to the CC Secretariat and in 1959 he became a substitute member of the Politburo. PKI policy statements issued at Peking invariably bear his name as "head of the delegation of the party's Central Committee." [43]

Adjitorop arrived in Peking at the head of a nine-man delegation on June 26, 1964—and he has never left, except briefly to attend the Albanian Party Congress in 1966.[44] He dropped out of sight shortly after his arrival in the Chinese capital and this prompted *Chen Hsin Hsin Wen Pao*, published at Taipei, to claim that Adjitorop had been placed under house arrest for apparently having engaged in "pro-Soviet activities." [45] Peking denied the report and announced that Adjitorop had suffered a nervous breakdown and had been confined to a hospital. "Adjitorop may have been sick," a former member of the Indonesian Embassy staff in Peking said.[46] "But nobody really knows. He never visited the Embassy; indeed, nobody ever saw him. I know he spent one winter in Canton, where the weather is milder. A friend saw him there and said he did not look sick."

The evidence suggests, however, that the Chinese Nationalist daily had been engaged in a bit of "black propaganda." The story no sooner appeared than Adjitorop reappeared in Peking and, on October 6, 1964, he was identified as the head of the PKI delegation attending the regime's fifteenth anniversary of its founding. Interestingly, before the October 6 announcement, the temporary head of the PKI delegation was Tjoo Tik Toen, an Indonesian of Chinese ethnic origin who was a member of the PKI Central Committee. Adjitorop, however, remained in Peking after the delegation returned to Jakarta. Yet there is no evidence that he was held involuntarily. On the contrary, the following year, Adjitorop attended the Aidit-Liu talks of August 3 and 4, 1965, and the Aidit-Mao conference of August 5.[47] We do not know what Aidit and the Chinese Communist leadership discussed at these lengthy sessions, but it is reasonable to speculate that the decision to move against the Indonesian general staff, in view of Sukarno's real or imagined illness, was made at this time. Little publicity was given to the talks, suggesting that they were working sessions. A brief communiqué reported that the two sides exchanged views on the world situation (doubtless Vietnam), the state of the international Communist movement (doubtless the Sino-Soviet schism), "and other matters of common interest to both parties." [48] The Chinese and Indonesian party chairmen also reached "complete unanimity (on) all questions." Two days later, Aidit, accompanied by a Chinese medical team, arrived in Jakarta.[49]

As the spokesman abroad for the PKI since 1965, Adjitorop has held that the "primary reason for the setback suffered by the Indonesian revolution is the failure of the PKI to master Mao Tse-tung's thought." This assessment, under the circumstances, may be little more than paying lip service to Mao in the midst of the all-embracing Cultural Revolution. Of greater interest is his implied criticism of the Aidit leadership despite the Aidit–Lin Piao relationship. Adjitorop has held that "the united front policy followed by the PKI leadership in the more than a decade before 1965, especially the policy of forming a united front with Sukarno, was in essence a policy of class collaboration." This, he contended, ran counter to Mao's teaching that the purpose of a united front is to carry out armed struggle. This is nonsense, since a united front may be developed under a Right or Left strategy. In any event, in Adjitorop's view, Indonesia's "liberation" can be achieved only if the country follows the road of people's war charted by Mao. This is the Lin Piao thesis, which would therefore bring us back to Aidit's "contribution" to Marxist-Leninist theory. Cearly, the PKI is in theoretical as well as physical disarray.

Realistically, the fact that the PKI must now openly depend on China as an operational base is likely to hinder rather than help the regrouping of the Communists in Indonesia. In addition to the stigma of Madiun and the Gestapu affair, the PKI today must bear the burden of identification with the power which, rightly or not, most Indonesians consider the long-term threat to the security of the Malay world.

13

Impact on Moscow

SIMILARITIES AND DISSIMILARITIES marked the Soviet response to the Gestapu affair, as compared to the reaction of its quondam ally China. The Russians, unlike the Chinese, immediately reported the events in Indonesia in their domestic news coverage, quoting Western news agencies. Tass, the state-controlled Soviet news agency, however, like its Chinese counterpart, NCNA, remained noncommittal. Like Peking, too, the first official Soviet reaction to the putsch was contained in a message to Sukarno congratulating him on his good health and expressing confidence in his continued leadership. Whereas the Chinese message was sent within seventy-two hours, the tidings from the Kremlin were delayed until October 10, possibly indicating uncertainty as to the role of Sukarno, the PKI and/or Peking in the affair. By then, the bodies of the generals had been exhumed, the Communist involvement in the murders exposed, Aidit was in hiding, and Sukarno fighting for political survival. The Soviet message bore three signatures: Leonid Brezhnev, the secretary of the Soviet Communist Party's Central Committee; President Anastas Mikoyan, a familiar visitor in Jakarta; and Premier Aleksei Kosygin.

From all appearances, the September 30 movement caught the Russians, like the Americans and British, by surprise. The knowledge that Aidit was at Halim and that the Pemuda Rakjat had taken part in the killings probably stunned the Soviet Embassy in Jakarta. So did the *Harian Rakjat* editorial, we can presume. The initial Soviet commentary on the purge appeared in *Pravda,* the party paper, on October 20. It endorsed Sukarno's appeal for a "normalization of the situation," cited the Kremlin's unswerving support of Indonesian independence (at a time when the putsch was being dubbed a second Madiun), and pointedly recalled the Soviet endorsement of Indonesia's Irian liberation campaign. *Pravda,* however, refrained from a direct comment on the affair other than to observe, in pedestrian fashion, that as Indonesia passed through "grave trial," the Soviet Union followed developments with "attention and great concern." The Kremlin was buying time.[1]

A second, and meatier, commentary emerged six days later. The party organ now observed that "the only established fact" was that Untung and a group of officers were the *"active* force behind the coup." *Pravda* then conceded a possibility that a PKI "adventurist clique" may have been involved. "Even if one assumes that individual members of left-wing organizations, succumbing to provocations, had something to do with the September 30 events, this cannot in any case justify reprisals against the three million strong PKI which has earned well-deserved glory as a genuinely patriotic and revolutionary party," *Pravda* said. It appeared that Moscow was trying to save the PKI by tarring an "adventurist clique" with Chinese feathers. In conclusion, the party daily stressed that "political adventurism, putschism and sectarianism are alien to Marxism-Leninism." As debatable as that may be, within a week Brezhnev, describing himself as a "sincere friend of Indonesia," expressed open concern about the anti-Communist drive and appealed to Jakarta to maintain "the unity of all progressive national forces." [2] Since Untung had claimed that he sought to abort a CIA plot and since the purge of the PKI had gained momentum, these Soviet reactions were relatively insouciant.

It was not until 1966 that the Russians put forth the view that the Indonesian Communists were being "unjustly accused" of playing a part in the affair.[3] Moscow sought to rationalize the presence of Aidit and the Pemuda Rakjat at Halim and explain away the incriminating *Harian Rakjat* editorial with the backhanded remark that "only a minor (Communist) group participated in the movement." [4] The Russians, however, continued to discount the PKI's official

version of the putsch as an "internal Army affair." Instead,
they maintained that "it is (still) not clear who was responsible for the *Gestapu*"—the acronym was Moscow's.[5] Once
again, the Russians contended that anyone familiar with
Communist strategy and tactics would know that the purge of
the Indonesian general staff had "nothing in common with
Marxism-Leninism, which rejects the road of terror and political gambles." [6]

A year later, the Soviet Union expounded its analysis and
for the first time tarred Sukarno, who had once received a
Lenin (formerly Stalin) Peace Prize. Moscow accused Sukarno
of having rejected "peaceful coexistence" (the Right strategy)
and of having "slipped towards dangerous adventures" (the
Left strategy).[7] By now, of course, the testimony developed at
the trials of Sudisman and Njono, Sjam and Supardjo, Dhani,
and the others had implicitly put the finger on Sukarno—
although Moscow, like Peking, denounced the tribunals as
stage-managed (which they doubtless were to some extent,
notably in skirting the question of the President's involvement).[8]

Privately, the Russians were more voluble. They told at
least one Indonesian general that the PKI deserved no better
fate than it received for having depended on Sukarno, thereby
deviating from Marxism-Leninism. This was rubbish; for,
after 1952, the Russians not only cultivated Sukarno but ordered the PKI to do likewise—this was, it must be recalled,
still the period of monolithic direction in the Communist
world. Moreover, although this is speculative, should Sukarno
ever return to power, Moscow doubtless would be among the
first to embrace and bolster his new regime. This assessment is
unlikely to be tested; while Indonesia may not be done with
Sukarnoism, it is done with Sukarno. In private, and to some
extent in public, the Russians also cite the PKI failure in
Indonesia as a singular example of how Mao's policies have
increasingly played into the hands of "imperialism and reaction." Moscow attributes the PKI debacle partly to the collapse of the monolithic international Communist movement.

The PKI's denouement in Indonesia, of course, prompted
some hard thinking in Moscow, as it did elsewhere. The effect

within the Kremlin itself is less clear than in the case of Peking, but undoubtedly the fall of the PKI strengthened the hand of the "hawks" (the Shelepin Group, at the time), who felt that Sino-Soviet disunity was being exploited by Washington to tip the world balance of power against Moscow. It also prompted a Soviet theorist to develop a thesis which has long been accepted, in reverse, in the Western world. Y. N. Guzevaty, a member of the Soviet Institute of World Economics and International Relations, concluded that "overoptimistic expectations," overpopulation, and economic difficulties—especially food shortages—in the developing world provided the West with the opportunity to discredit communism. In the West, of course, these problems are ritualistically cited as furthering the advance of communism.

In any event, throughout the post-Gestapu period, the Kremlin studiously maintained governmental relations with Jakarta. Brezhnev set the line at the Soviet party's Twenty-third Congress on March 29, 1966. Without referring directly to the putsch or the massacre, he emphasized that Moscow would continue to seek to develop "friendly relations" with Jakarta.[9] In effect, all was not lost. Moscow's subsequent policies did not belie his words.

The Kremlin rescheduled the debt of $1.2 billion which Indonesia owed the Soviet Bloc;[10] resumed the temporarily suspended shipment of spare parts to the Soviet-equipped Indonesian armed forces, including spares to maintain Indonesia's squadron of Soviet-built class W submarines; resumed new economic assistance, albeit on a scale so minimal as to be little more than symbolic; refrained from blocking Indonesia's re-entry into the United Nations; continued to provide Indonesian trade union leaders with five-year "scholarships" to the Soviet Union or short-term grants, both in unlimited numbers, despite the destruction of SOBSI; expelled the *Harian Rakjat* correspondent from Russia; ousted a clique of pro-Peking Indonesian students from Patrice Lumumba University in Moscow; and continued to maintain a huge Soviet mission in Jakarta, including fifty-one accredited diplomatic officers.[11] There were even hints that the Russians were helpful in "rooting out" some PKI members, though of this there is no confirmation.[12] Most important of all, Moscow abandoned, *for the present at least,* plans to abet the establishment of a new Marxist-Leninist PKI as a successor (or rival) to the old PKI.

This last development is deeply significant in terms of assessing the future of the Indonesian Communist Party—if, indeed, it has a future in this generation, which is strongly doubtful.

As a by-product of the Sino-Soviet split in the early sixties and the PKI's identification with Peking after 1963, the Russians entertained the idea of developing a counter, Marxist-Leninist PKI.[13] The founding of rival Communist parties in non-Communist states is not uncommon. As observed earlier, however, both Aidit and Peking denounced these Soviet machinations. The focal point of Soviet activity centered on Sumatra where the Russians belatedly opened a consulate at the end of 1964, giving rise to speculation that Moscow toyed with the idea of developing a rival PKI along ethnic, non-Javanese lines. There is no evidence to support this speculation, however, although it cannot be entirely discounted. The PKI debacle in 1965, however, provided the Kremlin with an unprecedented opportunity to put the blame for the putsch on the Chinese Communists—whether or not they were involved —and to regain control of a "clean" PKI. Thus, hard after September 30, the Kremlin openly expressed "confidence that the PKI will revive on the basis of Marxism-Leninism." [14] Indeed, in the period of October–December, 1965, there was widespread talk in Jakarta about the possible emergence of a new Communist Party. This was the period when Sukarno was struggling for his political life and the idea of a new PKI to replace the old PKI in the NASAKOM trinity was especially attractive. Sukarno, as well as the Russians, actively encouraged it.[15] The cow-catcher for this project was Semaun, the first chairman of the PKI who spent thirty-three years behind the iron curtain, where he acquired Soviet citizenship, became third premier of the Tadjikistan Soviet Republic, broadcast over Radio Moscow during the Madiun affair, returned to Indonesia in 1956 as a special adviser to Sukarno, and in 1959 was named by Sukarno to the Provisional Supreme Advisory Council.[16] Semaun's post-Gestapu maneuvers, however, were promptly and roundly denounced by the rump PKI leadership and by Peking.

Njoto, in his last public statement before his arrest and execution in December, 1965, decried the idea of establishing a new PKI. He declared that "it is not possible," and said such a party would only be "crypto-Communist or pseudo-Communist." [17] Peking, through the underground Malayan Communist Party—an ethnically Chinese-based party which Peking finances, arms, and directs—was equally derogatory. "Attention must be drawn to the fact that renegades from the Communist Party of Indonesia, Semaun and his like, are trying to piece together a pseudo 'Communist Party' while singing duets with Khrushchev revisionists in charging the Indonesian Communist Party, headed by Comrade Aidit, as 'betraying Marxism-Leninism,'" the Malayan Communist Party declared.[18] "These renegades have been given the role of fifth columnists to disrupt and crack the revolutionary ranks from within in coordination with the all-out attack of the reactionaries [from without]."

In the heady, anti-Communist atmosphere of the period, however, nothing overt resulted from Semaun's efforts. Not only did Jakarta reject communism, no matter how anti-Chinese a brand it was, but Indonesia outlawed the propagation of Marxism-Leninism, thereby short-circuiting the Semaun Plan. Nonetheless, Moscow remained openly interested in the scheme until at least 1967. That year, it circulated an "Appeal of the Marxist-Leninist Group of the Indonesian Communist Party," which proposed that the PKI return to a Right strategy. The appeal first appeared in the Soviet-controlled *Information Bulletin* published in Prague, which, until 1968, served Moscow as a subsidiary outlet in a fashion similar to Peking's use of Tirana today. It was subsequently republished in *l'Humanité*, the French Communist Party organ, and later in Soviet-influenced newspapers in India and Ceylon.[19]

In summary, the Appeal observed that since 1953 the PKI had successfully adopted a "cautious" (Right) strategy and profited from cooperation with Sukarno, although "this also

had some negative aspects." Under Peking's influence, however, the PKI had changed its strategy and adopted a " 'leftist'
revisionist" position. The PKI became an "experimental
ground for adventurist policy," abandoned Communist unity
for the Jakarta-Peking Axis, and embarked on "adventurism
pure and simple, which has nothing to do with the Marxist
theory of armed insurrection."

The Appeal then charged that the Aidit leadership "belatedly disassociated itself from the September 30 Movement"
and it accused many PKI functionaries of permitting themselves to be arrested "without any real resistance." This blend
of "passivity and panic" in the PKI leadership ended in the
party's destruction. "The PKI placed all its hopes in President
Sukarno and his political solution of the question, and not in
the power of the masses," the Kremlin said. Moscow then cata-
logued the "objective" reasons for the party's demise: irre-
sponsibility of certain party leaders; ideological, political, and
organizational confusion resulting objectively from petty
bourgeois revolutionary activity; excessive revolutionary zeal
and the desire to win as rapidly as possible; an unjustified
attempt to force the onset of the revolution; an inaccurate
estimate of the relationship of forces within Indonesia; impul-
sive and adventurist gambling, and so on.

The Russians conceded, perhaps unintentionally, that
they were not blameless for the disaster. They contended that
the PKI's efforts to find a solution to Indonesia's economic
decline was "sabotaged [by] unprecedented increases in military credits" to the Sukarno regime. This military burden
aggravated the economic crisis and the domestic opposition to
Sukarno profited from this situation. The opposition launched
a smear campaign against the Sukarno regime which "was not
without success among the masses with little political conscience."

The above is a self-indictment since Moscow was Sukarno's principal source of military credits between 1960 and
1965; indeed, 81 percent of Indonesia's credit from the Soviet
Union was spent on military hardware. The Appeal's analysis
is especially intriguing since many of Indonesia's leading economists have long felt that the PKI deliberately abetted the

collapse of the economy by disruptive "unilateral actions"—including the seizure of foreign properties—aimed at hampering production.

As Branko Lazitch has pointed out in *Est & Ouest,* the Parisian journal, a comparison of the Peking–Moscow lines on the Gestapu affair shows that both parties "recognize the role played by the [PKI] in the putsch." [20] The Chinese, he contends, implicitly admit Communist responsibility as an historical fact that can no longer be disputed, whereas the Russians do not question the PKI's role in the affair "but, rather, try to explain it." However, as soon as the question of responsibility for the failure of the putsch is raised, the Russians and Chinese disagree completely. It should go without saying that both Moscow and Peking exploit the PKI disaster to accuse each other reciprocally of the failure. Interestingly, however, both agree that at present the PKI should employ the tactic of the united front to recover lost ground. But while the Russians prefer to erect such a front within the guidelines of the Right strategy of "peaceful coexistence," without explicitly mentioning armed force, the Chinese advocate a front geared to the Left strategy and explicitly mention the armed seizure of power.

In some respects, 1968 became a testing ground for Moscow's low-key and Peking's high-key approach to the question of a PKI revival.

In the mountainous area of Blitar, East Java, the PKI moved to regroup its shattered forces into a "free zone" or liberated area. PKI organizations were set up, on paper at least, from the village to the provincial level.[21] A newly reformed underground Politburo, headed by a Sumatran, Olan Hutapea, pledged to "avenge the death" of murdered Communists and echoed the Peking line that "Indonesia's reactionaries must pay the blood debt they have incurred in blood." [22] In spring of that year, a number of terrorist acts were reported in the Blitar area, including the ambushing of a jeepload of Army officers.[23] The ambush was a mistake or, depending on your point of view, premature. As in the case of Che Guevara's abortive guerrilla campaign in the Andes, the incident acted as a magnet and invited massive Army sweeps.

Again, as in the case of Bolivia, the Communists lacked popular support. The Army operations were singularly successful; several Politburo members were slain, including Hutapea, and Rewang, the director of the PKI's intelligence operations. Also bagged was "General" Sukanto, the Pemuda Rakjat chairman, whose organization assisted in the murder of the generals at Halim on October 1. The Army took prisoners and their interrogation led to the disclosure of a sub rosa PKI network within the armed forces which maintained contact not only with Hutapea, but also with Sukarno.

As a consequence, several officers in the armed forces were detained, including a general, and Sukarno was interrogated for five days and then placed under formal house arrest. A new wave of anti-PKI hysteria, accompanied by a wavelet of murders, apparently followed.[24] Clearly, the PKI's persistent pursuit of a militant Left strategy is especially heartless since it places the lives of the fifty thousand Communist prisoners in jeopardy. In this connection, much has been made of the fate of the prisoners, and rightfully so (except in the case of the former Sukarno-PKI sympathizers who bleat over Indonesia's political prisoners of today but never publicly raised their voices about the prisoners of yesterday). However, for a country of about 125 million people and for a Communist movement which claimed more than ten million party and front members, the fifty thousand figure is not excessive. But it would defeat the Suharto government's design to rehabilitate Indonesia if they are not properly treated. Post-Gestapu Indonesia should not try to emulate the conditions of servitude which exist in the prison camps of the Communist states, notably Russia and China.

Returning to the Blitar affair: The Kremlin was furious. *Pravda* lashed the PKI for "another Communist disaster" and denounced the Blitar episode as an "irresponsible adventure" which, it said, was inspired by Peking.[25] In essence, the Russians did not dispute with Peking over whether or not a non-Communist Indonesia should be "buried" but, rather, the best way to go about the job. Thus, in attacking Peking, *Pravda* contended that armed struggle can only be successful when it has been *"carefully prepared* and is based on broad support."

In other words, the Kremlin accused the Indonesian and Chinese Communists of acting prematurely. This is especially worth noting because the PKI leaders captured, tried, and executed since September 30—Sudisman, for example—have invariably claimed that a reason for the failure of the power play was "prematurity." [26] This was also an excuse given for the Madiun failure. Interestingly, North Korea's Kim Il Sung, who spent three weeks in Indonesia in the spring of 1965 as the Korean—New Guinea power train was being assembled, has cited the failure of the PKI as a case of prematurity. He held that the Indonesian Communists misjudged "objective conditions," struck without being adequately prepared, and consequently were annihilated. Guerrilla warfare, Kim asserted, must follow careful, lengthy preparation. [27]

By contrast, Russia's low-key strategy in Indonesia since September 30 has proven more successful. Despite Moscow's interest in developing a Marxist-Leninist PKI, the Russians have recognized that Jakarta is not presently interested in this—however hostile to Peking. Displaying characteristic realism, the Russians shelved the Semaun Plan. Another example of ostensible Soviet inactivity on the Indonesian front was reflected in Moscow's unrelenting drive to mount a world conference of Communist parties, the first since 1960. Held in 1969, the organizing committee reported that "because of insurmountable obstacles" invitations could not be conveyed to four parties. Each of them—the Indonesian, Thai, Burmese, and Malayan [28]—are rooted in Southeast Asia; each operates underground; each tilts toward Peking; and in each case Moscow is actively wooing its government within the framework of its present anti-China policy. In the case of the PKI, as manifested by the "Appeal of the Marxist-Leninist Group," had the Kremlin desired, it could easily have arranged to have a representative of the Marxist-Leninist PKI group accept such an invitation. But apparently the Kremlin has placed a higher priority on friendly governmental relations with Indonesia at present than on the re-emergence of a friendly PKI at this juncture. Indeed, the PKI's absence at the conference can be construed as visible evidence of Soviet disinterest in a revival of the PKI *for the moment*. The Dutch

Communists, incidentally, also balked at attending the conference on the ground that Moscow betrayed the PKI.[29] There is other evidence of Moscow's "disinterest." The Soviet Union has assiduously avoided labeling the Suharto government "a fascist military regime," a commonplace Communist phrase for authoritarian, anti-Communist governments. Some of the sharpest Russian criticism of Indonesia has emanated not from Radio Moscow but from Radio Peace and Progress, ostensibly a Soviet nongovernmental station (a contradiction in terms), but actually an extension of Radio Moscow's external service, which began broadcasting in 1964. Indeed, Moscow's low-key posture has been pushed to amazing lengths, including, for example, a defense of the Suharto government against its domestic critics, particularly former Masjumi and Socialist Party members who complain that Suharto is moving too slowly to reform post-Sukarno, post-Gestapu Indonesia.[30] At the same time, the Russians have defended the NU and PNI, two of the three former NASAKOM pillars.[31] This suggests that the Soviets still nurture a hope that a "clean" Marxist-Leninist PKI may yet emerge and with it a rehabilitation of the NASAKOM trinity.

This is not the first time in the history of the Indonesian Communist movement that the Russians have displayed "disinterest" in Indonesia.[32] A prime example developed after the 1926 debacle, particularly in the thirties and early forties, during the period of the Right strategy when Moscow pursued a united front from above with Holland and Dutch colonialism as part of its world strategy against the Berlin-Tokyo Axis. Yet, during those years, it later developed, the PKI was active underground.

From his sanctuary in Moscow, Musso made clandestine visits to Indonesia; Gerindo, a youth organization, was formed as an above-ground PKI front; underground papers such as *Red Tower,* for which a youthful Djawoto worked, were circulated in the islands; and so forth. The PKI did not officially reemerge as an overt party until 1946, when the circumstances were favorable, and its membership, operating the bloc-within technique inside non-Communist parties, did not completely surface until 1948. It was a long wait—1926–46. Accordingly, the history of the PKI prompts the suggestion that there is presently in Indonesia a silent Marxist-Leninist PKI underground which Moscow is quietly nursing. Hanoi, for example, is confident about the PKI's future. "In the forty-five years and more of its history, the PKI twice suffered large-scale persecution and was compelled to carry out its activity under extremely difficult and clandestine conditions over long periods," *Hoc Tap,* the North Vietnamese theoretical journal, said.[33] ". . . Tempered in the furnace of revolutionary struggle, the Indonesian Communist Party will weather the severe tests of this period, and consolidate and develop its forces in order to continue to guide the revolutionary cause of Indonesia to new advances."

The wraps are likely to be removed from this silent underground at a propitious time, when there is a less hostile political climate in Indonesia toward the PKI and/or Marxism-Leninism or in the event that Indonesian foreign policy requires some future need to redevelop an intimate relationship with the Soviet Union. In such a case, the PKI might not return as the "PKI," but as a Worker's Party or with some such name, a device which has been employed in such Communist states as North Korea and North Vietnam. Whatever the outcome, it would be folly to think that Moscow has lost interest in the emergence of a Communist Indonesia. Given the Russians' concerted drive to develop a sea-power strategy, it is doubtful if the Kremlin is "disinterested" in the fate of the world's largest archipelago from "historical, political, economic, and geographic points of view," a phrase the Russians employed in clarifying their expanding naval policy in the Mediterranean.[34] The Soviet Union's silent underground must therefore wait a change in Indonesia's political atmosphere—even if it requires decades, as it may. If the Peking-oriented PKI, however, persists in pursuing a militant Left strategy, it will serve to delay the "rehabilitation" of the PKI even further and may lead the Indonesian Communists into the bottomless pit of white and red factions which destroyed the Burmese Communists.

Politically astute as usual, the Indonesians are aware of this state of affairs. A. Sjaichu, for example, the speaker of the house and third chairman of the NU, has drawn this conclusion in public. There are two kinds of PKI supporters at present, he observed, the activists associated with Peking and the passivists associated with Moscow.[35]

The Russians are far from happy about their posture of friendship with the Suharto government. They are embarrassed. "The fact that the Soviet Union maintains interstate relations with Indonesia does not mean that anyone in the Soviet socialist state can remain indifferent to terrorist acts against Communists, the ban on the Indonesian Communist Party, and the persecution of Marxist-Leninist ideology. . . ." *Pravda* said.[36] "Soviet policy is to support the Indonesian course toward national independence in the face of imperialist powers which are trying to exploit the political situation in Indonesia for their own neocolonialist aims." In substance, Moscow is seeking to check Indonesia's complete slide into the "Western" camp. Accordingly, Soviet post-Gestapu policy in Indonesia comes down to this: better half a loaf than none. In addition to ideological and political reasons for maintaining friendly relations with Indonesia, the Russians also have an appreciable economic motivation. It is a good and established banking practice that "sometimes the only way to save a loan may be to secure it by a further loan." [37] And *The Economist* asked: What else can the Russians do? "Well, they could have simply maintained their demand for money on the nail," the British weekly said.[38] "At which Indonesia would no doubt simply have defaulted on the debt, and the Russians would have lost both their money and their remaining Indonesian friends."

Jakarta is not that innocent. Indonesia has tempted the Russians into maintaining good relations. On his first visit to his old stamping ground in Moscow as foreign minister in 1966, as the Kremlin wavered in its Indonesian policy, Adam Malik came straight to the point. "One year ago something happened in Indonesia that gave you, so to speak, a 'shock' . . ." he said.[39] "The fault lies with the PKI itself, which assisted by the Chinese Communist Party, took steps which constituted a treacherous act against the Indonesian revolution." However, he stressed, the PKI problem is an internal

Indonesian affair beyond Moscow's pale. He said the initiative for good relations rested with Moscow since Indonesia genuinely wanted to maintain close relations with the Soviet Union. "We only want your understanding that *at the moment* we cannot accept communism in our country," Malik said. Later, Suharto himself said he would like to emphasize that the Indonesian people do not allow the development of Communist ideology on their soil, but that this does not imply that the Indonesian people do not desire friendly relations with Communist countries, providing they do not interfere in her domestic affairs.[40] This multiple bait was effective and, under the circumstances, Soviet-Indonesian relations have remained relatively unstrained. Indeed, relations were improving at an amiable pace when the Soviet occupation of Czechoslovakia in 1968 evoked memories of past Indonesian experiences with communism—both the Russian and Chinese-influenced varieties. After momentary hesitancy, Indonesia harshly denounced the Soviet-led invasion.[41] So did the undergound PKI.[42] Thus, the Czech crisis found the PKI and the Jakarta government sharing a political position for the first time since the Gestapu affair, although for different reasons.

In assessing Soviet policy toward Indonesia, one may paraphrase the opinion of Ivan Maisky, the former Soviet Ambassador to London at the time of Stalin's Right strategy, 1932–42. In international politics, states are guided not by sentiments, not by generosity, not by any ideals, but by crudely egotistical interests and infrequently by very ruthless calculation.[43] On Indonesia, nobody will ever accuse the Russians of sacrificing expediency for principle.

14

The "Cornell Paper"

A DISTURBING AND ALSO BEWILDERING aspect of the September 30 affair has been the apparent effort on the part of a small, but influential, group in the Western academic community to—as described in the *New Leader* [1]—"whitewash" the role of the Communists in the putsch and, in the process, also that of Sukarno.

The centerpiece in this effort was the putative "Cornell Paper," a paper written by some of the professional students of Indonesian affairs at the Modern Indonesia Project, Cornell University, though to this day it is not on the record which ones are responsible for the document. On the basis of its length and mixed writing styles, the so-called "Cornell Paper" appears to be the product of more than one author. But the Paper bears the name of no author, nor does it contain an identification mark, publication date, or catalogue number. It consists of 166 single-spaced, typewritten pages and it was apparently produced hurriedly because it was in circulation within ninety-odd days of October 1, 1965.

The theme of the Paper is contained in the opening paragraph of the foreward: "The weight of the evidence so far assembled and the (admittedly always fragile) logic of probabilities indicate that the coup of October 1, 1965, was neither the work of the PKI nor of Sukarno himself. Though both were deeply involved, it was after the coup plans were well under way. They were more the victims than the initiators of events."

In the Paper's estimate, the September 30 affair was more in conformity with a traditional Army coup, that is, as the PKI contends,[2] "an internal Army affair." The actual origina-

tors of the plan were, according to the Paper, middle-level
Army officers at the Central Java headquarters of the Seventh
Diponegoro Division. The main objective of the Diponegoro
group was the violent elimination of those generals on the
General Staff who in the plotters' view "had committed the
cardinal sins of succumbing to the corruptions of Jakarta elite
society, neglecting their former subordinates (General Yani
and several others had been former Diponegoro officers), and
consistently opposing and thwarting President Sukarno's external and internal policies. . . ." About half of the Paper is a
reconstruction of events—the abduction and murder of the
generals interspersed with a commentary on the social and
political milieu of the conspirators and their victims. The
principal Army plotters, according to the Paper, were General
Supardjo and Colonels Untung and Latief.

The second half of the Paper is an analysis of events.
According to the Paper, the Army plotters "attempted to use
both Sukarno and the PKI leadership for its own ends and
succeeded merely in irremediably damaging the moral and
political authority of the one, and causing the physical destruction of the other." In the opinion of the authors, the
officer clique "planned to exploit the PKI." Their reason for
doing so was "to ensure that Sukarno would go along with
them" since a Communist role would have committed his regime's main prop on the Left.

The language employed by the Paper is emotional. For
example, the *Harian Rakjat* editorial of October 2 is described
as "foolish"; the PKI is accused of making the "regrettable"
error of believing that it was more intelligent than the Army;
the omission of Sukarno's name from the list of the Revolutionary Council was also "foolish," when it was still in the
plotters' interest to make maximum use of his name. Untung
is the "wretched lieutenant-colonel"; General Pranoto is also
"wretched"; the *sub rosa* Communist leader and acting governor of Central Java, Sujono Atmo, is "attractive"; and Colonel Suherman led the "miserable" life of a fugitive until his
capture.

Throughout the Paper there is an effort to implant the
impression of some impending American intervention or in-

volvement at the time of the affair; for example, we are told that "suspicion and distrust of the General Staff was undoubtedly fanned by persistent rumors that some key Generals had been paid off by the CIA, regardless of the real truth of the charges."

The authors of the Paper also appear dismayed by the plotters' stupidity and lack of imagination. Take one example, the question of the disposal of the bodies of the butchered generals. Instead of stuffing the bodies down a well at a time when the conspirators controlled an air base, the Paper suggests that "it would have been no problem . . . to dump stripped bodies from a considerable height over the sea, which would have precluded their being identified." [3]

On substantive matters, the Paper collapses. According to the Paper, there is "good reason"—never provided—that the "brains" behind the affair were strongly anti-Communist. Yet this makes no sense at all if it was a coup by pro-Sukarno officers since Sukarno's external and internal policies, for all practical purposes, were almost identical with those of the PKI by 1965. Then, on page 20, the Paper says Aidit was told that a coup had started and that the President wanted him to join him at Halim air base immediately. Aidit suspected nothing and went. On page 107, however, the Paper terms this "the apparent kidnapping of Aidit." Yet the undisputed fact is that when the putsch collapsed, Aidit commandeered an Air Force plane and flew to Central Java where he freely joined other Communist leaders to enact the last act of the drama.

In political terms, a question never answered is why the conspirators felt it necessary to proclaim and install a "Revolutionary Council," laced with Communists and fellow travelers, among others, if the event was solely "an internal Army affair," a point which has been made with precision by Professor Victor M. Fic of Nanyang University, Singapore.[4]

As for the roles of the Pemuda Rakjat and other ancillary Communist organizations in the affair, the Paper concludes that they were "duped" into participating in the murders of the generals to incriminate and compromise the PKI. Yet, in inexplicable fashion, the Paper concedes that the Army pinned the blame for what happened on the Communists in part "because of *actual* PKI involvement, however confused [!]." [5]

Finally, in allegorical terms, the Paper exudes confidence about the future. It recalls the shadow play in which the noble Pandawa, the same Pandawa cited by Sukarno on the night of September 30,[6] are the unlucky victims of violence, treachery, and cruelty. Their forces are "forced to go underground or to travel in disguise to foreign parts," obviously a reference to the plight of the PKI today. But their day eventually comes when, "with the help of friendly allies abroad," they marshal their strength and join battle against the corrupt, vainglorious usurpers. In this "ultimate victory, all the suffering and misery of exile and persecution are fully recompensed."

Had the analysis been handled in established fashion as a seminar paper, openly distributed and discussed or published in any one of a number of scholarly journals, it would have retained a measure of paradigmatic value. The very nature of scholarship is the spirit of inquiry in a free and aboveboard manner. Anything may be said or written and then freely analyzed in the open. If it had been handled in this fashion, the "Cornell Paper" would have become an Indonesian curiosity piece. Instead, the authors classified it as "strictly confidential"—various pages so bear this chop—and then proceeded to distribute it to a select audience in the West and elsewhere. They said the recipients may "feel free to use it as you wish in publication, but please do not refer in any way to this document." [7] In this fashion, in the words of veteran Asia correspondent Sol Sanders, the whole thread of this Paper was "picked up and spread through academic and pseudo-academic circles." [8]

At this writing, the so-called "Cornell Paper" has not been made public and some graduate students and others, including Indonesians, who have visited Cornell University, have never seen a copy there. Yet at least eleven, perhaps fifty, copies of the "Cornell Paper" were circulated in the West, mostly in the United States. Copies turned up in Britain, The Netherlands, and Australia, and also in Sukarno's palace in late January, 1966, as Sukarno made his last move to retain power by dismissing Nasution as defense minister and installing a new, Communist-tainted cabinet. For the President, doubtless, the "Cornell Paper," in the vernacular of the news agencies, was a bell-ringer. It would have encouraged Sukarno if he read it, but it is doubtful that he did since he is not and never was a "reader."

The manner in which the Paper was handled raises many questions: Why wasn't the Paper dealt with in the open manner that is routine at colleges and in academic quarters? Why was it treated as black propaganda and turned into a political action document? Why did the Paper's authors rush to absolve the PKI and Sukarno in terms of scholarship when their motivation may have been ideological?

There are several explanations for this odd situation, which the author has gathered from a number of sources.

One explanation is contained in a covering letter which accompanied the Paper.[9] Dated January 10, 1966, it characterized the Paper as "provisional and incomplete" but said it was important to rush into circulation with it for fear that the tracks of what happened might be successfully wiped from the sands of time. However, the letter went on, because of the repercussions which knowledge of this report might arouse in some places, the authors did not wish it to receive further circulation. There was no elaboration of this point. However, the letter, which was attached to the Paper, said this copy is "for your eyes only" and added that the "material in it is common property." The letter said the recipients should feel free to use it as desired in publication but that they "should not refer in any way to this document."

The Paper, however, circulated in ever-widening circles after January 10. Part of the explanation is that one of the recipients of the original Paper was a member of the United States government. There is circumstantial evidence to indicate that a copy of the "Cornell Paper" was purloined from his office and photocopied by a person who had a clearance access to his filing cabinet. About fifty copies of the photocopied version, sans the covering letter, were then distributed among Western academicians and others, including members of the Indonesian government who were engaged in cutting short the efforts by Sukarno and the Communists to extricate themselves from the affair.

Whatever the case, a columnist for the Publishers Newspaper Syndicate, Joseph Kraft, based an article on the hypothesis contained in the Paper and identified it as "a study of recent Indonesian events by a group of scholars at Cornell University." [10] On the basis of this thesis, Kraft concluded (on his own) that the Communist debacle in Indonesia was "a true tragedy" because it meant that Indonesia would now be ruled by a jackboot regime holding power by terror, presumably the Suharto administration.

When the Kraft piece appeared in the *Washington Post*, the newspaper followed it up by publishing a letter from George McT. Kahin, the director of the Modern Indonesia Project, which sought to dispel publicly "any misleading impressions" resulting from the "tentative attempt by a few of the American Indonesian specialists at Cornell to reconstruct the confusing events surrounding the coup of October 1 and 2, 1965." [11] Thereupon, Kraft apologized for giving the impression that the conclusions he drew were those of the Indonesia specialists at Cornell. The *Post* published his apology.[12] It is painful to put these things down since George Kahin and I have been friends since Jogja days more than twenty years ago, when he was an aspiring young academician and I was an equally young foreign correspondent; as for Joe Kraft, we met and became friends more than a decade ago and worked together on the old news of the week in review section of the *New York Times*.

Following the publication of the Kraft article, various students of Indonesian affairs, journalists and others, wrote to Cornell to obtain a copy of the Paper. Some were turned away with the reply either that there was no such paper or that it was not available; some received a four-page summary of the Paper, entitled, "Hypothesis on the Origin of the Coup Analysis." Some thought the Hypothesis was the Paper.

Many Indonesians were disturbed by this development— not simply the military, but political leaders, students, and intellectuals. They felt, correctly or otherwise, that the Paper was designed to discredit post-Gestapu Indonesia by creating the impression that the destruction of the PKI was a "frame-up," an Asian Reichstag fire.[13]

"The authors of the Paper have abused their positions and they have forfeited their right to be called scholars," said Anak Agung Gde Agung, the former Indonesian Foreign Minister, who languished in a Sukarno prison at the time of the September 30 affair.[14] Similarly, other prominent Indonesians have held this Western "instant scholarship" up to ridicule. Rosihan Anwar, the writer and editor, dismissed the Paper with the thrust that it was the product of "social scientists who study and write about Indonesia . . . from their study rooms in the United States." [15] For that matter, many Westerners have also been disturbed. Denis Warner, the Australian author who has written about Southeast Asia for more than twenty years, termed the Paper "sheer fantasy." [16] In his book, Sanders described the Paper as "incredible." [17]

Perhaps the most devastating critique of all has been prepared by Mohammed Rum, a lawyer, former Home and Foreign Minister, and a principal negotiator for the Republic during the Indonesian revolution. Rum is fairly typical of those Indonesian leaders who, in their own lifetime, have been the victims of the extreme Right and the extreme Left. He was permanently crippled by a Dutch bullet during the war of independence and he was later jailed by the PKI-oriented Sukarno regime.

"If I were a member of the Communist Party, and not one of their brightest members, but with dedication to the principles of communism, I would make copies of the Paper, even translate it into Indonesian," Rum said.[18] "I would give it to other people in a very selective way, but to as many as possible. If someone asked me who is the author of the Paper, I would say that I am not entitled to mention the name of the author. I would say, however, that this Paper is from America or that it was written by scholars at Cornell. I would be truthful and act in accordance with the authors' desire for anonymity." And Rum added, "I don't think I exaggerate this presumption."

I do not think so either.

Rum believes the Paper betrayed itself immediately by conceding that both the PKI and Sukarno were "deeply involved" after the plans were well under way. "If the author knows what he says in that sentence and knows the criminal law of Indonesia, then Sukarno and Aidit are guilty," he said. "If they are involved, and deeply involved when the plan is 'well under way' or not 'well under way,' or from the beginning or at the end—they are involved." After citing other legal points, Rum grappled with the heart of the matter: "The problem is not only whether Sukarno and Aidit are guilty, in the sense of criminal law, but, more important, whether they are guilty in the political sense.

"I am certain," he said, "that the Indonesian Communists will base their efforts on a comeback on the line: The coup is *an internal affair of the Army—so'al dalam angkatan darat.*" And he added, "This time they will have at their disposal, intended or not, a Paper which they can present as a scholarly study to support their line."

Intentionally, or otherwise, the "Cornell Paper" may prove an ideological time bomb. Should the present-day benevolent, quasi-military government in Jakarta devolve into another narrowly based, chauvinistic, and corrupt "guided democracy" or a succession of such regimes, influenced by the military, the PKI will come alive again, and the so-called "Cornell Paper" may explode. The Communists will be in a position to say that "even" the Americans secretly admitted that both Sukarno, the Great Leader of the Revolution, and the PKI, the dedicated and devoted protectors of the people, were the victims of an imperialist conspiracy. In fact, some have already done so.[19] A generation from now, the Communist "evidence" in support of this claim may be the "suppressed" Paper of twenty or thirty years earlier. Given the generation gap which is likely to develop in Indonesia, the Paper will undoubtedly enhance the prospects of the Communist enterprise in Indonesia. The trouble with the younger generation, it has been said, is that it has not read the minutes of the last meeting.

The "Cornell Paper" was no sooner distributed in January, 1966, than the first article subscribing, knowingly or unknowingly, to the Paper's thesis was published. It appeared in the February issue of the *Asian Survey,* the only serious monthly journal on Asian affairs published in the United States, notwithstanding America's involvement in three wars in Asia within the past generation. The author of the article was Daniel S. Lev, a Cornell graduate and assistant professor of political science at the University of California, Berkeley.

"Barring some future incontrovertible proof that the PKI was behind the affair, it is quite possible that the October 1 coup represented a traditional putsch by an officer group willing to use whatever support it could get," Lev wrote.[20] In his view, the murder of the Indonesian general staff was "only an incident." According to Lev, the Army leadership, however, "would not let the incident pass . . . [and since] there was at least circumstantial evidence that the PKI was also involved in the coup," the Army turned on the Communists. Lev contended that "the PKI's reputation for honesty and dedication attracted respect and followers from among those sick of the hypocrisy of post-revolutionary politics.[!]" [21]

A month after the Lev article appeared, the view expressed in the "Cornell Paper" emerged in Britain. The March issue of the *New Left Review,* published in London, printed a précis of the "Cornell Paper," a service to the general reader or student of Asian affairs who might not otherwise have access to the Paper.[22] The article was not identified as a précis. However, it was generally faithful to the original and it remains the only version of the Paper currently available to the public. Entitled *Dossier of the Indonesian Drama,* it was written by "Lucien Rey," a cover name for someone who, on the basis of his article's content, must have had access to at least one version of the "Cornell Paper." [23]

In an editorial note, the editor, Perry Anderson, described the "Lucien Rey" account as unique and said, "We are fortunate to be able to print this first and full narrative, based on conversation with witnesses and study of the Indonesian press." [24] The general outline of the "Cornell Paper" emerged immediately. The note said the September 30 affair was initiated by Army officers and "the victims were the members of the Communist Party, caught totally unprepared by events of which it had no foreknowledge or warning but for which it was made to pay the penalty."

Then, in a sweeping statement, the note added, "The ill-concealed glee with which the Western press welcomed the ascendancy of the Army immediately after October 1st is a terrible reflection of our society." This is hyperbole. In general, Western statesmen and periodicals did not welcome the rise of the Army to power; on the contrary, the West was perturbed, but it did welcome the fall of Sukarno and the PKI.

Since the *Review* went to press as Sukarno made his desperate moves to retain power at the end of January and early February, the journal was ensnared by the same malign twist of fate which tripped *Harian Rakjat* on October 2. Thus, Perry Anderson concluded his editorial note with the observation that Sukarno's "dismissal of General Nasution, Minister of Defense, may prove another turning point, as important as October 1st, but inaugurating not terror and chaos, but a return to social justice and construction[!]."

As for the "Lucien Rey" article, the participation of the Communist fifth force in the murders at Halim is dismissed as "unauthorized." Moving a step beyond the so-called "Cornell Paper," however, the author contends that Aidit was "seized" and "arrested" and held "incommunicado."

The appearance of the *New Left Review's* version of events coincided with the eighteenth annual meeting of the Association for Asian Studies at New York which featured, among other seminars, a session on Indonesia.[25] Among the panelists were Ruth T. McVey, a research assistant at the Cornell Modern Indonesia Project, and Donald Hindley, an associate professor at Brandeis University. Miss McVey is the only American who is known to have lectured at the PKI's Aliarcham Academy of Social Sciences; her first full-length book, a richly informed and sympathetic account of the formative period of the PKI, ending with the 1926 revolt, entitled, *The Rise of Indonesian Communism*, was published in October, 1965.[26] As for Hindley, writing in the *Christian Science Monitor* shortly after the coup, he described the PKI as a "moderate, reformist and patriotic party," a description which may surprise many Indonesians.[27] Unlike the "Cornell Paper," however, Hindley considered Sukarno a "willing, if brief, participant" in the purge of the Indonesian general staff.[28]

In any event, the session on Indonesia was disconcerting. Much of the time was taken up in absolving the role of the PKI; there was not a single reference to Sukarno or any speculation whatsoever about Sukarno's possible role in the affair, an extraordinary feat for anyone with the most casual knowledge of Indonesian political history. The moderator, former Ambassador Jones, neither raised any question with the panelists nor entertained any serious challenges from the floor. Miss McVey's view, not surprisingly, reflected the posture of the Paper. She and Hindley tangled on the question of whether Aidit did or did not deserve "a lonely grave." Miss McVey thought not, given the spectacular growth of the party under his guidance; Hindley, however, felt he did since Aidit had misled the party and had not thought out clearly how to achieve power. Hindley observed, in this connection, that one of Lenin's virtues was that he knew how to flee.[29]

The theme contained in the "Cornell Paper" has traveled beyond Britain and the United States. W. F. Wertheim, a professor of sociology at the University of Amsterdam, for example, reflected the hypothesis in *Pacific Affairs,* currently published at the University of British Columbia, Vancouver. "Historical evidence available to Western scholars," Wertheim said, makes it highly probable that the September 30 affair was what its leader, Untung, claimed it to be—an internal Army affair.[30] This is speculation on my part, but if we assume Wertheim had access to the Paper, a fair assumption, we can appreciate how different a meaning and impact that conclusion may have had had it read: *"Western* historical evidence available to Western scholars." In Wertheim's opinion, "Serious students of Indonesian politics agree that there is little to prove that it was the PKI which started the whole affair—on the contrary, there are many more indications disproving such a possibility." [31]

On occasion, students must be puzzled. By illustration, Frederick P. Bunnel, a former research assistant at Cornell, expressed doubt about the PKI's participation in the affair in an article in *Current History*.[32] But with candor, he held, "As for the crucial question of authorship of the coup, that is likely to remain an open question for some time in academic circles." [33] Like all professional students of Indonesian affairs at this writing, however, he does not mention the existence of the Paper and this omission makes it difficult for students to appreciate the depth and accuracy of his remark. This situation has frequently arisen at seminars both in the United States and abroad since 1966. As late as 1969, at Boston, at the meetings of the Association of Asian Studies and the newly formed Committee of Concerned Asian Scholars, panels on the September 30 affair were held in which none of the participants cited the "Cornell Paper," although we can again fairly assume that they were all cognizant of its existence. The failure to bring this situation into the open is unfair to the new student generation, to emergent scholars, and to the students participating in the Modern Indonesia Project who have had nothing to do with the Paper.

For example, Roger K. Paget, the professor in charge of the Project's office in Jakarta at the time of the September 30 affair, concluded on the basis of his own research that "though the degree of PKI involvement may never be definitely ascertained, the fact of involvement is denied by few, even including all members of the banned PKI interviewed by this researcher." He also observed that the PKI's control of mass media "gave promise even on October 2 of branding the Thirtieth of September Movement as a purely intra-Army affair." [34] The authors of the Paper, however, apparently did not solicit his views from the vantage point of Jakarta.[35]

At this juncture, we must clearly distinguish between the efforts of some professional students of Indonesian affairs and the less sophisticated and less knowledgeable mythmakers identified with the Left. The former, by example, deftly skirt Untung's charge of a CIA plot. Not so the latter. "Few details are available at this writing about the coup and counter-coup that occurred in Indonesia," *The Minority of One,* which describes itself as an "independent monthly for an American alternative," said.[36] "With all that has been happening in South Asia, and with the CIA's history of an attempted coup

in that country in 1958, what is there to make one doubt that
whatever the specific machinations and cloak-and-dagger details, bloodshed in the general region is part and parcel of the
American conspiracy to subdue and rule every piece of land
accessible from the Pacific."

Another group associated with the Left is the Youth
Against War and Fascism (YAWF), which the *New York
Times* has termed "a militant Communist-dominated organization." [37] In 1966, YAWF organized a "public inquest into
the mass murders in Indonesia" at Columbia University's
McMillin Theatre. Among the meeting's sponsors were faculty
members from fourteen American universities.[38] The chairman of the session, Deirdre Griswold of YAWF, opened the
meeting with the observation that the organization's estimate
that three hundred thousand people were slain in Indonesia
may be wrong. A flyer circulated at the meeting termed the
massacre the "second biggest crime of the century." [39] Miss
Griswold said: "I was given a revised estimate only a few days
ago by a professor at the Modern Indonesia Project of Cornell
University. She had received her information from an Indonesian official, and the figure she cited to me was that about
one million Indonesians have been slaughtered since the right-
wing coup of last October." [40] The informant from the
Project was not otherwise identified.

According to Miss Griswold's information, she said the
CIA and the generals plotted a coup, Sukarno received a tape
recording of the plans and Untung decided to act. But when
Untung approached Aidit for support, the Communist leader
"flatly refused to believe him." [41] Untung went ahead, however, and when the preemptive strike failed the Army turned
on the Communists.

Just as the so-called "Cornell Paper" was lent stature by
its unauthorized association with the Modern Indonesia Project, YAWF's equally astonishing version of events was lent
credence by Lord Bertrand Russell, a man of great intellectual
attainment in his youth who is now approaching one hundred
years of age. Based on information from "close associates of
mine," Lord Russell claimed that as Untung moved to foil the
generals, the U.S. Seventh Fleet sailed into "Javanese wa-

ters." [42] "Let there be no doubt of the responsibility of the United States for this counter-revolutionary bloodbath," Lord Russell said. ". . . The massacres in Indonesia demand an international investigation and I congratulate those who have initiated it." [43] At its session, YAWF passed the hat around among the five hundred in attendance and collected $360, not enough to pay the meeting's advertising bill.[44]

What motivates these people? Some, of course, are simply naïve or innocent. Others are impressed by communism's "intellectual" pretensions and perhaps feel that, as "intellectuals," they will find the corridors to power more accessible in a monistic, elitist political system than in a pluralistic, egalitarian system. The most direct explanation for their behavior has been made by Professor Guy J. Pauker, the Harvard-trained head of the Asia Section of the Rand Corporation. He believes that the authors of the "Cornell Paper" whitewash simply possess an irrational sympathy towards the Communists.[45]

There is also the hypnotic effect of the Communist "wave of the future" thesis. This is fairly widespread. In Australia, for example, the Indonesians no sooner toppled the PKI along Australia's very borders, than the respected *Sydney Morning Herald* wrote that in developing Asia "communism still often appears not as a threat, but as a promise of a better life." [46] What about the Indonesian experience? Indeed, aside from China and Vietnam, where the Communists came to power by default and in the attire of strident nationalism, the Communists have never been popularly welcomed in Asia. That's the record. Yet even a professional student of Indonesian affairs, Harry Benda, a professor at Yale University, a year to the month of the September 30 affair, could still write a reflective paper on Asian communism without a single line or reflection on the Communist collapse in Indonesia.[47]

Whether it is an innocence of either experience or knowledge which contributes to this behavior, as the political analyst Louis J. Halle would say, is debatable. Of course, Asia may "go Communist," either by default, in the garb of racism and excessive nationalism, forcibly, or by popular acclaim. The point is that it is not inevitable. Nothing in politics is, and the Indonesian experience is a vivid lesson in our time.

In any event, while Moscow and Peking, and the hardcore professional Communists in Asia, viewed the fall of the PKI with remarkable restraint and realism, if not with callous disregard, a mixed bag in the West composed of adolescents and innocents, defeatists and apologists, interspersed with PKI admirers and sympathizers, sought to either forget or distort what happened in Indonesia on September 30–October 1, 1965.

Now, for the first time, this facet of the Gestapu affair is, in some detail, in the open—where it belongs. The hope is that in a generation or more, as the incubating PKI re-emerges, it will be robbed of the line, currently promoted by some European Communists,[48] that "even in the West" it was secretly known that the purge of the Indonesian general staff "was neither the work of the PKI nor of Sukarno himself." The Communists, in Indonesia and elsewhere, will be robbed of the contention that the "Cornell Paper" was "suppressed" in our era. Whether or not the Paper was intended as a time bomb, the hope here is that the mechanism has been defused.

15

Vietnam: Missing Link?

IS THERE A RELATIONSHIP BETWEEN the events in Vietnam and Indonesia in 1965? Invariably, the doves on Vietnam say no; the hawks, yes. Both, naturally, are anxious to use the Indonesian Communist debacle to justify their positions on Vietnam. The doves contend that the Communists were brought to bay in Indonesia because there was no American intervention there—and, in a sense, they are right. The hawks argue that the Americans intervened in Vietnam to buy time for Indonesia and Southeast Asia—and, in a sense, they are right. Accordingly, an observer analyzing what Gunnar Myrdal has described as the "undefined but real connection" between Vietnam and the tumult in the Malay world in 1965, is trapped between two stools.[1] Moreover, since there is no simplistic answer to the question, invariably the problem of spelling out the relationship between Indonesia and Vietnam is compounded.

The *New Republic,* whose opposition to American intervention in Vietnam narrowed its Asian outlook to the width of a laser beam, takes the extreme position that whichever way Vietnam goes, it has "no decisive effect" on the Communists in Indonesia or elsewhere in Southeast Asia.[2] Vietnam and Indonesia are, therefore, unrelated. "The blows recently rained on the Communist Party of Indonesia owe nothing to the way the tide is flowing in Vietnam, but are due to the Indonesian Communists' own blunders," the journal said. It is not that simple. Nor is it as simple as John Wayne, the folk hero and political activist, is wont to make it at the other end of the candle. "We went into Vietnam, and Indonesia got enough guts to throw the Communists out of Indonesia," he said.[3]

For a broader perspective, we must turn to other sources. In the House of Commons, a member of Parliament, M. R. Ridsdale (C–Nat. L), observed: "If there had not been the United States stand in Vietnam and Britain's in Malaysia, did anyone believe that change would have taken place so quickly in Indonesia?" [4] And the distinguished American critic, Max Lerner, pointed out that if the Chinese Communists gained a victory in both Vietnam and Indonesia "that could pretty much set their terms for Asia." [5]

Four American presidents have also established a relationship between Vietnam and the Malay world. "Whatever one may think of the 'domino' theory, it is beyond question that without the American commitment in Vietnam Asia would be a far different place today," Richard Nixon said.[6] Specifically, he believed that the American presence provided tangible and highly visible proof that communism is not necessarily the wave of Asia's future and that this was a "vital factor in the turn around in Indonesia" where a tendency toward fatalism is a national characteristic. His predecessor shared a similar outlook. Lyndon Johnson felt that "our fighting in Vietnam is buying time" [7] and that the Anglo-American defense in Southeast Asia jointly influenced the outcome of events in the Malay world. In his historic speech of March 31, in which he announced that he would not stand for re-election, Johnson cited Indonesia's experience in defense of his interventionist policy in Vietnam. He held that it would have been "far less likely—if not impossible" that Indonesia would be at peace with its neighbors today "if America and others had not made the stand in Vietnam." [8]

Shortly before his assassination, John Kennedy witnessed the first stirrings of the collaboration between Jakarta and Peking. Yet he had already intuitively envisioned an interrelationship between the Communist pressures on Vietnam and the Malay archipelago. Indeed, in September, 1963, Kennedy reversed his policy of appeasing Sukarno when the latter moved on to Malaysia after soliciting Kennedy's support on West Irian. "If South Vietnam went," Kennedy observed that month,[9] "it would not only give them an improved geographic position for a guerrilla assault on Malaya, but would also give the impression that the wave of the future in Southeast Asia was China and the Communists." This was, of course, the "domino" theory, and Kennedy endorsed it. "I believe it," he said.

Of all the presidents, Dwight Eisenhower, surprisingly, was the most brusque. "What do you think caused the overthrow of President Sukarno in Indonesia? What do you suppose determined the new federation state of Malaysia to cling to its hard-won independence despite all the pressure from outside and from within?" he asked.[10] "Well, I could tell you one thing: The presence of 450,000 American troops in South Vietnam . . . had a hell of a lot to do with it."

Presidents Nixon, Johnson, and Eisenhower, however, also believed that Indonesia found the "courage" to oppose a Communist takeover because of the American presence in Vietnam. This is open to question. The generals resisted the September 30 movement instinctively, as a matter of survival. It is doubtful if the American intervention on the other side of the South China Sea entered their minds that morning. In a firefight, one does not contemplate grand designs—anyone who has ever been shot at knows that.

Indeed, the "courage" issue should be laid to rest once and for all. When the former chairman of the United States Joint Chiefs of Staff, General Maxwell Taylor, paid a courtesy call on Simatupang, he implied that perhaps the American presence in Vietnam had given Indonesia the courage to resist the PKI. His Indonesian counterpart reacted sharply. Perhaps, he suggested, Indonesia's action had given the Americans in Vietnam the courage to resist.

Intrigued by this Indonesian perspective, in the spring of 1968, at a lunch in Danang, overlooking the South China Sea—or South Sea, as the Vietnamese call it [11]—I asked several senior American officials and officers what effect, if any, the Communist debacle in Indonesia had on the Americans in Vietnam. The spontaneous, unequivocal reply was that Indonesia's action "certainly encouraged us." A colonel, who had engaged in Indonesian staff studies, said, "It was a heartening development and everyone of us here in Vietnam felt that way, I can assure you." So much for the "courage" issue.

As for the substantive question of whether or not there is an Indonesian-Vietnamese relationship, it is noteworthy that the Eisenhower-Kennedy-Johnson-Nixon view is almost universally shared along the East Asian–Pacific perimeter. Malaysia, which considers Indonesia "the principal factor for peace and security in the region," is a case in point.[12] "A Communist Indonesia would have meant that Communist power would have spread like a giant nutcracker with one prong stretching southward from Hanoi and the other northward from Jakarta," Ismail bin Abdul Rahman, the former Malaysian home minister, said.[13] "It would have been difficult for Malaysia, Thailand, and Singapore to preserve their independence for long." In Singapore, a prominent academician of Chinese racial ancestry privately remarked, "If the PKI succeeded it would have imposed a long-term danger to our security for the simple reason that the Malayan [Chinese] Communist Party would have been in an ideal position to receive outside help." [14] The relationship between events in Indonesia and the future of Singapore is, of course, manifest. As Deputy Premier Toh Chin Chye once remarked to General Nasution, "I feel that Singapore's destiny is closely linked with that of Indonesia." [15] How could it be otherwise? And Rajaratnam, Singapore's foreign minister, quipped to Suharto during a post-Gestapu visit, "I can see more of Indonesia every day from my window than you can"—and he can, quite literally; Rajaratnam's office is in a multi-storied building overlooking the world's fifth largest port, a harbor whose horizon is dotted with Indonesian islands.

Unquestionably, Australia is another nation whose destiny is interlocked with that of the islands on its northern periphery. In 1965, as the United States intervened in Vietnam, the Australian Prime Minister, Sir Robert Menzies, held that "the notion that South Vietnam should be abandoned to communism is fantastic." [16] Such a development, he said, "would make Malaysia's position intolerable," and he added: "In the long run, and not so very long at that, we would find ourselves with aggressive communism almost at Australia's doors—just across the water." Menzies' successor, the late Harold Holt, proved as emphatic. "It is my own conviction," he said,[17] "that we would not have had the favorable turn of events in Indonesia had the United States not been present in strength in South Vietnam." Diosdado Macapagal, who played a cautious game of befriending Sukarno and then belatedly recognizing his expansionist tendencies, also felt that Malaysia "would be unable to resist falling to the Communists" if the United States had abandoned Vietnam in 1965. In the wake of such a development, the Filipino President asked, "How much more impatient would Sukarno's Indonesia be to bring the Philippine archipelago into its orbit?" [18] Significantly, each of the aforementioned leaders were popularly elected through a representative form of government.

In Vietnam, both in the north and south, there has been little doubt about the interrelationship between events in Vietnam and in Indonesia. The headline story in the Saigon *Daily News* of September 30, 1965, for example, was a dispatch from Pyongyang which reported that Indonesia and North Korea had reaffirmed "Sukarno's call for an anti-imperialist Axis linking Indonesia and Cambodia to Red China and her Korean and Vietnam allies." [19] Indeed, the South Vietnamese were so elated over the fall of the PKI that they could hardly believe it. "People say that the PKI collapsed," Ton That An, a director in Saigon's External Affairs Ministry, later remarked.[20] "I do not know if this is the proper word, however. I hope so, but based on our own experience, when the Communists feel objective factors are not favorable, they go underground." Wilfred Burchett, the Australian "journalist" and Communist sympathizer who was in Hanoi on September 30–October 1, 1965, reported that the North Vietnamese received the news of the failure of the September 30 movement with "great dismay." [21] They recognized, of course, that the second front in the American rear had dissolved.

The question of whether or not there is a relationship between Vietnam and Indonesia is a prickly issue in Jakarta. One must distinguish between official and unofficial positions. The belief that Vietnam and Indonesia are "somehow linked" is naïve, according to Adam Malik. The destruction of the PKI, in his opinion, had nothing to do with the presence of American troops in Vietnam and whether or not there are

American troops in Vietnam, Indonesia would not hesitate to crush the Gestapu and the PKI.[22] Malik's public position partly reflects Indonesia's justifiable pride in having destroyed the Communists from within. "What we've done," an Indonesian general said,[23] "we've done ourselves. We've saved this country from communism and we Indonesians did it. Nobody from outside had to help us." Not only is this a fair assessment, but Indonesia stands alone in Asia as the only nation which has turned back two armed Communist adventures without external assistance—in 1948 and 1965; indeed, in both instances, Western interests were at bay within Indonesia. Perhaps there is a lesson in this, too.

Indonesian sensitivity on this issue caused Vice President Humphrey, in the course of his post-Gestapu visit, to advise the small American community there that United States intervention in Vietnam did not lead to the overthrow of Sukarno. "We do not want it to appear that what happened here was because we made it happen," Humphrey said.[24] "That is not true." Humphrey, like Malik, was telling the truth. But these comments relate to only one aspect of the September 30 affair. *In positive terms,* there is no relationship between Vietnam and Indonesia. But *in negative terms,* the story is quite different.

For Indonesians imprisoned during the Sukarno regime, such as Mohammed Rum, the American presence in Vietnam meant "moral support for us, for non-Communist Asians." [25] Without much doubt, he said, an American withdrawal from Vietnam in 1965 "would have encouraged Sukarno and the PKI." The British, he felt, would have abandoned the defense of Malaya, Singapore, and northern Borneo because they "would feel themselves surrounded by Communist forces." Rum added: "A United States withdrawal in 1965 would have reassured Peking and Hanoi, and would have deepened Sukarno's commitment to the PKI. Sukarno moved closer to the Communists even after the American intervention. To Sukarno, communism was the wave of the future."

Another critic of Sukarno and the PKI, who was not imprisoned at the time and who maintained close relations during this period with Subandrio, felt differently. In a private conversation, he said, "It can also be argued that with a United States withdrawal from Vietnam in 1965 and with the Communists breathing down the archipelago, our general staff would have been frightened into taking an initiative against the PKI." He conceded, however, that Sukarno and the PKI would have been immeasurably encouraged by an American withdrawal.

Still another prominent Indonesian, with close Army connections, who was "retooled" (blacklisted) by the Sukarno regime, recalled that "in the summer of 1965 I told an American friend: 'Stay in Vietnam and save us.' " [26] In his opinion, if the United States permitted Vietnam to go Communist by default, the British would not be in a position to maintain their Malaysian defense. Sukarno would have scored another triumph and the Army would have had to go along with his latest victory. This view, interestingly, is shared by a Thai statesman, Pote Sarasin. "Everyone in Jakarta would be saying that Bung Karno was dead right all along," he said.[27] And Senator Gale McGee, a liberal Democrat from Wyoming, after a post-Gestapu visit to Indonesia, described Jakarta's political leaders as "candidly saying that United States intervention in Vietnam 'inspired confidence among tens of thousands of our people. . . .' " [28]

As for Indonesia's Communists, they had long been conscious of the link between a Communist victory in Vietnam and a PKI triumph in Indonesia. E. M. Mansjur, the chairman of the PKI-controlled Indonesian Organization for Afro-Asian Solidarity, viewed the Vietnam and Malaysian conflicts as "blows dealt upon the walls of imperialism and neocolonialism that besiege Indonesia." [29] The Fourth Plenary Session of the PKI Central Committee in 1965 adopted a resolution rejecting a negotiated settlement of the Malaysian dispute and calling for the defeat of the United States in Vietnam "this very year." [30] That same year, Aidit went on record opposing a negotiated settlement in Vietnam; [31] obviously, the Vietnam war served the PKI's interest by maintaining a second front in the north during the Malaysian confrontation. A link to Vietnam also briefly emerged during Sjam's trial. The director of the PKI's Special Bureau, in his defense, argued that the

United States sponsored the Council of Generals in the knowledge that the generals would make peace with Malaysia and the Philippines. The implication was that the generals would abandon the Jakarta-Peking Axis and dismantle one prong of the nutcracker, thereby wrecking the grand strategy of the Communists in Southeast Asia. Sjam said he believed the United States supported the Council of Generals to neutralize the "repeated defeats" the Communists were inflicting on the Americans in Vietnam in 1965.[32]

What then is the truth about the Vietnam-Indonesia relationship? Perhaps the most acicular analysis was developed by Ambassador Green, a former Deputy Assistant Secretary of State for Far Eastern Affairs, who was in Indonesia during the September 30 affair and who was tapped by the Nixon Administration to join the American negotiating team at the Paris peace talks. "The United States military presence in Southeast Asia emboldened the Army, but it had no decisive effect on the outcome," the Ambassador said.[33] "It is perhaps better to look at it in negative terms. If we hadn't stood firm in Southeast Asia, if we hadn't maintained a military presence, then the outcome might have been different."

This has long been my own view, and it was reinforced during a post-Gestapu visit to Indonesia and Vietnam, and in between. To appreciate the origins of the evaluation, we must turn the clock back to "a minute before midnight," [34] and survey the situation as it obtained in Southeast Asia in the weeks before the major American intervention in Vietnam on February 7, 1965.

Whether South Vietnam alone was worth the costly United States intervention is debatable. I, for one, doubt it.[35] Within the context of events that crowded the calendar at the beginning of 1965, however, the United States had no other option. The tragedy is that no serious or sustained effort was made by President Johnson to put the case for intervention in a historical context.[36] This failure cost America dearly, both in understanding and unity at home and in international support beyond the East Asian–Pacific perimeter.

Perhaps the most astonishing aspect of the continuing fallout over Vietnam is that Vietnam is invariably treated as an end in itself. Attention has been directed to almost every facet of the terrible conflict, except the core issue. Totally ignored is the compelling turn of events not only in but around Vietnam at the beginning of 1965 and the weeks immediately preceding it.

During this period, the military situation in South Vietnam was bleak, and deteriorating rapidly. Vietnamese Army units were being defeated daily; district capitals were falling weekly; village strongpoints were being overrun nightly.[37] Straining for the jugular, Hanoi sent its first regular North Vietnamese Army units across the demilitarized zone and into the South.[38]

The background to this development was ominous. From the non-Communist point of view, the region had been already hemorrhaging since the preceding October. That month, the Chinese Communists successfully tested their first nuclear bomb. Incredibly, on October 16, the day after the Chinese test, a team of American scientists at Bandung assisted the Sukarno regime in achieving its first sustained nuclear chain reaction, and Jakarta boasted that it would "explode its own bomb in 1965." [39]

In November, Sukarno was in Shanghai conferring with the Chinese Communist leadership, and at the end of the month Chen Yi flew to Jakarta to confer with Sukarno and Aidit.[40] At these conferences, the foundations were poured for the subsequent Jakarta-Peking Axis, amid strong indications that Peking had offered to assist Sukarno in making a nuclear test, probably a "dust-bin" device.

The following month, Subandrio attended his last General Assembly and briefed a meeting of Indonesian diplomats at New York during which he touched on the developing Sino-Indonesian alliance and suggested that its twin objectives were the expulsion of Anglo-American influence from Southeast Asia and the division of the region into respective spheres of Jakarta-Peking influence.[41] That same month, Sukarno announced Indonesia's withdrawal from the United Nations. At the United Nations, the impression was that Sukarno and his Asian Communist allies were planning to develop a rival U.N. organization, perhaps CONEFO, the Conference of New

Emerging Forces.

This impression deepened in January when Subandrio visited Peking and forged what could be considered a formal Axis relationship. During January, too, the PKI launched a series of anti-American actions and sounded the initial call for the formation within Indonesia of an armed fifth force.

Coincidentally, a "national liberation front" emerged in Thailand—the Thailand Patriotic Front [42]—and in January, at Peking, Ch'en Yi openly boasted that "Thailand is next." (Three months later, the Malayan National Liberation League emerged on the Malaysian peninsula; like the Thai front, it was patterned after the South Vietnamese Liberation Front.) [43] The Buddhist kingdoms of Laos and Cambodia were being used involuntarily as supply corridors by Hanoi's Army.

During December and January, too, Sukarno quickened the pace of his probing forays against northern Borneo and the Malay peninsula. During Christmas Week, 1964, Australian and Indonesian gunboats clashed off Singapore. In January, eighty British warships assembled around Singapore, perhaps the last major naval concentration in the history of the Royal Navy. By February, Australia's first combat troops landed on Borneo and joined up with a mixed Malaysian-British force. Against the backdrop of these major developments, Aidit hailed the Communist victories in Vietnam and described South Vietnam as "a political and military university for revolutionaries." [44] As for Sukarno, it was reported that the Communist successes in Vietnam "seem to have convinced him that the Chinese brand of communism is the 'way of the future in Asia.'" [45]

Clearly, a Jakarta-Peking crunch was in the making. Nor is this hindsight on the author's part. On December 23, 1964, for example, a Worldwide Press Service dispatch said: "As the war-racked region of Southeast Asia moves into the new year, two critical factors are Chinese Communist pressure from the north and Indonesian pressure from the south. . . . The Peking-Jakarta axis is pressing to achieve victory in the coming year. Thailand, a food surplus area, appears to be next on their list. The Chinese-backed Communists in Vietnam are already looking beyond the collapse of South Vietnam." [46] And on January 17, 1965, an article which appeared in the editorial section of the Lost Angeles *Times* observed: "A second front opened in Southeast Asia last week as China and Indonesia sealed a tacit alliance which aimed at dividing the rice-rich region into two respective spheres of influence. In the north, the pressure on South Vietnam intensified—the pitched battles at Bien Gia foreshadowing an escalation of the war. In the south, Sukarno's Indonesia launched three abortive landings against the Malaysian peninsula in a 36-hour period, massed its army along the nine hundred-mile border between Malaysian and Indonesian Borneo, and withdrew from the United Nations. For all practical purposes, the South China Sea became the focal point of the new crisis. The Americans and their South Vietnamese allies were pinned on its northern rim; the British and their Malaysian allies were pinned along its southern rim." [47]

Much later, Sukarno himself confirmed these strategic assessments. The strategy for defeating imperialism, Sukarno said, is for China to strike a blow against the American troops in Vietnam from the north while Indonesia strikes from the south against Malaysia. [48] There was also another, more subtle strategy built into the nutcracker. Indonesia's attacks on Malaysia prevented Britain from assisting the United States in South Vietnam—even if it wanted to do so—and the Vietnamese conflict prevented the Americans from committing themselves to the defense of Malaya, Singapore, and northern Borneo—even if they wanted to do so. [49]

Rightly or not, in January, 1965, a showdown was developing, and Peking-Hanoi-Jakarta gambled on the belief that the British and Americans lacked the will and desire to stay the course in Southeast Asia (they were not too far wrong). [50] Pyongyang waited on the sidelines, anxious to strike in Korea *after* the Anglo-American withdrawal from the south. [51]

Had the United States withdrawn from Vietnam at the beginning of 1965—and the question of withdrawal was debated in the highest councils of the Johnson Administration at that time—the British position to the south would have been untenable. A consolidation of the Jakarta-Peking-Hanoi-

Pyongyang Axis would have established a line of hostile, authoritarian, and expansionist states the length and breadth of the East Asian–Pacific perimeter—from Korea to New Guinea. It was to prevent this perimeter from falling into hostile hands that the Anglo-Americans fought Japan a generation earlier. Clearly, an Anglo-American withdrawal from Southeast Asia in 1965 would have doomed South Vietnam, Laos, Singapore, Malaya, and northern Borneo (Sarawak, Brunei, and Sabah); imperiled the Philippines and Thailand; jeopardized Australia's security; further eroded the ability of Burma and Cambodia to retain a modicum of independence; and exerted a baleful influence on Japan. It would have set the stage for the reopening of the Korean War. There would have been no need for Sukarno and the PKI to plot the removal of the Indonesian general staff. The generals would be preoccupied with new conquests. No general staff is apt to obstruct a popular authoritarian ruler while he is winning in the field.

Thus, the stake in early 1965 was far larger than Vietnam. Despite the cartons of books written about Vietnam since then, only rarely, if at all, are these developments mentioned, much less explored. Worse, many of the writers on Vietnam seem oblivious that this train of events was in motion at the time.[52] This is inexplicable. How can anyone hope to place Vietnam or the September 30 affair in perspective—as John Kennedy would say, "to inform, to arouse, to reflect, to state our dangers and our opportunities, to indicate our crises and our choices"—without giving these events consideration?

For example, Theodore Draper, a senior fellow at the Hoover Institution on War, Revolution and Peace, in his *Abuse of Power* quite correctly observes that early 1965 marked a turning point in United States policy toward Vietnam and that if there is one phase of the war that bears "the closest and most critical examination" it is this period.[53] But apart from observing that South Vietnam was in the process of complete disintegration and on the edge of military defeat, he does not review the events above, much less indicate that he was aware of the situation at the time. Another book, from which one expects more, *The Politics of Escalation in Viet-*

nam, is equally disturbing. The book termed January–February, 1965, the "ripe time, as it was not to be again, for decorous American disengagement" from Vietnam, but it never set out the options or lack of options confronting the Anglo-American powers and their allies in Southeast Asia at that time.[54] Especially disquieting is that John Kenneth Galbraith, in a jacket blurb, termed the book a "revealing history," and the authors solicited the assistance of six consultants "for this study," including two professional students of Indonesian affairs associated with the Cornell Modern Indonesian Project. The index contains no references to Sukarno, Australia, confrontation, Borneo, the PKI, Singapore, ad infinitum. The same may be said of upward of one hundred books on Vietnam printed in the United States between 1965 and 1968.

Such expertise notwithstanding, Washington—like a host of capitals, particularly London, Canberra, Kuala Lumpur, Singapore, Bangkok, Manila, Hanoi, Jakarta, Peking, and Tokyo—was acutely aware that Southeast Asia was in a vise at the beginning of 1965.[55] With Saigon on the verge of military collapse, the moment had arrived for President Johnson to make that fateful choice in Southeast Asia—to "get in or get out." The buck on Vietnam had been gingerly passed along from administration to administration since the Truman period and it came to rest with Johnson.[56] "In other parts of the world, where the Communists have shown expansionist tendencies, we have drawn lines and we are glad we did it," the *Washington Star* said, setting the tone in the American capital early in 1965.[57] "In Vietnam, it's a good bet another line will be drawn." Johnson himself conceded later that at the beginning of 1965 "we were forced to choose, forced to make a decision." [58]

In two significant statements, unreported in the American and foreign press, William P. Bundy, Assistant Secretary of State for East Asian and Pacific Affairs, spelled out the painful choice. In one analysis, Bundy said:

By 1965 (Indonesia) was hostile to us, engaged in a sterile but dangerous military confrontation with Malaysia and Singapore, and headed very shortly for Communist control and an effective alliance with Communist China. . . . The situation in Vietnam in 1965 stood, along side the trend in Indonesia, as the major dark spot in the area. And in early 1965 it became clear that unless the United States and other nations introduced major combat forces and took military action against the North, South Vietnam would be taken over by communist force.

If that had happened, there can be no doubt whatever that, by the sheer dynamics of aggression, Communist Chinese and North Vietnamese subversive efforts against the rest of Southeast Asia would have been increased and encouraged, and the will and capacity of the remaining nations of Southeast Asia to resist these pressures would have been drastically and probably fatally reduced.

So our actions in Vietnam were not only important in themselves . . . but were vital in the wider context.[59]

In a second analysis, Bundy observed that "as 1964 drew to a close, the situation in Southeast Asia was moving steadily downward in every respect" and "a review of policy was undertaken" from late November onward.[60] "All the indicators recorded increasingly shaky morale and confidence not only in South Vietnam but throughout the deeply concerned countries of Southeast Asia," he said. By late January, Bundy continued, it was the clear judgment of all those "familiar with the situation" that the United States had no option other than to intervene massively in Vietnam. The United States decision was far from a happy one. The Administration recognized that "had the choice been ours perhaps we would not have picked Vietnam" but that the Peking-Hanoi-Jakarta challenge had to be met where it developed. History and circumstances dictated Vietnam—it was too late to look for a "nicer, neater battlefield." Even so, Hubert Humphrey later observed, "I believe it's fair to say that no one really contemplated the depth of our involvement." [61]

On January 30, 1965, Peking analyzed the results of the Subandrio mission and concluded that it marked "the beginning of a new and higher stage in relations" between China and Indonesia—in area, the land and sea giants of Asia. A week later, the United States decided to intervene massively in Vietnam "to buy time." On February 7, the United States bombed North Vietnam.[62]

Aidit promptly recognized the strategic implications. "An attack on Vietnam," he said in a cable to President Johnson, "is an attack on Indonesia."

16

The Second Front Collapses

ANY FAIR HISTORIAN WOULD HAVE
to conclude on the basis of the available evidence in the preceding chapter that the American decision to intervene in
Vietnam was not reached in a vacuum, that it was bound up
with the general political deterioration in Southeast Asia at
the time, and that the situation in Indonesia was a factor in
American thinking. The evidence, moreover, suggests that the
joint Anglo-American defense of Southeast Asia, which probably had its origins at the 1962 Nassau Conference between
Prime Minister Douglas-Home and President Kennedy, upset
the strategy of both Sukarno and the Communists.

When Britain assumed a principal role in the defense of
Malaya, Singapore, and the northern Bornean territories in
1963, Sukarno was probably confident that he could repeat his
West Irian victory by conducting a vestpocket war while at-
tracting diplomatic support from the Sino-Soviet blocs and the
United States. Sukarno had grounds for optimism. Roger Hils-
man, the then Assistant Secretary of State for Far Eastern
Affairs, advocated appeasing what he misread as Indonesia's
"new nationalism." [1] The then United States ambassador in
Indonesia felt similarly. Jones felt that the sacrifices already
being made in Vietnam would be fruitless if Sukarno did a
Castro and joined the Communists.

By 1964, it became clear, however, that neither Britain
nor the United States was interested in appeasing Sukarno any
further. And shortly before the American intervention in
Vietnam, Aidit had recognized that Britain's defense of Malaysia was not to be taken lightly. "The increasingly stubborn
English attitude," he said,[2] "as the result of growing assistance

from United States imperialism, leaves Indonesia no other choice except that prescribed by President Sukarno, to wit, a stepped-up policy of confrontation."

The American aerial offensive against North Vietnam in 1965, however, had a sobering impact on Sukarno and his more ambitious generals. The Indonesian general staff was aware of Indonesia's vulnerability to air and sea attack. Sustained air strikes would not only destroy Indonesia's limited naval and air capacities but, unlike the situation in North Vietnam, they could reduce the Army to "pockets" on isolated, scattered islands, producing a logistic nightmare.

Clearly, then, it may be argued that the relationship between Indonesia and Vietnam—indeed, between Vietnam and the Malay world—is interwoven. The relationship is more accurately expressed in negative, rather than positive, terms. An American withdrawal from Vietnam in 1965 would have led to a British pull-out from Malaysia and would have left that country vulnerable to Indonesian conquest. We can only speculate, but it is reasonable to assume that the collapse of Malaysia would have strengthened Sukarno and the PKI immeasurably and might have precluded their necessity to plot the wholesale removal of the Indonesian general staff. Had Britain wavered, the London *Daily Telegraph* later commented, "the successful incursion into Malaysia would have rendered Sukarno and the Indonesian Communists irremovable." [3]

However, Professor Lea E. Williams, a Chinese specialist at Brown University, has suggested, in a private communication, that perhaps the British would not have withdrawn from Malaysia in the event of an American withdrawal from Vietnam. "American withdrawal from Vietnam would not necessarily have obliged the British to renege on their commitment in Malaysia," he said.[4] "On the contrary, the British might have been strengthened in their resolve had the Americans left Vietnam." In his view, an American withdrawal would not have signaled a retreat from Thailand and the Philippines and, indeed, might have led to a strengthening of the American presence in both countries. "The British, under those circumstances, would by no means have been outflanked or left defenseless in their rear," he said.[5]

This suggestion necessitates a fuller inquiry into Britain's position in Southeast Asia in 1965. At that time, in the event of an American withdrawal, all the pointers indicated that the British would have neither the will nor the desire—much less the military and financial strength—to continue the defense of Malaya, Singapore, and northern Borneo. Inside Malaysia the situation was hardly promising. Tension between Singapore and Malaya rose appreciably and in 1965 racial rioting erupted in Singapore for the first time. Hostility toward both the Malays and Chinese was mounting in Sabah and Sarawak where the Dyaks, Muruts, Kadazans, and other Bornean peoples were uneasy over their inclusion in the Malaysia federation. By 1965, only Sukarno's hostility and the British defense held the federation together. Even so, the strains within the country reached a breaking point and in August, 1965, Malaysia and Singapore secretly agreed to Singapore's exit from the federation and her emergence as a sovereign republic. The British public was jolted by these events and there was a rising public demand in London, encouraged especially by the left wing of the then ruling Labor Party, to appease Sukarno and end the Southeast Asian commitment. "The secession [of Singapore] raises new uncertainty about Britain's commitment to maintain a huge, and costly, defense establishment in the area," *Business Week* observed.[6]

The Malaysians and Singaporeans conceded as much. "Of course, the British were committed to our defense," a minister in the present Singapore government recalled.[7] "But our withdrawal shocked them. So did the prospect of more racial riots. These shocks, plus an American withdrawal from Vietnam that year, would have left the U.K. holding the bag. At least that is probably how they would see it. If it were only a question of Indonesia, they could easily deal with it. But it was more than that, and the psychological shockwaves in the region would probably undermine their resolve."

A senior Australian diplomat with Indonesian experience, who was in Canberra in 1965 and holds the rank of ambassador, privately expressed the opinion that had the Americans not made a stand in Vietnam, "the Brits would have sought to negotiate a compromise of sorts with Sukarno to effect an honorable withdrawal." He was convinced that Britain has pursued only one basic policy in recent years: entry into the Common Market. For Britain, he said, admission to the Market has become a question of national survival and every other aspect of British foreign policy has been submerged to achieve this objective. The British withdrawal from east of Suez is an essential ingredient of that paramount policy. "An American withdrawal and probable collapse of South Vietnam that summer, together with the rioting in Malaysia and Singapore's exit from the federation, would have put pressure on the Brits to break off the conflict with Sukarno," he concluded.

His emphasis on the economic underpinning of the political situation was the more noteworthy in view of Britain's 14.3 per cent devaluation of the pound in 1967 *after* an end to Sukarno and confrontation. The defense of Malaya, Singapore, and northern Borneo cost about $700 million annually before devaluation.[8]

The devaluation of the pound, moreover, marked the dividing point between the myth and reality of Britain's role in the world. Thus, "to make devaluation work"—as Prime Minister Wilson put it—Britain was compelled to cut back its global commitments.[9] Accordingly, London followed up the devaluation by announcing plans to withdraw from east of Suez by 1971, including from Malaysia and Singapore. Creighton Burns, in the *Melbourne Age,* put it crisply. "In terms of real world power, Britain is back where it was at the beginning of the 19th Century," he said.[10]

Against this screen of events, it appears a fair conclusion that had Britain been left in Southeast Asia as the only Western power engaged in hostilities in the area, it would have expeditiously sought to extract itself. A British withdrawal would have given Sukarno and the PKI the victory they sought. Their triumph would have eroded the position of the generals and precluded the necessity to remove them forcibly.

This line of reasoning brings us to another point: the role of the United States in Vietnam. Unquestionably, Indonesia's pull-back from the brink of the Communist abyss, the restoration of peace in the Malay world, and, in effect, the collapse of

Southeast Asia's second front, radically altered the geopolitical situation in the area. These developments presented the United States with the opportunity for a major strategic review.[11]

In addition to the collapse of the second front, another feature of the post-Gestapu period was the economic and political turmoil produced in China by Mao's Cultural Revolution. The turbulence effectively reduced China's influence in Asia. This can be demonstrated even in the Hanoi-Jakarta relationship. As a subtle sign of independence of Peking, Hanoi continued to maintain diplomatic relations with Indonesia following the fall of Sukarno and the PKI.[12] Another factor characteristic of the post-Gestapu period was that after months of systematic, pinpoint bombing of North Vietnam, the economy of the Ho regime was strained and hopefully his missionary zeal tempered vis-à-vis Laos and Cambodia.

Taken together, the moment was ripening in 1966 "for decorous American disengagement" from Vietnam.

The suggestion that the time had arrived for a judicious reassessment of United States policy in Southeast Asia is not an isolated judgment. The disorder inside China and the collapse of the putsch in Indonesia "have created a new situation and they have opened up new opportunities," Walter Lippmann wrote in the *New York Herald-Tribune*.[13] Across the street, C. L. Sulzberger observed, "Now, since Indonesia's policy switch and the erosion of Chinese power, one wonders if the time hasn't come to promote [a] general settlement." [14] Another commentary concluded that "the Vietnam intervention has already paid off" and "by the same token, the shift in Indonesia's fortunes places Vietnam in a new setting, and justifiably, in terms of power politics, sets the stage for a phased deescalation of the conflict." [15]

Rightly or not, it appeared that Washington may have arrived at a similar evaluation. Thus, at 6:00 P.M. on Christmas Eve, 1965—within one hundred days of the Indonesian upheaval—President Johnson ordered a halt to the bombing of the North in an effort to move the war off dead center and to the negotiating table.

Hanoi did not respond, however. Could it have done so?

Could Hanoi ignore the sacrifices it had made to promote five years of guerrilla warfare in the South? Could Hanoi accept the continued existence of a non-Communist South after exposing the North to air raids for almost a year? In truth, could the Communist dictatorship survive a third betrayal of Vietnam? Twice before—at Fontainebleau in 1946 and Geneva in 1954—Ho Chi Minh had settled for less than total victory only to launch a new war. Indeed, could the Communists in general accept a compromise settlement in South Vietnam so soon after the debacle in Indonesia?

Hanoi remained silent. On February 1, 1966, the bombing resumed. Perhaps it should not have.

During the bombing pause, Professors Seymour Lipset of Harvard University and Irving Horowitz of Washington University, among others, proposed the convocation of a condominium of Asian nations, including Indonesia, to help work out a Vietnam settlement.[16] But, from Hanoi's standpoint, this was probably asking too much, although post-Gestapu Indonesia was not unsympathetic toward Ho Chi Minh's regime. Most Indonesians recalled the blurred lines between nationalists and communists before Indonesia attained complete independence and, therefore, appreciated the complexity of the Vietnamese political situation.[17] Of course, it was relatively easier for Indonesians to espouse this view when the war in Vietnam no longer served their own immediate interests, however negatively or indirectly. In any event, the Suharto government repeatedly sought to play the honest broker between Washington and Hanoi without success. In Hanoi's opinion, and justifiably so, post-Gestapu Indonesia was hardly in a position to assay such a role.

17

The Overview

IN RETROSPECT, THE GESTAPU AFFAIR is one of the great watersheds of contemporary Asian history. The events which took place in Indonesia on September 30– October 1, 1965, altered the course of history in Indonesia, the whole of the Malay archipelago, and, in turn, Southeast Asia. Their impact was felt the length and breadth of the East Asian–Pacific perimeter. Insofar as the outcome shaped the trend of events in Asia, it influenced world affairs. Clearly, too, the consequences arising out of the failure of the September 30 movement were as varied and profound as the consequences would have been had it succeeded.

The catalog of developments springing from Indonesia's night of the generals embraces a broad spectrum. In world affairs, it upset the grand design of the Asian Communists: the establishment of an array of contiguous, like-minded, authoritarian regimes from Korea to New Guinea—coincidentally, the writ of the Japanese Empire at its apogee. If it was inimical to American interests to have this region fall into hostile hands in the forties, perforce, this should be equally true in the sixties. In Asian affairs, the Gestapu affair led to the decimation of the oldest Communist Party along the East Asian–Pacific perimeter, and the largest in the non-Communist world at that time. In Southeast Asian affairs, it brought peace to the Malay world and restored peace between Indonesia and her closest neighbors—Singapore, the Philippines, Brunei, Australia, Malaysia, and Portuguese Timor.

Within Indonesia, it brought about the eclipse of a senescent demagogue and put an end to his arid nationalist regime. It revived the fortunes of Indonesia's democratic socialists, and it reawakened within a new student generation the high ideals pursued by the Republic during the 1945 war of independence: the pursuit of political liberty—general elections, unfettered freedom of thought, press, and public meetings, untrammeled political discussion. As Rosa Luxemburg expressed it, "Political liberty is as necessary to society as breath to a human being." But it also put the Army in power and framed a question for the seventies: When and how will the Army get out, however timely and benevolent its indirect rule.[1] This central question is compounded by other legacies, notably the failure of the Sukarno era to resolve the latent issue of federalism (the word "regionalism" is controversial in Indonesia but closer to the point) and the resurgence of orthodox Islam following the collapse of the PKI. The latter development has produced veiled tensions vis-à-vis the secular Army and tensions with other, non-Moslem religious groups in the competition to fill the vacuum left by the Communists. Finally, it gave rise to that horror of human horrors—mass murder.

The Gestapu affair shattered—or at least should have shattered—the notion that communism in Asia is necessarily the wave of the future. It discredited—or at least should have discredited—the thesis that "nationalism" is necessarily the antidote to communism in Asia. In Indonesia, nationalism and communism were comrades-in-arms. "We will keep close to Sukarno," Aidit once said.[2] "He is our best friend." As Indonesia demonstrated, the political struggle after independence is not so much between the forces of nationalism and communism but, within a much wider compass, between the forces of authoritarianism and political liberty. Indeed, one of the great ironies of the Gestapu affair is that the PKI was destroyed soon after it had proclaimed its independence for the first time in its history. That independence was short-lived. The greatest irony is that the destruction of the party has destroyed the PKI's independence and returned it to foreign manipulation in order to survive.

Frequently, and hopefully among Communists and "the specially motivated,"[3] the suggestion is heard that just as the Communist disaster in China in 1927 was a prelude to the party's takeover almost a generation later, perhaps the Communist disaster in Indonesia is the forerunner of a new, pruned, and sturdier PKI. Peking apparently makes this assessment in the light of its own experience. Yao Wen-yuan, a member of the Chinese Communist Party's Central Committee, for example, has described Indonesia thusly: "Indonesia today is like China in 1927." [4] Indeed, it has been correctly said that the PKI moved in 1965 in part to avoid a repetition of what happened in China in the twenties, when Sun Yat-sen's death precipitated the confrontation between the Communists and Chiang Kai-shek.[5]

But the analogy between the Indonesian and the Chinese Communist disasters is strained. By 1929, the Chinese Communists had sufficiently recovered to re-establish a clandestine Politburo and occupy a "liberated area" with the nucleus of a Red Army—in a sense, a Blitar. Yet long ago Aidit himself recognized that "there are specific differences in geography and political development between Indonesia and China." [6] Most of these are obvious. China is a land mass; Indonesia is insular. China is lacking a cohesive religious force; Indonesia is nominally Moslem. And so forth. Accordingly, the analogy between China and Indonesia is "hardly fitting." [7]

The question persists, however: Can the PKI regroup, rebuild, and recover its lost ground? If PKI rhetoric is a measure, the party is already committed to a "Three Banner" policy borrowed from Mao Tse-tung: rebuild the party along Marxist-Leninist lines (whatever that may mean); lead a "protracted armed struggle" with emphasis on agrarian revolution (for the PKI, a new approach which, however, is unlikely to dissociate it from a Java-centric policy); and establish "a united front of all the forces that are against the military dictatorship of the right-wing Army generals." [8]

There is also strong evidence that the Communists have jettisoned their traditional dependence on Java and are trying to free themselves from their disastrous reliance on Java in the past. As observed earlier, the PKI was founded in Java, recruited most of its membership there, and carried out its principal adventures on that island. In fairness to the Javanese, however, it has been Java which has borne the brunt in blunting the Communist power thrusts.

The evidence that the PKI is currently laboring to abandon its Java-orientation is contained in the second most *important* (their word) document issued by the underground Communist Party since the collapse of the Gestapu affair.[9] Clandestinely distributed in late 1967, the "program," as it is called, indicates that the Communists have broken ground for a new departure, that is, for the development of an "ethnic" or "regional" policy based on the outer, non-Javanese islands.[10] This is the most illuminating element in the program, which placed emphasis on Indonesia's non-Javanese minorities. The PKI program, for example, holds that every Indonesian, "irrespective of his or her ethnic group or descent shall enjoy equal rights" and that in "the regions . . . broad autonomy shall be given to ethnic groups." [11] Furthermore, "all the ethnic groups are entitled to use their own language in schools, courts and elsewhere" in addition to the national Indonesian language.[12]

In pursuit of that elusive paramilitary organization, or fifth force, the Communist program declared that in addition to a standing People's Liberation Army, "the state shall arm the people and organize [a] people's militia." Finally, the PKI pledges that "in places where the revolution is already victorious and the revolutionary political power established"— presumably including the outer or non-Javanese islands as well as Java—the main points of the program will be implemented, *ergo*, autonomy.

To appreciate the profound character of this aspect of the program it is worth underlining the "third banner" described above in which the PKI sounds the call for a united front against the Army's "military dictatorship."

Should the present quasi-military government retain power for an inordinate period or devolve into a genuine military regime, the PKI's chances, however, slim, would obviously improve. It is in this light that the PKI's new emphasis on "regionalism" should be analyzed, especially since the Army is largely Javanese in ethnic composition. Accordingly, the Communists may be inviting the outer islands to link up at some future date in a united front against "Javanese military domination." Conceivably, this would be an application of the Aidit-Lin Piao thesis, based on Mao, in which the rural areas are seized as a prelude to the capture of the cities. In this instance, the outer islands would be the "rural" areas and Java the "city."

Many, many years ago the author expressed concern that one of the dangers inherent in the Sukarno era was that the PKI would one day be driven underground by the Army and from this half-world would wage a campaign of "liberation." The Indonesians themselves, of course, are not oblivious to the possibilities. They recognize that the Communists are striving to create a "Vietcong situation." [13] They also recognize that if the economy fails to recover from the ravages of the Sukarno era, if people continue to do without while the agencies of power live in a relatively prosperous, corrupt environment, then the PKI may find a basis for discrediting the Suharto government and/or its military successors. But the Communists currently have four strikes against them. The Army is attuned to the problem, as are most able and articulate Indonesians. Power is in the Army's hands and it is therefore in a political position to prevent such an eventuality by a judicious, gradual restoration of civilian authority. Time is on the Army's side since the Communists are identified with Peking and, moreover, the PKI persists in traveling "on the road of armed struggle."[14] Finally, the ghastly September 30 affair is still fresh in everyone's mind. Indeed, the specter of a "third Madiun" runs so deep in Indonesia as to preclude a return of the PKI within the memory of the present generation.

Twenty-five years from now, the forecast may be different. The recovery of the PKI, or a reasonable facsimile, would appear to depend on two factors. One factor, beyond Indonesian control, will be the success or failure of the Communist enterprise in the immediate north—notably in the Philippines, Singapore, Brunei, and Malaysia. The other factor, of transcending importance, is the success or failure of Indonesia's leadership in the years ahead in restoring political liberty largely for the benefit of the country's growing number of educated and politically sophisticated people, and promoting economic growth largely for the benefit of the country's uneducated, politically unsophisticated masses.[15]

Many lessons may be drawn from the outcome of the Gestapu affair, as noted in these pages. Some were obvious; others have not yet emerged and will not until the event recedes further into history. The most obvious exercise is that the Gestapu affair provided an object lesson in the uncertainties of power politics whether the game is played at home or abroad.

Another: All of us die but each has his own grave.

Notes

Introduction: The Time Frame

1. Malaysian Prime Minister Rahman registered this point at the Commonwealth Prime Ministers' Conference, London, September 14, 1966. See Malaysian Information Service, No. NB, 55, October, 1966.
2. William P. Bundy, Assistant Secretary of State for East Asia and Pacific Affairs, in an address before the Commonwealth Club of California, San Francisco, January 20, 1967.
3. By 1965, both Communists and non-Communists increasingly foresaw the likelihood of such a development.
4. Sukarno, *Sukarno: An Autobiography*, as told to Cindy Adams (New York: Bobbs-Merrill, 1965), p. 118. A distorted political history.

1. The Mephitic Climate

1. Seymour Topping, *New York Times*, August 26, 1965. The second in a series of three penetrating articles on this period.
2. Adam Malik, "Promise in Indonesia," *Foreign Affairs* 46, no. 2 (January, 1968). An East Sumatran, Malik was born in 1917 and helped found Antara, Indonesia's first national news agency, in 1937. On the eve of World War II, he was a member of the executive board of Gerindo, a PKI-influenced nationalist grouping. In 1945 he participated, with Aidit among others, in the kidnapping of Sukarno (and Hatta) to speed Indonesia's proclamation of independence. By now, Malik was identified with the National Communists led by Tan Malakka, a former Comintern agent who broke with Stalin in the late twenties. In 1946, Malik was jailed as a participant in Tan Malakka's abortive coup. Upon his release in Jogjakarta in August, 1948, Malik helped found the Murba. In 1959, he became ambassador to the Soviet Union and Poland, and in 1963 he held a trade portfolio in the Sukarno cabinet. Within a year, however, he joined in organizing the BPS against the PKI in the guise of defending Sukarno's teachings. Modest, unassuming, self-educated, his experiences have left him a pragmatist.
3. O. G. Roeder lists as many as seven in the *Far Eastern Economic Review*, May 25, 1967.
4. *Economist*, July 9, 1966.
5. Clarence E. Pike, "Indonesia Striving to Pull Out of Economic Tangle," *Foreign Agriculture*, February 6, 1967. Pike is an agronomist with the U.S. Department of Agriculture. He revisited Indonesia in 1969 in the course of a general Asian tour and held that "the level of living of the bulk of the population appeared to be the lowest of that of any country visited.

Evidences of unemployment and underemployment appear everywhere. Consumer goods are in extremely short supply. Nevertheless, conditions seem to be somewhat improved over those of November 1966—the time of a previous visit to Indonesia by the author." *Foreign Agriculture,* June 9, 1969.

6. Sukarno launched a drive to raise corn in 1964 as the economy crumbled. That same year, October 10, *Harian Rakjat* (People's Daily), the official Indonesian Communist daily, proposed that people consume mice; indeed, Aidit later claimed that he and Sukarno tasted rat flesh and found it palatable.

7. Antara News Agency, August 12, 1966—hereafter cited as Antara. The Communists were obviously also aware of the rapidly deteriorating economic situation. E.g., Lukman's defense of the regime in *Harian Rakjat,* June 23, 1965. Lukman implied that the weakening of the economy strengthened the regime (and therefore the PKI) politically.

2. The Rise of Indonesian Communism

1. For a fuller discussion, see John H. Kautsky, *Moscow and the Communist Party of India* (New York: John Wiley, 1956).

2. "Madiun" is a household word in Indonesian politics. See also Burhan and Subekti, *Facta dan Latar Belakang G-30-S* (Jakarta, 1966). In the foreword, written by Nasution, he observes that "on two different occasions, I myself have experienced uprisings by the Indonesian Communist Party." This is true of most Army officers in his age group. An unpublished English version is entitled, "The Red Coup That Failed"—hereafter cited as Burhan and Subekti.

3. Suripno, "Why We Lost," *Mutiara,* June, 1949. Suripno returned to Indonesia in 1948 with Musso and played a prominent role in the Madiun affair. His memoir was written in prison. Suripno and many other Communist leaders were executed in December, 1948, when the Dutch attacked the Republic for a second time.

4. In the Malay world, mysticism has a deep hold on both the educated and uneducated. Darsono, a founder of the PKI and its first vice chairman, observed as late as 1957 that many PKI branch leaders are "still dominated by superstition [and] traditional mysticism." See Darsono, "The Indonesian Communist Party," *Eastern World,* December, 1957. Indonesia's mystic mood is magnificently captured by Maria Dermoût, *The Ten Thousand Things* (New York: Simon & Schuster, 1958), trans. Hans Koningsberger.

5. The *razzia* was named for prime minister, Sukiman Wirjosandro. Sukiman was a leader of the Masjumi's conservative wing. In 1948–49, during the second Dutch military action, he was hunted by PKI bands. He eluded them by surrendering to the Dutch. Toward the end of the Sukarno era, he was imprisoned by the regime.

6. New China News Agency, May 27, 1965—hereafter cited as NCNA. Peng Chen, head of the Chinese Communist Party delegation to the forty-fifth PKI anniversary celebration, made the estimate. Peng was purged during the Great Proletarian Cultural Revolution.

7. Draft program, Fifth Party Congress, prepared by the plenum of the Central Committee of the PKI, October, 1953. The congress was held at Jakarta in 1954.

8. Antara, December 12, 1965. The "proper settlement" was apparently

the liquidation of the PKI. Despite Madiun, the PKI avoided being out-lawed in the chaotic period of the second Dutch military action which followed. During this period the Republic was being battered by the extreme "right" and extreme "left."

9. Draft program.

10. Aidit's statistics. See *Harian Rakjat*, August 20, 1965.

11. Interview at New York, September 15, 1961. At the time, Aidit accompanied Sukarno on his first visit to President Kennedy. "Are you still writing about my company?" Aidit opened. "Yes," I replied, "how's business?" Aidit said, "Very, very good." His opening referred to a lengthy biographical interview at New York, October 3, 1960, when Aidit accompanied Sukarno to the so-called "circus summit" at the United Nations attended by Khrushchev, Nasser, Tito, *et al.*

12. NCNA, October 4, 1963.

13. *Harian Rakjat*, August 20, 1965.

14. Many correspondents on the scene reported this in detail, e.g., Roeder, *Far Eastern Economic Review*, June 17, 1965.

15. Norman Sklarewitz, *Wall Street Journal*, June 3, 1964.

3. List to Port

1. Sklarewitz, *op. cit.* This was also the considered judgment of thoughtful Indonesians, during this period.

2. John Hughes, *Christian Science Monitor*, January 21, 1965.

3. *Harian Rakjat*, June 14, 1965. Njoto drew this conclusion after analyzing what the PKI considered Sukarno's seven most important statements since 1955, four of them—or more than half—between January 1, 1964, and June 1, 1965, another tell-tale indicator of which way the wind was blowing in this period.

4. Sukarno policy address at the third session of the Provisional People's Consultative Council, Bandung, April 11, 1965—hereafter cited as MPRS. Kim Il-sung, the head of the Workers' (Communist) Party of Korea and Premier of North Korea, attended as Sukarno's state guest. Sukarno termed the Korean Stalinist "our comrade-in-arms and our close friend." The following month, May 5, 1965, Ho Chi Minh, the head of the Lao Dong (Communist) Party of Vietnam and President of North Vietnam, in an interview with Antara's correspondent Suwargono Wirjono, described Sukarno as "my own brother."

5. United Press International, May 23, 1964—hereafter cited as UPI. Lukman spoke at the forty-fourth anniversary celebration of the PKI. Lukman boasted that the Communists "possess the most experienced and influential leaders in Indonesia today."

6. UPI, May 26, 1964.

7. *Facts and Figures: The Special Military Tribunal Tries Dr. Subandrio, 1–22 October, 1966*, issued by the Department of Information, Republic of Indonesia, no. 4/FF/Penlugri, vol. II, April, 1967—hereafter cited as The Subandrio Trial. One in a series of mimeographed English summaries of the trials conducted by the Special Military Tribunal (Mahmillub), which will hereafter be cited as The Sudisman Trial, The Untung Trial, and so on. The Indonesian transcripts of the trials are being issued in a series of books, e.g., *G-30-S Dihadapan Mahmillub* 1, Perkara Njono (Djakarta: P. T. Pembimbing Masa, 1966). This first volume covered the Njono trial and subsequent volumes will cover the remainder.

8. The PKI take-over of Antara was gradual, although such Communist adherents as Djawoto and Suroto held important editorial posts within the agency for more than a decade. Malik was quietly pushed aside following the return to Indonesia of Go Gien Tjwan, the director of Antara's Amsterdam branch. Go was expelled from The Netherlands as a PKI agent in 1952. In this period, the Antara office in Holland was a hotbed of PKI activity.

9. The Western expression, "community of fear," probably best fits the description.

10. Denis Warner, *Reporter*, January 27, 1966.

11. Antara, November 23, 1964. In a message to the Third Congress of the South Celebes (Sulawesi) chapter of the Party of the Upholders of Indonesian Independence, IPKI, a Nasution creation.

12. *Ibid.*

13. Sukarno, Independence Day address, August 17, 1965. Peking conspicuously avoided using the word "Axis" until much later suggesting, perhaps, Sukarno's unilateral decision to use it. However, both Njoto and Subandrio had a hand in the draft. (The Subandrio Trial.) In addition, the author confirmed this through private palace sources in the Spring, 1968. After the collapse of the September 30 movement, however, in an apparent bid to bolster the tottering Sukarno regime, Peking formally endorsed the "Axis" for the first time. Observing that the "Axis" concept was proposed by Sukarno, Peking declared that it strengthens the "common cause of opposing imperialism." See NCNA, October 7, 1965.

14. Tan Malakka had always envisioned the long-term threat to Indonesia as coming from the north, although he collaborated with the Japanese before and during World War II, doubtless on the basis that Holland's enemy is my friend. Sukarno assumed a similar position, based more on personal opportunism. Sjahrir and Hatta opposed collaboration with the Japanese. The PKI followed the Moscow line, cooperative during the period of the Hitler-Stalin pact and thereafter hostile.

15. Antara, January 13, 1965.

16. Roeder, *op. cit.* June 17, 1965.

17. Indonesians generally agree that this was almost the universal consensus at the time.

18. See also *Harian Rakjat,* August 20, 1965.

19. Aidit ended his report thusly: "Nobody intends to turn back, though death is awaiting." See Guy Pauker, *The Rise and Fall of the Communist Party of Indonesia* (Santa Monica: Rand, 1969), a monograph prepared for the U.S. Air Force. Pauker quotes Dr. Walter Slote of Columbia University as suggesting that Aidit subconsciously expected the failure of his drive to power.

20. Hatta interview, Spring, 1968—hereafter, unless otherwise cited, all interviews in this period took place in Indonesia in the Spring, 1968.

21. Pemuda Rakjat (People's Youth) declared itself at the Fifth Party Congress, 1954, "the loyal and trusted assistant" of the PKI. At the Sixth Party Congress, 1959, the organization was formally incorporated into the party's structure. See Chapter X, Article 68, Draft Revision of the Constitution of the C.P.I. (c.q.) in *Materials of the Sixth National Congress of the Communist Party of Indonesia* (Jakarta: Agitation and Propaganda Department, C.C., C.P.I., 1959).

22. This Indonesian viewpoint, however, was an exception making the

general rule that most people in Jakarta were cowed by the display of apparently mass-based Communist power.

23. Presented September 15, 1965. Sukarno simultaneously conferred a similar medal on the late Major General Wilujo Puspojudo, thereby delicately maintaining the impression of a PKI-Army balance of power. Wilujo, who mistrusted the PKI, was conveniently enticed out of the country, as were hundreds of others, by an invitation from Peking to attend the sixteenth anniversary celebrations of the Communist assumption of power in China, October 1, 1949. On July 5, 1966, the MPRS revoked Aidit's award. See MPRS Decision No. XXX/MPRS/1966. (That same day, the MPRS stripped Sukarno of the title "Great Leader of the Revolution.")

24. *Straits Times,* Singapore, May 7, 1965. See also Antara for that same date.

25. *Harian Rakjat,* February 19, 1965. Shortly before, Aidit proposed four "Articles of Association" designed to avoid "a showdown between groups within NASAKOM" whereunder one group "may not interpret the teachings of another group in a manner detrimental to that group." *Harian Rakjat,* December 7, 1964.

26. *Current Activities of the Partai Komunis Indonesia (PKI),* n.p., n.d., circa August 10, 1965. Cyclostyled typescript, 7 pages.

27. *Straits Times,* May 24, 1965. Italic added.

28. E.g., the Council on Posts and Ranks for Senior Officers (WANDJABTI) which, on the eve of August 17, 1965, considered the promotion of colonels to the rank of brigadier general. See "Selected Documents Relating to the 'September 30th Movement' And Its Epilogue," *Indonesia,* April, 1966, p. 165.

The reference to WANDJABTI was contained in a strait-laced speech by Suharto on October 15, 1965, to Sukarno's National Front that avoided any discussion of political ramifications. *Indonesia* does not give the source for this apparent tape recording. At the end, Suharto raised the question of whether the affair was really simply an internal Army affair or politically connected and introduced General Sujipto to give "the facts which connect this affair with political questons." *Indonesia,* however, did not print Sujipto's analysis.

29. The Subandrio Trial. The witness, Air Rear Marshal Muljono Herlambang went on to say that Sukarno then asked Yani: "Are there some who still have relations with the United States?" Yani replied, "Individually, yes. General Parman and General Sukrendro, on my orders, were assigned to collect informative materials." This contact was apparently used by Defense Secretary Robert McNamara before the Senate Foreign Relations Committee, May 11, 1966, to justify past United States appeasement of the Sukarno regime with military aid. McNamara implied that such aid enabled Washington to maintain contact with the Indonesian general staff. The following month, June 19, 1966, James Reston, a columnist on the *New York Times,* wrote that "there was a great deal more contact between the Indonesian high command and Washington before September 30 than is generally realized." The relationship between military aid and political influence is invariably exaggerated. See Chapter IV, footnote 13.

30. Alamsjah interview.

31. The *Pantjasila* or Five Principles were framed by Sukarno, with an

assist from Mohammed Yamin, on June 1, 1945, and later became the
code of the Republic. The principles are nationalism, internationalism,
democracy, social justice, and God, in that order. Later, God was placed
first. In October, 1964, Aidit was widely criticized for having said that the
Pantjasila was only an instrument to unite the people and would no
longer be needed once Indonesia had achieved "socialist unity." Aidit
later denied making the remark. See Antara, October 28, 1964.
32. The Subandrio Trial.
33. Umar Seno Adjie, interview. A democratic socialist, Adjie later joined
the Suharto administration as justice minister.

4. The Masterplan

1. *Act No. 5 Of The Year 1960 Concerning Basic Regulations on Agrarian
Principles* (Jakarta: Department of Information).
2. Among others, Aidit made this remark to Wangsawidjaja, a Hatta aide.
3. Asmu, general chairman of the central council of BTI, chided its East
Java branch for engaging in terrorism, *"even killing,"* to push the unilateral action policy (*aksi spihak* or *sefihak*). *Harian Rakjat,* December 11,
1964. (Italics added.)
4. Hatta interview.
5. Natsir interview.
6. This, of course, was the PKI version. See *Harian Rakjat,* May 31, 1965.
The author of the affair, the chairman of a local BTI branch, was apprehended, tried, and sentenced to death after the collapse of the September
30 movement. See *Duta Masjarakat,* August 1, 1966.
7. Draft program.
8. Antara, July 13, 1953.
9. Antara, January 14, 1965.
10. *Indonesian Herald,* January 16, 1965—hereafter cited as *Herald.* Sukarno's PKI-influenced National Front unanimously supported the proposal on January 18.
11. The Subandrio Trial.
12. *Ibid.*
13. Dhani's career is one of many stunning examples which puncture the
widely held notion that there is necessarily a connection between military
aid and an officer's politics. Dhani received his initial flight training in
California and graduated in 1952. Five years later, for good measure, he
graduated from the Staff College in Britain. In 1958, he directed operations against the anti-Sukarno, anti-PKI PRRI rebels on Sumatra,
Ambdon, and the Moluccas. In 1962, Sukarno named him chief of staff
of the Air Force. That same year, he directed air operations against West
Irian and a year later against Malaysia. See also Jacques Decornoy, *Le
Monde,* August 17, 1965. He quotes Dhani as scoffing at the idea that the
arming of the people would "start internal battles." Decornoy suggests
that the Chinese concept of a "fifth force" was possibly "the first step
towards a popular army" and that the PKI was preparing for the post-
Sukarno period. He held that Aidit was "too intelligent to go straight into
open revolt" but that, mindful of the 1926 and 1948 PKI disasters, he
was bracing himself for the future.
14. Antara, July 9, 1965. Suwardi emphasized that "our enemy does not
come from the north," an interesting comment since Indonesia was then
engaged in a miniwar with Malaysia "north" of Indonesia. Of course, like

all Indonesians in the contemporary period, Suwardi meant China in referring to the "north."

15. *Harian Rakjat*, June 9, 10, 1965.

16. Antara, December 7, 1965, as retold by the manager of the government-controlled Krumput rubber estate near Banjumas.

17. Sutopo interview. Sutopo recalled that at about 6 A.M., October 1, 1965, he left Jakarta's Kemajoran airport for Bandjermasin, South Borneo, via Surabaya in the company of General Panggabean, who was going to East Java. On their arrival at Surabaya, at around 8:00 A.M., "we learned that something had happened in Jakarta," Sutopo said. He continued: "I was puzzled by the radio report of a 'Council of Generals' because there was no such thing and I told Panggabean that something must be wrong." Sutopo decided to continue to Bandjermasin and induced Panggabean to accompany him. On their arrival in Borneo, shortly after noon, Bandjermasin had already received a message from Suharto reporting that Nasution and others had been kidnapped and that he had taken command of the Army. "I had a feeling that the PKI may be behind the whole thing, but we did not know at the time," he recalled.

18. Umar interview. Incidentally, as in the case of Sutopo above, the kidnappings also took him by surprise. Umar said, "I retired about 11:00 P.M. the night before and everything was 'normal.' Let me explain the word 'normal'—things were not. There were constant rumors that something would happen but nobody knew what. About 4:20 A.M. I received a telephone call from the police that Nasution had been kidnapped. I dressed quickly and drove directly to Nasution's house. The house was shot up and the police were there. I then drove to Yani's house and found that it was also shot up. The Madiun affair came to mind; I was a battalion commander in Solo (Surakarta) in 1948 and we had the same kind of situation, with kidnappings. My next thought was: What has happened to Bung Karno?"

19. *Herald*, June 21, 1965, established Yani's position. As for Nasution's, see Antara, July 26, 1965.

20. Sukarno Independence Day speech, August 17, 1965.

21. *Harian Rakjat*, January 1, 1965, in a report by the Information Bureau of the Central Committee, PKI, entitled, "Make 1965 the Year in Which We Crush Bureaucratic Capitalists." Aidit's analysis was prescient. The collapse of the PKI was followed by the rise of the Army (Suharto) and, with a little stretch of imagination, the Murba (Malik).

22. Antara, January 16, 1965.

23. Green interview.

24. Antara, January 3, 1965.

25. UPI, March 17, 1967.

26. The suggestion is from a resident in psychiatry, Bellevue Hospital, New York.

27. *Reuters*, August 20, 1967. However, Sukarno appeared physically fit when he attended a daughter's wedding and appeared in public for the first time in almost a year in 1969, attired in mufti. A photograph of the occasion appeared in the *Asian Student*, March 29, 1969.

28. *Sinar Harapan*, August 20, 1967.

29. The Subandrio Trial.

30. Leimena interview.

31. Alamsjah interview.

32. The Subandrio Trial.

33. E.g., September 16, 1963, when Sukarno unleashed his "crush Malaysia" campaign, Aidit was abroad. There have been other such instances.

34. There is no doubt about some manipulation of the Jakarta trials, particularly with a view to protecting Sukarno. These trials, however, lacked the jigsaw precision of the Moscow purge trials. See *Report of Court Proceedings in the Case of the Anti-Soviet "Bloc of Rights (c.q.) and Trotskyites"* (Moscow: People's Commissariat of Justice of the U.S.S.R., 1938). By illustration, Njono retracted statements attributed to him during preliminary interrogations because they had been made in an "atmosphere of Communist-phobia." Lt. Col. Heru Atmodjo, a Dhani aide, charged from the dock that in prison he had been humiliated, tortured, and coached. PKI defendants also frequently misled the prosecution by citing, for example, Aidit's role at secret deliberations in June and July, 1965, when in point of fact he was abroad, a reflection on the Army's lack of intelligence on even overt PKI activities. The Mahmillub also permitted Sudisman and Njono to talk freely over the heads of the court to the underground, remnant PKI, steeling them for the future. Much of the testimony was windy and irrelevant. See also Sheldon W. Simon, *The Broken Triangle—Peking, Djakarta and the PKI* (Baltimore: Johns Hopkins, 1969)—hereafter cited as Sheldon. "With representatives of the Suharto government serving as both prosecutors and judges, the results of the 'trials' could easily be predicted," Sheldon said. But, he added, "Their political function was to serve as well-publicized negative examples for future Indonesian political aspirants (by borrowing a technique from the Chinese People's Republic) and to lay bare the incredible corruption of the Sukarno era" (pp. 155–56). In effect, Indonesia sought to cauterize the Communists by sunlight.

35. *Anti-Soviet Bloc, op. cit.*

36. The Sudisman Trial.

37. The depth of Communist penetration and disunity within the armed forces is illustrated by the links between the PKI and senior officers from the three divisions on Java—Siliwangi, Diponegoro, and Brawidjaja— publicly disclosed since the September 30 affair. Further, senior officers in the Air Force, and Navy and Marine officers have also been linked directly either with the affair or the post-1966 attempt by the PKI to regroup its shattered organization.

38. The Sjam Trial. Sjam testified that the search for PKI sympathizers within the armed forces was actually begun in 1957, which would place the start of the recruitment operation at the eve of the ill-fated PRRI rebellion. Sjam claimed that his network embraced about seven hundred officers, about five hundred stationed in Central and East Java.

39. The Njono Trial.

40. *Duta Masjarakat*, October 10, 1966. This may partially explain Aidit's frequent cryptic remarks in August–September, 1965. E.g., *Harian Rakjat*, August 21, 1965, wherein Aidit openly declared that "people must not be surprised if conflict bursts out to destroy the luxurious living of corruptors and thieves."

41. The Subandrio Trial.

42. *Los Angeles Times*, October 7, 1965.

43. Brian Crozier, "Indonesia's Civil War," *New Leader*, November 8, 1965.

44. Other prominent nationalist figures, such as Sjahrir and Hatta, were sent to West Irian. In 1968, Hatta publicly disclosed what had long been rumored in Indonesia, i.e., that Sukarno had "cooperated" with the Dutch and therefore received better treatment. Hatta did not go into detail. See Antara, February 17, 1968. In the "inner circle" of the nationalist leadership during the revolution, there was a long-standing undocumented report Sukarno "cooperated" to the extent of informing on the nationalist movement.

45. Since 1945, this has occurred frequently in Indonesia; the "Sukiman Razzia" is a case in point.

46. TRI (Army of the Republic of Indonesia) was one of the Army's early designations; in those days, it was mixed force including armed bands, and so on. In 1947, on the eve of the first Dutch military action, in a bid to improve discipline and "rationalize" the Army, TRI was changed to TNI (the designation in use today). Nasution was known as a "TNI man"; Supardjo, for example, as a "TRI man."

47. Private sources at the presidential palace.

48. The Untung Trial. Robert Shaplen, however, reported that "according to evidence obtained by Indonesian authorities late in 1968, following the arrest of additional officers who had played a role in the coup, Sukarno was told, on September 30, that the Generals would be arrested and might be eliminated, and he raised no objection." See Robert Shaplen, *Time Out of Hand* (New York: Harper & Row, 1969). p. 99.

5. Enemies of the People

1. *Harian Rakjat,* September 29, 1965.

2. Antara, September 28, 1965.

3. Antara, September 14, 1965. Aidit made the statement following a meeting with Sukarno and several leaders of the '45 Revolutionary Group. In another statement, Aidit called for the "elimination" of the PKI's adversaries. See *Herald,* September 14, 1965.

4. Another illustration: Lukman, who concurrently held the position of MPRS vice speaker, acquired a house by arranging to pay off the family which lived there with 250 million rupiahs withdrawn without approval from the MPRS treasury by Islan, the parliament's vice secretary general and member of the PKI. There are numerous other examples; the point is that no party was unstained by corruption in this period, although the PKI arrogated to itself the mantle of incorruptibility.

5. Antara, September 25, 1965.

6. *Ibid.* The HMI, the Islamic student organization, was also attacked.

7. *Ibid.,* September 28, 1965. At a rally Aidit applauded the decision of "engaged" schoolchildren to exchange their books for guns.

8. *Ibid.,* September 29, 1965. (Italics added.)

9. *Ibid.*

10. Antara, September 14, 1965. Italics added.

11. Antara, September 28, 1965. See also *Herald,* September 24, 1965, in which Subandrio charged that many heroes of the war against the Dutch had "turned traitors in the present stage of the revolution" (presumably Army officers).

12. *Herald,* September 18, 1965.

13. Interview with private source at Saigon, Spring, 1968.

14. Antara, September 24, 1965. That same day several Communist or-

ganizations—including peasant (BTI), women (Gerwani), and labor (SOBSI)—hailed the dissolution of the Murba, "the tool of the CIA."

15. The Army had 68 battalions on Borneo within the framework of Sukarno's "crush Malaysia" campaign. Supardjo, a KOSTRAD brigadier, was a Borneo field commander.

16. These were the arms offered by Peking to Subandrio in January, 1965. With literally hundreds of Indonesians arriving in China for the October 1 celebrations, Dhani was conveniently "lost" in the shuffle. In this connection, having helped seed the "fifth force" idea in the Chou-Subandrio talks, the Chinese Communists later applauded "the PKI's fighting call for arming the workers and peasants and for 'holding a rifle in one hand and a spade in the other.'" See NCNA, May 26, 1965.

17. The Subandrio Trial.

18. Antara, September 26, 1965. Major General Achmadi, Sukarno's "progressive" information minister, took part in the ceremonies. Later, he was tried by the Suharto government.

19. Sultan interview. This Suprapto should not be confused with General Suprapto, who was murdered October 1.

20. Tasning interview.

21. Sjafruddin interview.

22. Taihija interview.

23. Sudjatmoko interview.

24. Sugandhi interview.

25. For that matter, so did several other officers on the general staff.

26. *Herald*, September 28, 1965.

27. Antara, September 29, 1965.

28. Antara, September 29, 1965.

29. Nugroho Notosusanto and Ismail Saleh, *The Coup Attempt of the "September 30 Movement" in Indonesia,* unpublished paper, n.d., 167 pages, typescript—hereafter cited as Nugroho and Saleh. Nugroho is head of the Department of History, University of Indonesia, Jakarta, and Saleh is a Colonel in the Army. In Indonesia and abroad, this paper is frequently called the "White Paper." On September 28, Njono placed the "fifth force" at Halim on alert and the following day received a note from Sukatno, the Pemuda Rakjat commander, which read: "On Friday, October 1, 1965, near dawn, at about 4 A.M." p. 141.

30. Antara, September 30, 1965.

31. Sukarno transcript, September 30, 1965, Sekretariat Negara, Kabinet Presiden Republik Indonesia. Nst. 1182/65, 13 pages.

32. The allusion may have been to Sakirman, a member of the Politburo's "inner five," the brother of General Parman, who was murdered the following morning.

33. Antara, September 30, 1965, quoting the Information Bureau, Central Committee, PKI. Antara that same day reported that SOBSI also refused to participate in the conference.

34. Sukarno invariably talked down to his audiences, e.g., when Sukarno reshuffled the cabinet February 23, 1966, he lectured Indonesian newsmen on the spelling of "reshuffle." He said: "'Reshuffle' is written with 'ffle.' [A newspaper] on one occasion wrote it with 'fel,' which is wrong, and on another occasion with one 'f'—'reshufle.' This is why I have always urged that our journalists be upgraded. Reshuffle—'uffle,' not 'uffel,' and not 'reshufle' with only one 'f.'"

35. Elison interview.
36. *Ibid.*
37. Sukarno transcript. It should be recorded that many Indonesians recall that at the end of Sukarno's speech he observed that he must cut it short because it was late and he had a lot of work to do while the audience went home to sleep. This statement, however, was made on September 29, 1965, at the end of his speech before the CGMI congress. See Sukarno transcript, Sekretariat Negara, Kabinet Presiden, Republik Indonesia, Nst. 1219/65. 8 pages. According to some sources, Supardjo conferred with Sukarno on September 29, 1965. See *op. cit.* Shaplen, p. 98-99.

6. Night of the Generals

1. The Sjam Trial. Sjam claimed the order to slay the generals came from Aidit.
2. Wilopo interview.
3. Leimena interview.
4. Nugroho and Saleh, p. 28.
5. *Harian Rakjat*, October 2, 1965.
6. *Ibid.*
7. The formation of such a network of Revolutionary Councils across the country, almost on the pattern of "Soviets," coupled with the announcement that the Council would adhere to Indonesia's foreign policy, i.e., the Jakarta-Peking Axis, completely demolishes the contention that the affair was "solely an internal Army movement."
8. *Straits Times,* September 29, 1967.
9. *Harian Rakjat*, October 2, 1965.
10. Anak Agung interview at Honolulu, Spring, 1968.
11. Budiman interview. Of ethnic Chinese origin, Budiman was among the student leaders at the University of Indonesia who helped organize the anti-Sukarno campaign over Radio Ampera, 1966. Their broadcasts were mimeographed and widely distributed among students, academicians, and intellectuals. Another prominent leader thrown up by events was Adnan Buyung Nasution, who founded the Intellectuals' Action Command (KASI), which cooperated with the KAMI-KAPPI student organizations in toppling Sukarno.
12. Hatta interview.
13. The diplomatic community was caught flat-footed, e.g., the Philippines ambassador was abroad, the Australian ambassdor at a West Java hill station for the weekend, and the Japanese ambassador was touring Wonosobo. Sukarno's Senajan speech was attended by virtually nobody from the diplomatic group other than two newly arrived diplomatic officers from Yugoslavia and Australia whose motivation was to see for the first time Sukarno in action.
14. Sastroamidjojo interview. He recalled that this was Saleh's first reaction. The *Malay Mail*, October 17, 1965, quoted the *Ceylon Daily News,* October 16, 1965 as reporting that Saleh planned to set up a government in exile at Hong Kong if the September 30 movement succeeded. The article was based on a report by Gerald Delikhan, managing editor of *Asia Magazine.* However, this is unlikely. According to private sources, Saleh planned to set up such a government at Pnom Penh, although it is doubtful that Prince Sihanouk would have consented since Cambodia would have been firmly clamped in the Jakarta-Peking vise if the move-

ment succeeded and, therefore, would have enjoyed no room for political maneuver.
15. Goh interview at Singapore, Spring, 1968.

7. *Sukarno Miscalculates*

1. Natsir interview.
2. Without exception, this was the reaction of scores of Indonesian political personalities, both friendly and unfriendly toward Sukarno, who were interviewed between 1965 and 1969.
3. Radio Jakarta, October 3, 1965.
4. Antara, October 14, 1965. Sukarno gave his first interview after the affair to Mohammad Nahar. Sukarno initially claimed he had been at the palace that morning, which was patently untrue.
5. Roeder interview. He amplifies these remarks in O. G. Roeder, *The Smiling General: President Soeharto of Indonesia* (Jakarta: Gunung Agung, 1969), pp. 16–20.
6. Willard Hanna, *Eight Nation Makers* (New York: St. Martin's, 1964), p. 292.
7. *Angkatan Bersendjata,* October 17–20, 1965.
8. Suharto MPRS speech.
9. The Heru Atmodjo Trial.
10. The Omar Dhani Trial.
11. *Ibid.*
12. Repeatedly Indonesians have made this point, e.g., after learning of the murder of the generals, Suharto charged that "the President did not take any steps to condemn that movement or to evacuate the Halim area and then take measures to punish and to crush it [the movement]." (Suharto MPRS speech.) And Nasution pointed out that on October 1 Sukarno failed to contact the Army but, in fact, contacted the Air Force, adding, "The President felt safe with the Gestapu at Halim and not with KOSTRAD." (Cited in Sheldon, p. 160.) Shaplen also makes the point that "significantly," Sukarno went to Halim *after* the Untung broadcast announced the success of the September 30 movement. Shaplen, *op. cit.*
13. Denis Warner, "Indonesia's Communists: Down But Not Out," *Reporter,* November 18, 1965. And *The Times* (London), April 12, 1966, concluded that the day was lost—"narrowly."
14. Sukarno, *op. cit.,* p. 85.
15. Antara, February 25, 1967. See also the Supardjo Trial. From the dock, Supardjo pointed out with bitter irony that in the aftermath of the putsch, "the Council of Generals got what they aimed for."
16. Leimena interview.
17. *Djakarta Times,* February 26, 1968, quoting The Sjam Trial.
18. Radio Jakarta, October 16, 1965, at ceremonies swearing in Suharto as the new Army chief of staff.
19. Antara, January 27, 1967. Nasution interpreted the "stand fast" as a device to forestall Suharto's counterattack.
20. Radio Jakarta, October 3, 1965.
21. Budiardjo interview.
22. Radio Jakarta, October 16, 1965.
23. *Ibid.*
24. Radio Jakarta, December 22, 1965. Sukarno said: "I can say this:

The PKI's sacrifices in the struggle for Indonesian independence are greater than those made by other political parties or groups." This statement infuriated many Indonesians; among other things, Sukarno conveniently overlooked, for example, the PKI stab-in-the-back at Madiun, 1948.

25. Antara, January 11, 1966. Interestingly, Sukarno referred to the PKI's Politburo, not simply to the party.

26. Another question, why Sukarno sought to change the name of the "September 30 movement" to that of the "October 1 movement," is discussed in Chapter IX.

27. Antara, January 27, 1967.

28. See also Nugroho and Saleh, p. 61.

29. Antara, February 18, 1967.

30. Antara, December 22, 1966.

31. UPI, February 13, 1967. The court specifically accused Sukarno of the theft of $7 million and charged that part of the money was deposited in Dutch and Japanese banks.

32. Peter Polomka, *Washington Post*, February 10, 1967.

33. "Sukarno: Enigma on the Southern Flank," ABC-TV, April 2, 1966.

34. Antara, November 12, 1968.

35. Chalmers M. Roberts, *Washington Post*, October 13, 1965.

36. See Antara, December 23, 1966.

37. Donald Kirk, "Indonesia's Revolutionary Justice," *New Leader*, November 7, 1966.

38. Prawoto interview.

39. Suharto MPRS speech. It should be added that, in character, Sukarno stepped aside when he sensed danger to his own person. In his Presidential Order of March 11, 1966, handing over *de facto* power to Suharto, Sukarno specifically states that Suharto pledges to secure Sukarno's "personal safety." See *Presidential Order 11 March 1966 to General Soeharto*, Department of Information, Special Issue 002/1966. The booklet contains eight key documents relating to the change of power.

40. Unimpeachable source. (See page 111.)

8. Gestapu or Gestok?

1. The term "Gestapu," of course, is meaningless to the average Indonesian; however, it is a highly emotive word among educated people, both Indonesians and foreigners alike. General Sugandhi, who directs the armed forces daily, *Angkatan Bersendjata*, is generally credited with minting the acronym. Muljono bin Nglai, a member of Sjam's Special Bureau, is credited with coining the plot's code name, "September 30 movement."

2. Suharto interview.

3. Private sources.

4. *Pikiran Rakjat*, Bandung, February 27, 1964.

5. *Ibid.* The source was Lt. Col. Soedharsono, the fifth assistant chief of staff, KOSTRAD.

6. Suharto interview.

7. *Ibid.*

8. *Ibid.*

9. Latief was the commander of the First Infantry Brigade, Jakarta Garrison, and was in charge of the killer squads at Halim.

10. Roger K. Paget, "The Military in Indonesian Politics: the Burden of Power," a paper delivered at the annual meeting of the Association for Asian Studies, Chicago, March, 1967.

11. In an imaginative reconstruction, Professor Victor Fic suggests there was a coup and countercoup interwoven within the putsch itself among the principal protagonists at Halim that morning, i.e., Sukarno, Aidit, Supardjo, and so on. See Victor M. Fic, "September 30th Movement in Indonesia; 1965 Gamble That Failed," a paper presented at the International Conference on Asian History, August 5–10, 1968, at Kuala Lumpur.

12. Antara, March 6, 1967.

13. Simatupang interview.

14. Herald, October 11, 1965.

15. Sukarno at a news conference, October 14, 1965.

9. Debacle on Java

1. Nugroho and Saleh, p. 52.

2. Thus, the Politburo's "inner five" were divided as follows on the night of Sept. 30: Aidit in Jakarta; Sudisman at Rawasari; Njoto in Sumatra; Lukman and Sakirman in Central Java. Jakarta and Central Java were the keys to the control of Java, and Aidit realized that whoever controlled Java controlled Indonesia. See Nugroho and Saleh, p. 124.

3. Reuters, October 7, 1965. For the text, see Indonesia, April, 1966, p. 188.

4. Ibid.

5. Gani interview at New York, Autumn, 1967.

6. The Subandrio Trial. See also Arthur Dommen, Los Angeles Times, November 15, 1965.

7. Radio Jakarta, October 14, 1965. The Supreme Operations Command, KOTI, issued the order.

8. Radio Jakarta, October 20, 1965. Similar action was taken that same day in North Celebes (Sulawesi) and in South Celebes the day before.

9. Antara, October 20, 1965.

10. Radio Hanoi, October 20, 1965.

11. Antara, March 14, 1965.

12. Nugroho and Saleh, p. 78.

13. Burhan and Subekti.

14. Dommen, Los Angeles Times, November 11, 1965. As early as October 29, 1965, the Straits Times, in a front-page headline, reported the Communists massacred political opponents and this in turn unleashed "anti-Communist violence," especially clashes between Muslims and PKI members.

15. Ibid.

16. Dommen, op. cit.

17. Harald Munthe-Kaas, "Searching for Aidit," Far Eastern Economic Review, November 11, 1965.

18. Unimpeachable source. In connection with Aidit's capture, it is worth emphasizing that he and most of the other PKI leaders remained at large for as relatively brief a period as Musso and his aides after the Madiun debacle. This must partly reflect a lack of popular support for the PKI since the Communists were never able to behave, according to Mao's guerrilla model, as fish in a sea of people. Yet the leaders of extremist Islam, the Darul Islam, and others, in a series of uncoordinated revolts,

remained at large for a dozen years or more, although under intense Army pressure—certainly indicative of a broader popular base of support than that ever enjoyed by the Communists—e.g., Kartosuwirjo in West Java, Kahar Muzzakhar in South Celebes, Ibnu Hadjar in South Borneo, and Daud Bereuh in Atjeh (North Sumatra). Their feats were unmatched by the PKI in 1926, 1948, 1951, 1965. By comparison with the PKI, these revolts and movements received relatively scanty and insignificant attention (publicity) abroad. Most Western writers, including the author, are seriously at fault. For that matter, non-Communist nationalist leaders also showed a far greater stamina for remaining at liberty than the PKI, e.g., during the second Dutch military action and in the aftermath of the abortive PRRI rebellion. I am grateful to Oejeng Soewargana for bringing this failure to my attention.

19. *Asahi Evening News,* February 7, 1966.

20. See the *Straits Times,* Malaysian edition, September 18, 1965, which quoted the *Manila Evening News* as reporting that "China was smuggling arms into Indonesia for use by the Indonesian Communists." This was one of any number of dispatches *before* September 30 which indicated that a PKI showdown was in the making. E.g., see C. W. Huang, *Malay Mail,* June 21, 1965, who held that a PKI-Army conflict "is sure to come —it is only a question of time."

21. *Asahi Evening News.*

22. *Asahi Evening News,* December 2, 1965.

23. By now this distinction was no longer valid; for, the PKI was completely identified with the Peking wing in the Sino-Soviet schism. Had the Communists come to power, however, there is a reasonable possibility that Aidit would have veered back to Moscow as a source of air and naval weapons to strengthen an Indonesian Communist sphere of influence in the Malay world against Peking. Maps published in Peking in 1954 showed segments of the Malay triangle as former Chinese territories, including Malaya, Singapore, and the Sulu islands of the Philippines. No claim, however, was made to any Indonesian territory, although the Chinese once set up "republics" in Indonesian West Borneo (Kalimantan).

24. *Djaja,* December 20, 1965. See Antara, December 21, 1966. Mrs. Aidit is still in detention.

10. A Final Solution?

1. *Statement of the Politburo of the Central Committee of the PKI, Indonesian Tribune,* November, 1966. The statement was dated, Jogjakarta, May 23, 1966.

2. Sukarno's figure was based on the findings of a board of inquiry established by KOTI December, 1965. The board reported 54,000 persons killed in East Java, 12,500 in Bali, 10,000 in Central Java, and 2,000 in North Sumatra. *Angkatan Bersendjata,* February 10, 11, 1966, published the findings.

3. An American academician during a panel discussion on Indonesia at the annual meeting of the Association of Asian Studies, New York, 1966.

4. William Glenn, *Far Eastern Economic Review,* August 8, 1968. This view persists, e.g., Roger A. Freeman, *Socialism and Private Enterprise in Equatorial Asia* (Stanford: Stanford University 1968), p. 52.

5. By the spring, 1968, this figure was generally provided by a wide-ranging number of sources within and without the government. Several foreign

embassies had also reduced their previous estimates following reports by church groups and others that many of those who "disappeared" in the holocaust was gradually filtering back to their villages.

6. Charles Mohr, *New York Times,* March 17, 1967.

7. Bridget Mellor, *New Statesman,* August 5, 1966.

8. Miroslav Oplt, who is also a philologist. See his *Bahasa Indonesia Ucebnice Indonestiny Indonesian Lanauge* (Prague: Statni Pedagogoicke Nakladatelstvi, 1966).

9. Sukarno address, August 17, 1966. Department of Information. See also Antara, August 19, 1969.

10. *New York Times,* December 19, 1965. Two days earlier, Antara quoted Sukarno as declaring that the culprits in the affair must be tried, sentenced, and "if necessary, shot."

11. *Economist,* July 27, 1968. See also M. Lewin, *Russian Peasants and Soviet Power* (London: Allen & Unwin, 1968).

12. Fall's figure, as in the case of the Indonesian statistic, was a "reasonable" estimate.

13. See Joseph Buttinger, *Vietnam: A Dragon Embattled* (New York: Praeger, 1967).

14. Mononutu interview at Jakarta, Autumn, 1954. See also Stephen S. Rosenfeld commentary on Han Suyin, *Washington Post,* February 8, 1962.

15. Jean Contenay, "Heritage of Blood," *Far Eastern Economic Review,* December 14, 1967.

16. Natsir interview.

17. *Economist,* January 29, 1966. In some instances, the Army protected PKI cadres against popular outbursts. E.g., Antara, April 4, 1969.

18. *Angkatan Bersendjata,* October 9, 1965, however summed up the attitude generally found within and without the Army: "For the inhuman savagery they showed, we will take reprisals in accordance with the existing laws of revolution. . . . If we do not do this, later on it won't be seven generals, eight generals, or ten generals who will be subjected to terrorism, but hundreds and even thousands of people who will be wiped out. . . . [The PKI] has no right to continue to live."

19. Burhan and Subekti.

20. Radio Jakarta, October 26, 1965.

21. *Herald,* November 15, 1965.

22. Antara, December 10, 1965.

23. The order was issued November 15, 1965, and broadcast over Radio Jakarta. Similarly, Radio Jakarta broadcast on March 31, 1966, Suharto's directive which ordered that the implementation of ABRI KOTI No. 22/KOTI/1965 be intensified.

24. "Reign of Terror in Java," *Times* (London), April 13, 1966. See also *Times,* January 2, February 8, 1966, and *Guardian,* January 17, 1966, for other British reactions. The *Guardian* noted that Sukarno's figure of eighty-seven thousand was higher than the number of deaths resulting from the atomic bomb at Hiroshima, which brought World War II to a swift close and ended the repressive Japanese occupation of East Asia and the Pacific, including Indonesia.

25. Many Indonesians felt that Sukarno's refusal to take a strong political lead against the PKI led to the massacres of Communists and others that began in late October, after the details of the generals' murders and pictures of their exhumed bodies had been well publicized. See *External*

Affairs Review, August, 1967, a publication of the New Zealand Ministry of External Affairs.

26. A South Asian who experienced the India-Pakistan massacres accompanying partition distinguishes between spontaneous mass murder and state-organized mass murder. He feels the former applies especially to economically and educationally "backward" countries where ideology is increasingly simplified as it extends further from the country's political center or urban areas and where the level of political sophistication is either low or nonexistent. However, this does not preclude state-organized mass murder in relatively "backward" countries, e.g., the Soviet Union in the twenties and thirties, and China in the fifties.

27. The celebrated French case of Daniel Hugon, tried for the murder of a prostitute on September 4, 1965, is a case in point.

28. Horace Sutton, "Indonesia's Night of Terror," *Saturday Review,* February 4, 1967.

29. Jean-Francois Steiner, *Treblinka* (New York: Simon & Schuster, 1967). Steiner points to cases where Jews not only let themselves be killed without a gesture of revolt, but even assisted their killers with their work of extermination.

30. Antara, September 21, 1966, in a dispatch from Belgrade.

31. NCNA, December 14, 1966.

32. Interview at Saigon, Spring, 1968.

33. Or the photographed summary execution of a Vietcong prisoner by General Nguyen Ngoc Loan, February 1, 1968, at Saigon, during the Communist "Tet" offensive.

34. *The Silent Slaughter,* a pamphlet prepared and sponsored by Youth Against War and Fascism, 1966.

35. Kennedy speech, University of Capetown, South Africa, June 6, 1966. Kennedy was probably prompted to equate these "differing evils," given the location of his address.

36. John Hughes, *Indonesian Upheaval* (New York: McKay, 1967).

37. Sutton, *op. cit.*

38. *New York Times,* May 22, 1966.

39. *Ibid.,* January 23, 1966. The author was Francis B. Randall.

40. *Ibid.,* June 19, 1966.

41. Moscow periodically attempts to pin Westerling to the United States, an example of the Kremlin's gross propaganda in Indonesia, e.g., Radio Moscow, in Indonesian to Indonesia, Mikhail Marinov commentary, July 30, 1965, which claimed the Pentagon recruited Westerling for "new adventures" in Indonesia. See also Raymond ("Turk") Westerling, *Challenge To Terror* (London: Kimber, 1952).

42. *Life's* pictorial spread, July 1, 1966, is frequently cited as an example of photographic evidence. In fact, there is not a single photograph of the massacre in the photographic essay which senior *Life* combat correspondents such as Carl Mydans, or producer Lothar Wolff, agreed was inexplicable.

43. Experienced correspondents on the scene were unable to explain why they did not see a single body in Jakarta or, for that matter, anywhere else, during their travels in this period. By contrast, my wife Aggie landed on Java for the first time as a member of the Allied forces in September, 1945, during the so-called "bersiap period," and saw bodies floating in Jakarta's (Batavia's) canals.

44. I.e., verbal or photographic.

45. *Christian Science Monitor,* May 5, 1966.
46. Jeff T. Williams, the former Indonesia correspondent of the Associated Press, made this point. Virtually all non-Communist and non-Indonesian correspondents in the area between 1965 and 1966 are skeptical about the massacre figures. All agree, however, that thousands of persons disappeared and were probably murdered.
47. *Sinar Harapan,* February 3, 1966.
48. *Angkatan Bersendjata,* September 26–30, 1966.
49. *Indonesian Tribune,* August–September, 1967.
50. Frances L. Starner, *Far Eastern Economic Review,* August 17, 1967. The late Donald Fagg, a brilliant young American scholar made a similar estimate as early as 1953 and was convinced that tension on Java would explode one day in a murderous orgy. Another lethal outburst in the distant future, this time perhaps nihilistic in content, cannot be precluded.
51. This viewpoint was put forth by thoughtful Indonesians in Jakarta at the time of the "Tet" offensive.
52. Suharto MPRS speech, August 16, 1968.
53. See *No Massacre in Purwodadi,* Department of Information, no. 041/H.O./3/69, March 3, 1969. Mimeographed, 4 pages.

11. Why the Communists Failed

1. Arthur Dommen, *Los Angeles Times,* January 19, 1966.
2. Antara, December 28, 1965.
3. Subadio interview.
4. Goh interview.
5. Marpaung interview, Summer, 1968, at Brookfield Center, Conn.
6. Sumitro interview.
7. Khrushchev address at Gadja Mada University, Jogjakarta, February 22, 1960.
8. Darsono, *op. cit.*
9. Soetan Sjahrir, *Out Of Exile* (New York: John Day, 1949), trans. Charles Wolf, Jr., p. 73. Sjahrir died at Zurich, April 9, 1966, at the age of fifty-six. Only when his health was completely broken, following long neglect in various Sukarno prisons, did the Sukarno regime permit him to go to Switzerland for medical care. See Roeder, "Darkness At Noon," *Far Eastern Economic Review,* April 21, 1966. His wife, Poppy, and a number of his aides, recounted in the Spring, 1968, how Sjahrir remained mentally alert to the end and how he understood that the Sukarno regime, and what it represented, had collapsed with the PKI, although he could neither speak nor write at the time. Sukarno, in effect, had transferred power to Suharto March 11, 1966. Sjahrir, perhaps, was the greatest figure produced by the Indonesian revolution. His horizon and influence extended far beyond the rim of the Malay world.
10. Hatta interview.
11. Gani interview, at New York, Summer, 1968.
12. Lubis interview.
13. Tobing interview.
14. Invariably, this was the estimate of any number of different Indonesian sources.
15. Mellor, *op. cit.*
16. Leimena interview.

17. Prawoto interview.
18. Natsir interview.
19. Wilopo interview.
20. Simatupang interview.
21. Burhan and Subekti.
22. Gani interview.
23. Anak Agung interview at Honolulu, Spring, 1968.
24. During this period, the Indonesian general staff was in contact with its Malaysian counterpart. The most biting commentary on the Army appeared in *U.S. News & World Report,* March 26, 1966, which described Indonesia's military leaders as largely bright, but arrogant and corrupt. See also Antara, July 18, 1967, in which Nasution agreed with public criticism of the abuse and misuse of authority by some members of the armed forces. He further called for a "cleaning up" of corrupt elements within the armed forces.
25. Aidit interview at New York, Autumn, 1960. See also S. M. Ali's interview with Aidit, *Far Eastern Economic Review,* April 16, 1964. Aidit said, "There will be no armed struggle, unless there is foreign intervention." In Aidit's view, "When we complete the first stage of our revolution, which is now in progress, we can enter into friendly consultation (*mushawara*) with other progressive elements in our society and, without an armed struggle, lead the country toward Socialist Revolution." Aidit frequently interspersed such comments in this period with calls for general elections, e.g., *Herald,* May 27, 1964.
26. Once again Aidit and Sukarno shared the same motives. Sukarno probably realized that he could not assert "great influence on the ranks" until he first replaced the general staff.
28. Adjie interview.
29. Draft program. See also *Tentang Tan Ling Djie-ism,* Central Committee, PKI, Jakarta, 1954.
30. Sjam and Olan Hutapea, the rector of the Aliarcham Academy, and the leader of the reorganized Politburo in 1968, are cases in point. Both were sub rosa members of the PKI when they became members of the Socialist Party in 1945. There are numerous other examples of this type of PKI infiltration. See, e.g., *Duta Masjarakat,* September 6, 1966.
31. Interestingly, since the collapse of the PKI, Peking has accused the "Suharto-Nasution fascist military regime"—not Sukarno—of "traveling the previous path of Chiang Kai-shek." See *Chung Kuo Hsin-win,* Canton, November 3, 1967. JPRS 44:085. In this connection, see also Sheldon, *op. cit.,* p. 16, who suggests that the Communist betrayal by Chiang Kai-shek in 1927 "may have precluded total reliance on revolution from above," the policy Aidit pursued in Indonesia. Yet, Sheldon observes, the Chinese leadership was in a dilemma since the party learned the necessity for such a policy during the alliance with Chiang Kai-shek during the Sino-Japanese War.
32. This maneuver came into the open during a party conference, July 3–5, 1964, at which Aidit warned that the PKI's "internal contradictions" must be resolved quickly by criticism and self-criticism to avoid the disintegration of party unity. Peking promptly exploited his public disclosure. In a note to the Central Committee of the Soviet Communist Party, July 28, 1964, the Chinese party's Central Committee declared, "We resolutely support the struggle of the Indonesian Communist Party and other

fraternal Marxist-Leninist Parties against your disruptive activities." In early 1965, Aidit renewed his warning and said that among the PKI's opponents are those who "even acknowledge themselves to be Marxist-Leninists, and, in fact, even more so than the very leaders of the PKI." Then he added, "They even once thought they would set up a 'Communist Party' along modern revisionist lines." See *Harian Rakjat,* January 6, 1965.
33. In this manner, Moscow apparently sought to usurp the "Marxist-Leninist" label, which the Chinese have used to identify "true" Communist parties. They have also engaged competitively in accusing each other of fostering "splittism" within the PKI. During the Sino-Soviet border clashes, March, 1969, Moscow listed the failures of Chinese Communist "adventurism" and said, "But the most tragic events occurred in Indonesia in 1965 where hundreds of thousands of democrats perished as a result of the rash policies of the Chinese splitters and their followers." See Radio Moscow commentary, March 12, 1969. Peking replied in these terms: "The Soviet revisionist renegade clique has carried out a series of criminal activities in an attempt to split the Indonesian Communist Party." See NCNA, March 14, 1969.
34. Surjotojondro interview.
35. E.g., Donald Hindley, "President Sukarno and the Communists: the Politics of Domestication," *American Political Science Review* 56 (1962). There are numerous other examples. Justus M. van der Koref, *The Communist Party of Indonesia* (Vancouver: University of British Columbia, 1965), p. 296, suggests that such an interpretation is "quite misleading."

12. Impact on Peking

1. Seth King, "The Great Purge in Indonesia," *New York Times Magazine,* May 8, 1966. See also Robert S. Elegant, *Los Angeles Times,* January 9, 1966.
2. Aidit's acceptance speech, NCNA, September 6, 1963. Italics added. NCNA gave the event broad coverage and carried the speeches of Ku Mo Jo, Peng Chen, and others at a dinner in Aidit's honor.
3. That is, in the same year. Sukarno visited China for the first time in 1956; Mao, then head of state, did not reciprocate.
4. Antara and NCNA, January 23, 1965. Also, see The Subandrio Trial.
5. Sastradinata interview. "Baron" is Sastradinata's given name. See also a series of articles by W. W. Tjokro, "An Account of Events in Peking at the Time of the 30 September 1965 Abortive Coup" in *Angkatan Bersendjata,* September 20–21, 24–28, 1968. JPRS 46:880.
6. Subandrio-Ch'en Yi Joint Statement, January 28, 1965.
7. Antara, January 28, 1965.
8. Antara, September 23, 1965. In Indonesia, meanwhile, on September 24, Subandrio conferred with Chinese Ambassador Yao Chung Ming on Jakarta-Peking cooperation in "*all* spheres." Emphasis added. See Antara, September 24, 1965.
9. Antara, September 23, 1965. Italics added. The agency also quoted an Indonesian Air Force spokesman in Peking as praising the People's Liberation Army for practicing "military democracy."
10. Sastradinata interview.
11. Sastroamidjojo interview.
12. Arthur J. Dommen, "The Attempted Coup in Indonesia," *China Quarterly,* January–March, 1966.

13. Sastroamidjojo interview.
14. H. R. Trevor-Roper, "Understanding Mao; or, Look Back to Stalin," *New York Times Magazine*, February 12, 1967.
15. The number of Indonesians in sanctuary in Peking may number as many as seven hundred, discounting the tens of thousands of Overseas Chinese who have returned to the mainland. About four hundred Indonesians are known to be in refuge in the Soviet Union and Eastern Europe.
16. NCNA, October 4, 1965.
17. Jacques Marcuse, *The Peking Papers* (New York: Dutton, 1967), p. 334.
18. NCNA, October 19, 1965.
19. *The Great Cultural Revolution in China,* compiled and edited by the Asian Research Center (Tokyo: Tuttle, 1968), p. 493.
20. See *Wen Hui Pao*, December 2, 1968, and Ting Wang, "Profile of Wang Kuwang-mei," *Far Eastern Economic Review*, June 22, 1967. Actually, such leaders as Premier Chou En-lai, who survived Mao's "Cultural Revolution," were as lavish in their praise of Sukarno as Liu, e.g., NCNA, April 16, 1965.
21. Antara, November 25, 1966.
22. NCNA, September 2, 1965. The Foreign Languages Press, Peking, has also published the thesis under the same title in 1966.
23. Peng Chen, at the head of a Chinese Communist Party delegation to the forty-fifth anniversary celebration of the PKI, delivered a speech at the Aliarcham Academy of Social Science, which was attended by Aidit, Lukman, Hutapea, Suijono, Mrs. Sukiman Aliarcham, and others. "As Comrade Aidit has said," Peng Chen said, "Asia, Africa, and Latin America are the rural areas of the world taken as a whole while Europe and North America are its cities." And Peng Chen continued: "In order to win victory in the world revolution, the proletariat must attach great importance to the revolutions in Asia, Africa, and Latin America, that is, to the revolutions in the world's rural areas, and there is no other path." See NCNA, May 28, 1965.
24. NCNA, December 2, 1965, discounted reports that Aidit was dead. As late as March, 1966, the Peking-operated *Malayan Monitor* still referred to Aidit as alive.
25. *Hung Ch'i* (Red Flag), the Chinese party's theoretical journal, editorially endorsed Sudisman's "auto-critique" November 11, 1967. The critique, which bears no name but is generally considered to have been written by him, was dated and circulated in Indonesia September, 1966, under the title, "Self-Criticism by the Political Bureau of the Central Committee of the Indonesian Communist Party."
26. Antara, April 21, 1967.
27. Suharto, in an address before the MPRS, August 16, 1967.
28. Antara, December 18, 1965.
29. NCNA, December 29, 1966. This became a recurrent Chinese theme in a series of statements and notes protesting the mistreatment of Chinese nationals in Indonesia.
30. A strain between Jakarta and Peking developed from the outset when China—and Cuba—refused to fly their embassy flags at half staff to pay tribute to the murdered generals. The Indonesians were incensed. The Chinese, however, exercised a diplomatic prerogative and in a note, October 20, 1965, held that the Chinese Embassy's flag would be flown at

half mast only if the head of state or "leader of the fraternal party of a Socialist [Communist] country passes away." The note said that "no foreign country has ever raised any objection to this practice."

31. *Melbourne Herald,* August 29, 1967.

32. Suharto MPRS address.

33. Suharto issued a Cabinet Presidium Instruction No. 37/U/IN/6/1967, June 7, 1967, entitled, "The Basic Policy for the Solution of the Chinese Problem." Article 14 read: "In regard to the substance of the double citizenship agreement between the Republic of Indonesia and the People's Republic of China, a rearrangement will be made on the basis of national interest." *Dawn,* April 14, 1969, quoted the Indonesian Embassy in Pakistan as reporting that the agreement had been revoked.

34. Antara, August 15, 1967. For the texts of a series of presidential directives treating with the "Chinese problem," see *Presidential Instructions Concerning the Chinese Problem,* Department of Information, Jakarta, December, 1967. *Sinar Harapan,* June 28, 1969, quoted an official announcement that the Special Staff had been disbanded on the grounds that it was "no longer necessary." See also Antara for that date.

35. More than one hundred thousand fled to China aboard vessels provided by Peking in the aftermath of anti-Chinese measures, 1958–60. In 1958, thousands left for Taiwan aboard ships provided by Taipeh following repressive measures against "stateless" Chinese.

36. Sastradinata interview.

37. *Statement of the Government of the Republic of Indonesia,* September 15, 1966. The statement accused China of "giving protection to fugitives of the Gestapu-PKI movement and of even inciting them to carry out political activities against the Republic of Indonesia."

38. For examples, see the *Malayan Monitor,* December, 1965, and January–April, 1966.

39. *People's Daily,* October 29, 1967. This has been a persistent theme in Chinese Communist commentaries and in underground PKI circulars since the Gestapu affair.

40. *Ibid.* The Russians, however, contend that Mao Tse-tung drew no lesson. "The Communist Party of Indonesia which came under the influence of Mao Tse-tung's 'Leftist' and reactionary ideas, suffered a tragic defeat as a result of which millions of Communists and non-Party workers, peasants, and intellectuals suffered horribly," Moscow said. "Mao Tse-tung drew no lesson whatever from this. Instead, he imputed the blame to the leaders of the Communist Party of Indonesia, who died heroically." Wang Ming, *China: Cultural Revolution or Counter-Revolutionary Coup?* (Moscow: Novosti, 1969), p. 62.

41. *Malayan Monitor,* March, 1966.

42. See also footnote 15. Fourteen persons seeking sanctuary in Singapore from Indonesia were barred by the Singapore government. See *Agence France Press,* February 12, 1967. The Barisan Sosialis Malaya, a Peking-oriented opposition party in Singapore, has denounced the Singapore government for "collaboration with anti-Chinese Indonesian generals." See *Plebeian,* February 13, 1968. In the aftermath of the Gestapu affair, between fifty and sixty Communists also sought sanctuary in The Netherlands. See *Nederlandsche Rotterdamsche Courant Overseas Weekly,* February 8, 1966. Interestingly, after the collapse of the Madiun affair in 1948, many PKI adherents sought safety behind the Dutch lines. The

Indonesian Communists apparently felt they would be accorded better treatment in Western hands than in the hands of their compatriots.

43. *People's Daily*, February 23, 1968. The *Indonesian Tribune*, November, 1966, has also described him as "a member of the Political Bureau and deputy head of the secretariat of the central committee of the PKI."

44. *Indonesian Tribune*, December, 1966.

45. Chen Hsin Hsin Wen Pao, September 29, 1964, cited in *Free China Weekly*, October 4, 1964. See also the *Hong Kong Express*, September 30, 1964.

46. Sastradinata interview.

47. NCNA, August 4–5, 1965.

48. *Ibid.*

49. The names of the doctors in attendance or whether they were in fact doctors—although there is no reason to doubt their authenticity—is not known.

13. Impact on Moscow

1. Aidit had visited Moscow the previous July and a question which will probably never be answered is whether or not Aidit discussed the "Council of Generals" with the Russians. As far as can be ascertained, the Soviet Embassy, and the embassies of the East European countries, were surprised by events. The Russians had long been running scared on Indonesia as Sukarno and the PKI became increasingly Peking-oriented. Georgiy Afrin, the *Tass* correspondent in Jogjakarta and Batavia, 1947–48, commented hopefully over Radio Moscow, July 31, 1965, shortly after the Aidit visit: "We are comrades-in-arms—this was the statement once made by President Sukarno. Indeed, this is true. . . . This means that our friendship is based on unshakable foundations."

2. East German News Agency (ADN), November 1, 1965, Kiev dispatch.

3. Radio Moscow, March 19, 1966.

4. *Ibid.*, February 26, 1966.

5. *Ibid.*, March 19, 1966. Thus, the Kremlin also dismissed the Untung claim of a CIA intrigue. However, by 1968, Moscow charged that "the U.S. and its CIA inspired the mass murders of Indonesian Communists and patriots." See Radio Moscow, September 10, 1968.

6. Radio Moscow, August 6, 1967.

7. *Komsomolskaya Pravda*, March 19, 1967.

8. A. Lavin, "In Defense of Indonesia's Democrats," *Trud*, March 2, 1966. Their schism notwithstanding, Sino-Soviet publications launched a concerted drive to save Sudisman and Njono from the death penalty handed down by the Mamillub. The Kremlin went so far as having President Nikolai V. Podgorny write Suharto a letter requesting that the lives of the PKI leaders be spared. Earlier, Hanoi had sought to provide lawyers for their defense.

9. *Tass*, March 29, 1966.

10. Soviets credits totaled $800 million, the remainder was drawn from Czechoslovakia, East Germany, and so on. Irate Peking declared, "In these slaughters, the Indonesian fascist military group was provided with arms by Soviet revisionists." NCNA, December 1, 1967.

11. *Los Angeles Times*, October 9, 1965.

12. *Sunday Straits Times*, October 24, 1965. See also the *Christian Science Monitor*, September 18, 1968.

13. See Chapter 11.
14. Radio Moscow, March 19, 1966.
15. This was common gossip in Jakarta in this period.
16. The ageing Semaun remained in the background during the consolidation of the Sukarno-PKI alliance and the Jakarta-Peking Axis.
17. *Asahi Evening News,* December 2, 1965.
18. *Malayan Monitor,* February, 1966.
19. *L'Humanité,* December 9, 1967. In a rare JPRS mistranslation, this document is described as the "Appeal *to* the Marxist-Leninist Group of the Indonesian Communist Party." JPRS 10:944. (Italics added.) In translation, the document may also be termed a "Call of the . . ."
20. Branko Lazitch, "Declaration of Indonesian Communists," *Est & Ouest,* January 1–15, 1968. JPRS 44:580.
21. Suharto Independence Day address, August 17, 1968.
22. *Indonesian Tribune,* August–September, 1967. The document indicated a further downgrading of Aidit since it referred only to the loss of such "leading members" of the PKI as Sudisman, Anwar Sanusi, and Djokosudjono and, by implication, Njono.
23. NCNA, February 8, 1968, reported an "uprising of revolutionary people . . . in a place near Blitar." By late March, there were numerous reports of such activity reported in the Indonesian press, e.g., *Djakarta Times,* March 26, 1968. See also *Asia,* Spring, 1969.
24. *Economist,* November 30, 1968. The dispatch was not from a staff correspondent, however. See also Chapter 9, footnote 53.
25. *Pravda,* September 14, 1968. For additional details, see "Indonesia: Another Communist Disaster," *Current History,* March, 1969.
26. Aidit is said to have offered a similar explanation in the "Asahi Confession."
27. Kim Il-song, in an address before the Central Committee of the Korean Workers' (Communist) Party, October 5, 1966.
28. Peking and its allies, including the PKI, do not recognize the existence of either Malaysia or Singapore as separate political entities. Chinese Communist (and PKI) documents always refer to "Malaya," which they define as Malaya and Singapore combined. Such a combination gives "Malaya" a Chinese racial dominance. By excluding the Bornean territories of Malaysia (Sarawak and Sabah) from their definition, the Chinese Communists (and the PKI) imply that these areas either belong to Indonesia outright or are within an Indonesian sphere of influence.
29. Radio Budapest, February 11, 1968. Invitations to the Moscow-sponsored conclave were issued by the Hungarian Communist Party. The Hungarians said that "owing to circumstances over which we have no control," the invitation could not be forwarded to the PKI. They also reported that the Dutch Communists declined to attend. This was not surprising since the Netherlands Communist Party (CPN) had repeatedly assailed Moscow for "selling out" the PKI. Like the Chinese, the Dutch Communists endorsed a course of armed struggle for the PKI following the abortive September 30 affair. E.g., Joop Moorier, "Generals' Rule, PKI and Growing Resistance," *Politiek en Cultuur,* November 11, 1968. The journal is a CPN organ.
30. *Pravda,* January 13, 1967. See also *Moscow Radio Peace and Progress,* August 3, 1967. The latter came into operation November, 1964, not as a state organ but ostensibly as a "voice of public opinion" in the Soviet

Union. It has been employed to attack countries with which Moscow maintains friendly and/or diplomatic relations. Among its board members is B. G. Gafurov, who visited Burma in 1957 as a member of a delegation from the Supreme Soviet and is believed to have offered Soviet support for the Burmese Communist underground in the competition with Peking. Radio Moscow, October 24, 1967.

32. Ruth Thomas McVey, *The Development of the Indonesian Communist Party and its Relations with the Soviet Union and the Chinese People's Republic* (Cambridge: M.I.T., 1954), p. 2. She held that Indonesia's "geographic isolation" minimized the opportunity for Soviet guidance and aid to the PKI.

33. *Hoc Tap*, April, 1966—the theoretical journal of the Lao Dong (Communist) Party of Vietnam.

34. "The Russians are in Southeast Asia," *Los Angeles Times*, March 5, 1968. Admiral Muljadi led a naval mission to Moscow in 1967 and reported on his return that the Russians agreed to provide the largely Soviet-built Indonesian fleet with spare parts. On December 11, 1967, at formal ceremonies at the Surabaya naval base, the Soviet Navy transferred to Indonesia equipment used for charging submarines. However, the Russians apparently insisted on cash and by 1969 the flow of spare parts was reduced to a trickle. The Indonesians accused Moscow of failing to live up to its purchase agreements with Jakarta whereunder spare parts for warships delivered in 1963 were guaranteed for three to five years. See *Antara*, May 19, 1969.

35. *Antara*, July 26, 1966. See also *Antara*, December 19, 1968, in which Lt. Col. Sitorus accused both Moscow and Peking of engaging in "subversive" activities at Medan, North Sumatra. The Russians formally requested permission to open a consulate in Medan in November, 1964, amid speculation that they were trying to develop a "Sumatran wing" of the PKI as opposed to a Peking-oriented "Java wing." There has also been agitation in Bandjermasin, South Borneo, to have the Soviet consulate there removed. There are no Soviet nationals in the area. See *Antara*, January 28, May 2, 1969.

36. *Pravda*, November 24, 1966.

37. However, the Soviets have imposed strict "cash and carry" terms in contrast to their former policy of lavish credits. See footnote 34.

38. *Economist*, November 26, 1966.

39. *Antara*, October 18, 1966. The dispatch originated in Moscow.

40. Suharto, in an address before the MPRS, August 16, 1967.

41. The Soviet Union occupied Czechoslovakia August 20, 1967. Two days later, Jakarta reacted with a mild statement expressing "deep concern" and invoking the "five principles of peaceful coexistence." On August 24, Malik issued a stronger statement "deploring" the invasion and calling for a Soviet withdrawal. Student and labor groups, political parties, and the press, however, harshly denounced the Soviet invasion and occupation.

42. *Indonesian Tribune*, 2, 8, 1968. (Some issues are dated by months and others by numbers.) The PKI said the "barbarous armed aggression of the Soviet modern revisionists . . . have exposed their true features before the peoples of the world."

43. Ivan Maisky, *Memoirs of a Soviet Ambassador* (London: Hutchinson, 1967). Maisky held that was true only of "capitalist" states, however.

14. The "Cornell Paper"

1. *New Leader,* March 28, 1968.
2. *A Preliminary Analysis of the October 1, 1965 Coup in Indonesia,* n.d., n.p., 162 single-spaced typewritten pages, plus *Synopsis of the Coup Analysis,* 4 pages—hereafter cited as "The Cornell Paper."
3. This is pure Alfred Hitchcock. In his Hollywood thriller, *North by Northwest,* a Dutch Communist by the name of Van Dam decides to dispose of an adversary and confides to an aide: "These matters are best disposed of over great heights—at sea."
4. Fic, *op. cit.*
5. "The Cornell Paper." (Italics added.)
6. For background on Javanese mythology, see Benedict R. O'G. Anderson, *Mythology and the Tolerance of the Javanese* (Ithaca: Modern Indonesia Project, 1965).
7. The mimeographed covering letter was dated January 10, 1966. The form letter contained no letterhead, a blank salutation, and no signature.
8. Sol Sanders, *A Sense of Asia* (New York: Scribner's 1969), p. 185.
9. Covering letter.
10. *Washington Post,* March 5, 1966.
11. *Washington Post,* March 10, 1966.
12. *Ibid.*
13. "The Cornell Paper" avoids so pedestrian an example and, instead, compares the PKI's destruction to the Christian martyrdom in pagan Rome at the time of Nero, citing Edward Gibbon, *History of the Decline and Fall of the Roman Empire,* vol. 2 (New York: 1958), p. 86.
14. Anak Agung interview, Honolulu.
15. *Kami,* September 26, 1966.
16. Denis Warner, in a conversation at New York, Winter, 1967.
17. Sanders, *op. cit.*
18. In a private analysis which Roem permitted the author to use.
19. Soviet and East European diplomats have employed this gambit in both Jakarta and at the United Nations, New York.
20. Daniel S. Lev, "Indonesia 1965: The Year of the Coup," *Asian Survey,* February, 1966.
21. Some months later, the *Asian Survey* redressed the balance by the publication of an analysis of the affair by a former Cornell student, John O. Sutter. In his article, Sutter put responsibility on Sukarno, the PKI, and their progressive coconspirators in the military. See John O. Sutter, "Two Faces of Konfrontasi: 'Crush Malaysia' and the *Gestapu,*" *Asian Survey,* October, 1966.
22. Lucien Rey, "Dossier of the Indonesian Drama," *New Left Review,* March–April, 1966.
23. Sutter, *op. cit.,* who employs quotation marks around Lucien Rey's name.
24. *New Left Review.*
25. Eighteenth Annual Meeting, Association for Asian Studies, New York, April 4–6, 1966. The session was entitled, "Reflections on Indonesian Guided Democracy."
26. Ruth T. McVey, *The Rise of Indonesian Communism* (Ithaca: Cornell University Press, 1965). The book's publication was announced in an advertisement in the *Reporter,* October 21, 1965.

27. Donald Hindley, *Christian Science Monitor*, October 21, 1965. For an Indonesian definition, see Mochtar Lubis, "Report from Indonesia," *Current Affairs Bulletin*, University of Sydney, January 1, 1968. Lubis described the Sukarno regime as "unreasonable, narrow and aggressively nationalistic." In an interview, 1968, Lubis said the same description applied to the PKI. An editorial in the *Monitor*, January 18, 1966, reestablished a balance by characterizing the PKI as a "model of ruthlessness, trickery and a lack of patriotism." The *New Left Review* notwithstanding, the same editorial expressed glee over the uprooting of the PKI and simultaneously condemned the "ghastly bloodbath" in the aftermath, appealing to Jakarta to halt the fratricide.

28. Hindley, *op. cit.*

29. This exchange recalled to mind Major General Hans Oster's defense of Marshal von Manstein's refusal to take part in the July 20, 1944, plot of the German general staff against Hitler. "Failure in a great hour," Oster said, "is an historical not a personal fault."

30. W. F. Wertheim, "Indonesia Before and After the Untung Coup," *Pacific Affairs*, Spring–Summer, 1966. Despite Sukarno's repeated public statements and the mountain of evidence that he went to Halim of his own free will, and that Aidit freely flew to Central Java after the collapse of the movement, Wertheim insists that Sukarno, and Aidit, were "taken" to Halim.

31. His "serious students" are Lev, "Lucien Rey," and an unsigned article in *Current Affairs Bulletin*, May 30, 1966.

32. Frederick Bunnel, "Indonesia's Quasi-Military Regime," *Current History*, January, 1967.

33. *Ibid.*

34. Paget, *op. cit.* The October 2 reference, of course, was to *Harian Rakjat*.

35. See also R. E. Stannard, Jr., "Indonesia: Frustrated Giant," *War/Peace Report*, April, 1969. Stannard, a graduate of the Modern Indonesian Project and a veteran UPI correspondent in Southeast Asia, who blends his academic background with rice-roots reportorial experience, holds that the PKI leadership was convinced that the party's survival after Sukarno hinged "on achieving a neutral or friendly military structure before he died" and that the solution was a "preemptive putsch against the Army high command passed off as the crushing of a military plot against the President discovered by loyal members of his own palace guard."

36. *The Minority of One*, November, 1965.

37. *New York Times*, October 22, 1966.

38. *Ibid.*, June 1, 1966. A YAWF advertisement lists the names of the meeting's sponsors.

39. Second? See Robert Conquest, *The Great Terror: Stalin's Purge of the Thirties* (New York: Macmillan, 1968). Conquest suggests that twelve million people perished in the Soviet Union in the thirties and that "this killing has every right to be called the crime of the century."

40. *The Silent Slaughter: The Role of the United States in the Indonesian Massacre.* A pamphlet prepared and sponsored by YAWF. See also "Special Indonesian Supplement," *The Partisan*, October, 1968.

41. *Ibid., The Silent Slaughter.*

42. The myth about the presence of the Seventh Fleet was apparently put into circulation by *Harian Rakjat*, September 28, 1965. The PKI daily

declared that the rise of a NASAKOM cabinet "cannot be prevented, not even by the Seventh Fleet nor, as Bung Karno said, by the empty head in a General's uniform."

43. *The Silent Slaughter, op. cit.*
44. The figure solicited was announced at the meeting.
45. *Indonesian News and Views,* March, 1968. A Bulletin of the Indonesian Embassy, Washington, D.C. In a statement at Bandung rejecting "The Cornell Paper's" thesis, March 4, 1968. Pauker's remark was widely quoted in the Indonesian press.
46. *Sydney Morning Herald,* November 7, 1967.
47. Harry J. Benda, *Reflections on Asian Communism,* Reprint Series 17 (New Haven. Yale University, 1966). The reflections first appeared in the *Yale Review,* October, 1966.
48. See footnote 19.

15. Vietnam: The Missing Link?

1. Gunnar Myrdal, *An Asian Drama,* 1 (New York: Pantheon, 1968), p. 381.
2. *New Republic,* January 8, 1966.
3. *New York Times,* December 24, 1967.
4. Max Lerner, *New York Post,* March 14, 1966.
5. *Times* (London), April 27, 1966.
6. Richard M. Nixon, "Asia After Viet Nam," *Foreign Affairs,* October, 1967.
7. Lyndon B. Johnson address at Omaha, Nebraska, July 1, 1966.
8. Lyndon B. Johnson address from the White House, March 31, 1968.
9. David Brinkley interview with John F. Kennedy, NBC September 16, 1963.
10. *New York Times* interview with Dwight D. Eisenhower, December 24, 1967.
11. For that matter, so do the Chinese.
12. Mohammad Ghazali, Malaysian permanent secretary of foreign affairs. See Antara, December 24, 1968.
13. Malaysian Information Service, July 18, 1966.
14. The source currently holds a sensitive diplomatic post.
15. Deputy Premier Toh Chin Chye, in a speech welcoming Nasution to Singapore, October 12 ,1960. Singapore Government Press Statement, JK/MC. OC 44/60.
16. *Australian Daily News,* July 13, 1965. A Bulletin of the Australian News and Information Bureau, New York.
17. Prime Minister Holt, in an address before the Far East–American Council, New York, June 9, 1967.
18. Oscar S. Villadolid, *Manila Daily Bulletin,* September 13, 1965.
19. *Saigon Daily News,* September 30, 1965.
20. Ton interview, Saigon, Spring, 1968. Ton served in the Republic of Vietnam Embassy, London, during Sukarno's "crush Malaysia" campaign.
21. Wilfred Burchett news conference, at the United Nations, New York, December 2, 1968.
22. Antara, July 11, 1967. Malik, however, felt Peking put pressure on the PKI to organize the September 30 affair partly "for the purpose of lessening pressure on itself arising from the concentration of United States military power in Vietnam." See Radio Jakarta, May 17, 1967.

23. John Hughes, *Christian Science Monitor,* January 27, 1967.
24. *New York Times,* November 5, 1967.
25. Roem interview, New York, Winter, 1967.
26. The American he told this to, a correspondent, later confirmed this in an interview.
27. Cited by Joseph Alsop, *Washington Post,* September 9, 1966.
28. *Congressional Record,* June 12, 1967.
29. Antara, January 11, 1963.
30. *Harian Rakjat,* May 14, 1965.
31. NCNA, August 19, 1965. Aidit warned North Vietnam against what he termed the peril of the Western "peace offensive." He added, "What is most heartening is that the Vietnamese people and their leaders are on the alert for this 'peace offensive.' "
32. The Sjam Trial. See *Djakarta Times,* February 27, 1968.
33. Sutton, *op. cit.* Thereafter, Green was named assistant secretary of state for East Asian and Pacific Affairs. He was replaced in Jakarta by Francis Galbraith, the first United States ambassador to Singapore.
34. This is the view of a British correspondent, John Manders.
35. See the *Saturday Review,* October 28, 1967.
36. At his last news conference as President, January 17, 1969, Johnson lamented, "I would be less than candid if I failed to say I am troubled by the difficulties of communicating with and through the press."
37. *Senate Republican Policy Committee White Paper,* May 3, 1967. For the text, see *Congressional Record,* May 9, 1967.
38. One regiment entered South Vietnam by December, 1964, and several others by the Spring, 1965, on infiltration timetables that "can only have reflected command decisions" taken in Hanoi prior to February. See Bundy address at University of Maryland, August 15, 1967.
39. The statement was issued by General Hartono, in charge of nuclear operations in Indonesia, November 14, 1964. Other than receiving direct Chinese nuclear aid, this statement was largely bombast.
40. Aidit set up his Special Bureau under Sjam at this time.
41. Arnold Beichman, *New York Herald Tribune,* February 7, 1965. Against this background, see also Chapter II, footnote 1.
42. Preceded by the formation of the Thailand Independence Movement in November, 1964. See *Asia,* Autumn, 1966.
43. The MNLL established its headquarters in Jakarta under Ibrahim Mohammed. Following the collapse of the PKI, Hanoi granted political asylum to the MNLL. See Vietnam News Agency, Hanoi, January 9, 1967.
44. *Harian Rakjat,* September 15, 1965.
45. Tad Szulc, *New York Times,* January 8, 1965. This article, together with the Topping series and the Beichman piece in pre-Gestapu 1965, provides a penetrating insight into the situation obtaining within Indonesia and Indonesia's relationship to the rest of Southeast Asia just prior to the putsch.
46. The author's "Peking–Jakarta Axis Seen Pressing for 1965 Victory in S.E. Asia," *Worldwide Press Service,* December 23, 1964.
47. The author's "Second Front Opened in Southeast Asia," *Los Angeles Times,* January 17, 1965.
48. *New York Times,* September 7, 1966.
49. Villadolid, *op. cit.,* March 24, 1966.
50. The situation had a parallel at the time that Japan was staking a

claim to an empire extending from Korea to ultimately New Guinea. See *The Far Eastern Crisis, 1931–32* (London: Foreign Office, 1965). The British ambassador in Washington, Sir Ronald Lindsay, wrote on March 3, 1932: "I know the American people are dreadful people to deal with. They cannot make firm promises, but they jolly you along with fair prospects and when you are committed, they let you down."

51. *Los Angeles Times,* January 5, 1969.

52. *Saturday Review.*

53. Theodore Draper, *Abuse of Power* (New York: Viking, 1967), p. 63. Draper also believes "there is just enough truth in the 'domino theory' to make it, for some, a persuasive fallacy." p. 118.

54. Franz Schurmann, Peter Dale Scott, and Reginald Zelnik, *The Politics of Escalation in Vietnam* (New York: Fawcett, 1966), p. 51.

55. A reading of radio and press reports in these various capitals during this period unquestionably confirms this estimate.

56. The origins of the war can be traced to Charles de Gaulle, who ruled out independence for Vietnam in 1945 and dispatched the first expeditionary force to reestablish French rule in Vietnam in August, 1945. See Ellen J. Hammer, *The Struggle for Indochina* (Stanford: Stanford University, 1954), p. 42–43.

57. Richard Fryklund, *Washington Star,* February 11, 1965.

58. Address before the Tennessee Legislature, March 15, 1967. Johnson amplified his remarks in "Agenda for the Future: A Presidential Perspective," *Britannica Book of the Year 1969* (Chicago: Encyclopaedia Britannica, 1969). The former President said that although the PKI putsch failed, this "does not change the Communists' intent or the consequences that would have flowed throughout Asia and the Pacific from their victory." Johnson reiterated that given the situation obtaining in Southeast Asia in 1964–65, "we had no acceptable option" other than (massive) intervention.

59. *Department of State Bulletin,* May 22, 1967.

60. Bundy, *op. cit.*

61. *New York Times,* June 23, 1968.

62. The PKI promptly organized demonstrations in front of the United States Embassy, raising the slogan, "Hands Off Vietnam!"

16. The Second Front Collapses

1. Roger Hilsman, *To Move a Nation* (New York: Doubleday, 1967), p. 379.

2. *Harian Rakjat,* December 7, 1964. The occasion was the December 8 second anniversary of the independence proclamation of the State of North Borneo (NKKU).

3. *Daily Telegraph* (London), March 14, 1966.

4. In a private communication, dated November 7, 1967, following the author's colloquy at Brown on the interrelationship between Indonesia and Vietnam.

5. *Ibid.*

6. *Business Week,* August 14, 1965.

7. In a private talk at New York, 1966.

8. *Economist,* June 4, 1966.

9. Wilson, in a statement before the House of Commons, January 16, 1968.

10. *Melbourne Age,* November 21, 1967.

11. Jakarta was also attuned to the new situation. Thus, Radio Jakarta, May 8, 1966, observed that the secession of Singapore from Malaysia, the change of government in the Philippines (Ferdinand Marcos defeated Diosdado Macapagal's bid for re-election in the presidential balloting in Novembef, 1965), and the political shift in Indonesia as a result of the failure of the September 30 movement, "were far from being insignificant in the political constellation of the Maphilindo countries." Maphilindo referred to Malaysia, the Philippines, and Indonesia. The organization by that name, comprising Malaya, the Philippines and Indonesia, is now defunct. See also *New York Times,* May 30, 1966.

12. The new Indonesian ambassador to North Vietnam, Nugroho, presented his credentials at Hanoi to Acting President Ton Duc September 4, 1967. His predecessor, Sukrisno, is presently a member of the PKI emigré colony at Peking. Suharto's direction to Nugroho was to tell Hanoi that Indonesia does not hold a negative attitude toward the Democratic Republic of Vietnam, but that friendship is not a one-way street. See Antara, July 8, 1967, and September 4, 1967. *Nhan Dan,* the official Hanoi daily, had branded the Suharto government a "reactionary lackey of United States imperialism." E.g., *Nhan Dan,* February 15, 1966.

13. Walter Lippmann, *New York Herald Tribune,* January 31, 1967.

14. C. L. Sulzberger, *New York Times,* February 12, 1967.

15. *Newsday,* September 30, 1967.

16. *New York Herald Tribune,* December 27, 1965.

17. E.g., Malik, in an address before the MPRS, May 5, 1965, said Indonesia continued to firmly support the struggle of the "Vietnamese people" and that Indonesia "maintains her demand that the United States withdraw its military forces from Vietnam. . . ." But in 1969, with the United States moving toward disengagement and possibly a neo-isolationist phase in Asia—amid demands on all sides for "no more Vietnams"—Malik held that the American withdrawal from Vietnam should not be precipitate since this could be "dangerous." He favored a gradual withdrawal, Malik said, and cited Korea as an illustration. At the request of the Seoul government, the United States still maintains fifty thousand troops in South Korea.

17. The Overview

1. The Army leadership is aware of the problem. The Army's first test will come between 1971 and 1973. On March 27, 1968, the MPRS installed Suharto as President for five years. Later, it adopted a bill that fixed a general election for July, 1971, and the selection of a President February, 1973. Thus far, Indonesia has had only one general election, in 1955. It is unlikely at this writing that elections can be held in 1971. The Army's sensitivity is reflected in such pamphlets by the Department of Information as *The Truth of (the) Civic Mission as Carried Out By Indonesia's Armed Forces is Not Militarism* and *Participation in State Affairs of the Armed Forces of the Republic of Indonesia Is Not Militarism,* both published in 1967.

2. Alex Josey, "The Eclipse of the PKI," *Nation,* February 11, 1967.

3. Clifford Geertz and Herbert Luethy, "Are the Javanese Mad?," *Encounter,* August, 1966.

4. Yao Wen-yuan, in an address before the Shanghai Revolutionary Committee, cited by Afro-Asia News Service, May 14, 1968.

5. Transcript of an interview with Professor Robert A. Scalapino, re-

corded in the studios of Television Singapore, October 11, 1967. See also
C. P. Fitzgerald, "Present Trends in China," *Royal Central Asian Journal,*
February, 1967. He feels the Chinese Communists view the PKI failure on
a level with their experience in 1927. Of course, in 1927 the nationalist
leadership in China turned on the Communists; in 1965, in Indonesia, the
nationalist leadership was an active ally of the Communists, a rather important distinction.   6. Draft Program.   7. Lazitch, *op. cit.*
8. Sudisman "Self-Criticism," *op. cit.* Adjitorop, at the Albanian party
congress, endorsed the "Three Banners." See *Indonesian Tribune,* December, 1966—the month Sudisman was captured. This should not be confused with Aidit's "Three Banner" policy restated in *Peking Review,*
September 13, 1963. This previous policy embraced the banner of the national front, the banner of party building, and the banner of the August,
1945 revolution. Sudisman has described the new three-banner policy
as "the way out" for the PKI. The Kremlin, however, sees another "way
out." The Russians concede that "the Communist movement in Indonesia
has entered into a difficult stage," but offers this remedy: "Communists
see the outcome in the revival of the Communist Party of Indonesia on a
genuine Marxist-Leninist basis, in disassociating themselves from the Mao-
ists, and in restoring the ties of friendship and cooperation with the world
Communist movement." In mid 1969 there was a dramatic development.
Moscow proposed creating a new "Marxist-Lenninist PKI" with its own
"armed units" to prepare for the eventual overthrow of the Indonesian
government. The proposal was apparently designed to undercut Peking in
the competition for control of the remnant PKI and to restrain the PKI
from new, premature "Blitars." See *Horizont,* East Berlin, June, 1969.
JPRS: 48462. See also *Far Eastern Economic Review,* July 20, 1969. There
is speculation that some PKI immigrees find this approach receptive,
among them, Djawoto, although there is no firm evidence as this book
goes to press.
9. The underground PKI has described only two party documents as
"important" since 1965—the Sudisman auto-critique and its new program.
See footnote below.
10. The text of the "Program of the Communist Party of Indonesia For
People's Democracy in Indonesia," dated November, 1967, appeared in the
Indonesian Tribune, 2, no. 9, 1968.
11. In a sense this is sugar coating since the program specifically states
that an Indonesian People's Democracy will be governed on the basis of
"democratic centralism," that is, solely governed by the leadership of the
unopposed, ruling Communist Party.
12. Since the program refers to Indonesians of not only different ethnic
groups but also of different "descent," this would presumably offer the
Overseas Chinese community protection and would permit the reopening
of former Chinese-language schools and other institutions.
13. See Rosihan Anwar, *Angkatan Bersendjata,* March 4, 1968.
14. See "PKI's Consolidated Position Has Thrown The Suharto-Nasution
Fascist Regime Into Utter Panick (c.q.)," *Indonesian Tribune,* 2, pp. 6–7.
15. One legacy of the abortive Communist effort of October 1, 1965, is a
"witch-hunting" atmosphere in Indonesia which is likely to take several
years to dissipate and which is sometimes conveniently used to cover other
tensions, such as between the Moslem and Christian communities. E.g.,
Sinar Harapan, November 7, 1967.

Bibliography

Additional sources of material may be found in the Notes.

Aidit, Dipa Nusantara. *Pilihan Tulisan.* Jakarta: Pembaruan, 1959. 2 vols. An English-language translation, entitled, *The Selected Writings of D. N. Aidit,* is available from the Joint Publications Research Service, Washington, D.C. See JPRS below.

————. *The Indonesian Revolution and the Immediate Tasks of the Communist Party of Indonesia.* Peking: Foreign Language Press, 1964.

Ali, S. M. "Interview with Dr. D. N. Aidit." *Far Eastern Economic Review,* April 16, 1964.

Allen, Richard. *Malaysia: Prospect & Retrospect.* London: Oxford University Press, 1968. Sir Richard, former British ambassador to Burma, considered Antara by mid-1965 "little more than a tool of the New China News Agency."

Anderson, Benedict R. O'G., *Mythology and the Tolerance of the Javanese.* Ithaca, N.Y.: Modern Indonesia Project, 1965.

Angkatan Bersendjata. A daily newspaper published by the Director of Information, Indonesian Armed Forces. First published in 1965.

Antara News Bulletin. Jakarta. Published in two editions daily by Indonesia's national news agency.

Anti-Soviet Bloc of Rights [sic] and Trotskyites. Moscow: People's Commissariat of Justice, USSR, 1938. The Moscow purge trials.

Basic Policy for the Solution of the Chinese Problem. Jakarta: Department of Information, Republic of Indonesia. Special issue 024/1967.

Benda, Harry J. *Reflections on Asian Communism.* Southeast Asia Studies. Reprint Series, no. 17. New Haven, Conn.: Yale University, October, 1966.

Brackman, Arnold C. *Indonesian Communism: A History.* New York: Praeger, 1963. The first full-length history of the party to appear in the West. Traces party from origins in 1920 through Indonesia's recovery of West Irian in 1963.

————. *Southeast Asia's Second Front: The Power Struggle in the Malay Archipelago.* New York: Praeger, 1966. Continues the development of the party from West Irian to the September 30 affair.

————. "The Malay World and China: Partner or Barrier?" In A. M. Halpern, et. al., *Policies Toward China: Views from Six Continents.* New York: McGraw-Hill, 1965. Published by the Council on Foreign Relations.

Bunnell, Frederick. "Indonesia's Quasi-Military Regime." *Current History,* 52, No. 305 (January, 1967).

Burhan and Subekti. *The Red Coup That Failed.* (n.d.). Photocopy of English typescript. Published in the original Indonesian in Jakarta.

Butwell, Richard, "Indonesia's Leaders Have a Surplus of Opponents," *The New Republic,* October 8, 1966.

Conquest, Robert. *The Great Terror: Stalin's Purges of the Thirties.* New York: Macmillan, 1968.

"Current Activities of the Partai Komunis Indonesia." Translated from the original Indonesian. Typescript, stenciled. One of a series of analyses prepared by the democratic socialist underground during the Sukarno period. Pp. 7. August 10, 1965. Compare with their report titled, "Situation in Java." August 7, 1964.

Decornoy, Jacques. "The Fight for Power in Indonesia—Will Sukarno Arm the Workers and Farmers?" *Le Monde,* August 17, 1965.

Dommen, Arthur J. "The Attempted Coup in Indonesia." *The China Quarterly,* January–March, 1966. Contains text of Aidit's "Asahi confession."

External Affairs Review. Indonesia in 2 parts. Wellington: Ministry of External Affairs, July and August, 1967. Unsigned but probably the work of Paul Edmonds, a senior member of the New Zealand Embassy, Jakarta, 1965.

Facts & Figures. Jakarta: Department of Information, Republic of Indonesia, 1967–69. A series of irregularly published summaries in English of the Special Military Tribunal. Mimeographed.

Fic, Victor M. "September 30th Movement in Indonesia: 1965 Gamble that Failed." Kuala Lumpur: Department of History, University of Malaya, 1968, p. 164; stenciled paper. The author is on the faculty of Nanyang University, Singapore, and is executive secretary of the Institute of Southeast Asia.

40 Hari Kegagalan "G. 30. S" Jakarta: Staf Angkatan Bersendjata, 1965. The first in a series of monographs by the Army, covering the period October 1–November 10, 1965.

Freeman, Roger A. *Socialism and Private Enterprise in Equatorial Asia.* Stanford: Hoover Institute, 1968.

G-30-S Dihadapan Mahmillub. Jakarta: Oembimbing Masa, 1966–68. 3 vols. and more to come. Transcripts of the Special Military Tribunal (*Mahkamah Militer Luar Biasa* or *Mahmillub*).

Geertz, Clifford, and Luethy, Herbert. "Are the Javanese Mad?" *Encounter*, August 1966.

Geertz, Hilda. "Latah in Java: A Theoretical Paradox." *Indonesia* 5 (April, 1968).

Great Cultural Revolution in China, The. Tokyo & Rutland, Vt.: Tuttle, 1968. Compiled and edited by the Asian Research Centre, Hong Kong.

Hanna, Willard A. *Bung Karno's Indonesia.* Washington: American Universities Field Staff, 1961. By an outspoken academic and critic of the Sukarno regime.

Harian Rakjat. Jakarta. The official daily newspaper of the Indonesian Communist Party.

Hartowardjojo, Harijadi S. "Mental Conditioning Process in Troubled Indonesia." *Solidarity* 3, no. 9 (September, 1968). The situation on the eve of September 30.

Hassan, Faud. "Prospects for Relations Between Indonesia and Communist China: An Indonesian View." *Current Scene*, November 4, 1968.

Hastings, Peter. "Java Journey." *The Australian*, July 9, 1966.

Hidaja, S. "The Mystery in the G. 30. S." *Ampera Review*, June 2, 1968. Edited by Mrs. Supeni, formerly ambassador-at-large and close associate of Subandrio.

Higgins, Benjamin. *Indonesia: Crisis of the Millstones.* Princeton: Van Nostrand, 1965. By the Canadian economist.

Hindley, Donald. *The Communist Party of Indonesia 1951–63.* Berkeley and Los Angeles: University of California, 1964.

———. "Political Power and the October 1965 Coup in Indonesia." *The Journal of Asian Studies* 26, no. 2 (February, 1967).

Hughes, John. *Indonesian Upheaval.* New York: McKay, 1967. First-hand reporting on the student campaign against Sukarno in the Gestapu aftermath.

Indonesia. Ithaca, N.Y.: Modern Indonesia Project, Cornell University. Biannual. First issued in April 1966. Generally high-calibre, technical articles on Indonesia.

Indonesian Armed Forces and the New Order, The. Jakarta: Department of Defense and Security, Institute of History, 1968.

Indonesian Herald. A Jakarta daily published by the Foreign Office during the Subandrio period.

Joint Publications Research Service (JPRS). Clearinghouse for Federal Scientific and Technical Information, National Bureau of Standards, U.S. Department of Commerce. Springfield, Va. JPRS provides invaluable translations of Indonesian material for the public. E.g., *see* JPRS 33-287. No. 105. *Harian Rakjat*, October 2, 1965.

Josey, Alex. "Indonesia: The Guru and the Coup." *The Nation*, September 11, 1967.

Karnow, Stanley. "Indonesia: Aftermath of Collapse." A series in the *Washington Post*, December 1966.

King, Seth. "The Great Purge in Indonesia." *The New York Times Magazine*, May 8, 1966.

Kompas. A Jakarta daily newspaper published by the Catholic Party and widely considered Indonesia's most reliable journal.

Lazitch, Branko. "Declaration of Indonesian Communists." *Est & Ouest*, January 1–15, 1968. An analysis of the Moscow/Peking polemic in relation to September 30.

Lev, Daniel S. "Indonesia 1965: The Year of the Coup." *Asian Survey* 6, no. 2 (February, 1966).

Lin Piao. *Long Live the Victory of People's War.* Peking: Foreign Language Press, 1966. Originally published in *People's Daily*, September 3, 1965.

Lubis, Mochtar. "Report from Indonesia." *Current Affairs Bulletin* 41, no. 3 (January 1, 1968).

"Lucien Rey." "Dossier of the Indonesian Drama." *New Left Review*, March–April, 1966. With an introduction by the editor, Perry Anderson.

Luethy, Herbert. "The Indonesian Mystery." *The New York Review of Books*, May 26, 1966. By a professor of economic history, University of Zurich. The collapse of G. 30. S., he holds, "brought down the whole fictitious structure of Sukarno's state philosophy and balance of power."

Lukman, M. H. "Overcoming Difficulties in the National Economy." *Harian Rakjat*, June 24, 1965.

McVey, Ruth T. *The Rise of Indonesian Communism.* Ithaca, N.Y.: Cornell University Press, 1965. A detailed study of the party up to the abortive 1926 revolt.

———. *The Development of the Indonesian Communist Party and Its Relations with the Soviet Union and the Chinese People's Republic.* Cambridge: Massachusetts Institute of Technology, 1954.

Malayan Monitor. A monthly which often contains Communist documents on the Malay world. Mimeographed. The Peking line down to the last comma.

Malik, Adam. *Sovjet Russia sperti jang saja liaht.* Jakarta: Pustaka, 1954.

———. "Promise in Indonesia." *Foreign Affairs* 46, no. 2 (January, 1968).

Marcuse, Jacques. *The Peking Papers.* New York: Dutton, 1967.

Marsudi, Djamal. *Peristiwa Madiun.* Jakarta: Merdeka Press, 1965.

Mortimer, Rex. "Indonesia: Emigre Post-Mortems on the PKI." *Australian Outlook,* December, 1968.

Nasution, Abdul Haris. *Menegakkan: Keadilan Dan Kebenaran.* Jakarta: Seruling Masa, 1967.

———. *Towards A People's Army.* Jakarta: Delegasi, 1964.

Nugroho, Notosusanto and Saleh, Ismail. *The Coup Attempt of the "September 30 Movement" in Indonesia.* Photocopy of typescript. Pp. 167. (n.p., n.d.) Generally known in academic circles as the "White Paper." Nugroho is head of the History Department, University of Indonesia. Saleh is a colonel in the Indonesian Army.

ORBA: A Guide to the New Order Government Policy. Jakarta: Department of Information, Republic of Indonesia, 1966. Sets out conflict between Sukarno and the Army over the PKI's role in the putsch.

Paget, Roger K. "The Military in Indonesian Politics: the Burden of Power." Paper delivered at Association of Asian Studies annual meeting, Chicago, March 1967. Mimeographed. Pp. 22.

Pauker, Ewa T. "Has the Sukarno Regime Weakened the PKI?" *Asian Survey* 4, no. 9 (September, 1964).

Pauker, Guy J. *The Rise and Fall of the Communist Party of Indonesia.* Santa Monica: RAND Corporation, February 1969. Memorandum RM 5753 PR. Prepared for the U.S. Air Force.

People of Indonesia, Unite and Fight to Overthrow the Fascist Regime. Peking: Foreign Language Press, 1968. Contains a severely edited version of Sudisman's 1966 autocritique (e.g., the suggestion of PKI "adventurism," an epithet Moscow hurls at Peking, is deleted). Also contains the November 11, 1967, *Red Flag* commentary.

Plebeian. Singapore: Barisan Sosialis Malaya. A newsletter published in Chinese and English.

Preliminary Analysis of the October 1, 1965, Coup in Indonesia, A (n.p., n.d.). Pp. 162. Photocopy of a typescript. Two versions, one containing a covering letter requesting no attribution and another without a covering letter. Marked on various pages "strictly confidential." Known in Indonesia and in Western academic circles as the so-called "Cornell Paper."

Ra'anan, Uri. "The Coup That Failed: A Background Analysis." *Problems of Communism,* March–April 1966.

Ray, Sibnarayan. *Vietnam: Seen From East and West.* New York: Praeger, 1966. One of the extremely few books on Vietnam to view the conflict in a broad Asian perspective.

Results of the Fourth MPRS Session in 1966. Jakarta: Antara. Mimeographed. Pp. 111. Contains texts of documents relating to the withering away of the Sukarno regime in 1966. With an introduction by the late Adinegoro.

Roeder, O. G. "Death of a Rebel." *Far Eastern Economic Review,* December 23, 1965. One of any number of brilliant articles on Indonesia for the period 1963–66. See *all* his dispatches.

———. *The Smiling General: President Soeharto of Indonesia.* Jakarta: Gunung Agung, 1969. The first biography of Suharto.

Rostow, W. W. "The Great Transition: Tasks of the First and Second Postwar Generations." *Department of State Bulletin,* March 27, 1967.

Saleh, Miriam. "Parliamentary Government In Indonesia, Parties and Parliament." Thesis. Georgetown University, 1955.

Samson, Allan A. "Islam in Indonesian Politics." *Asian Survey*, December, 1968.

Sanders, Sol W. *A Sense of Asia*. New York: Scribner's, 1969. Impressionistic vignettes.

Scott, James C. "An Essay on the Political Functions of Corruption." *Asian Studies* 5, no. 3 (December, 1967).

"Selected Documents Relating to the September 30 Movement and Its Epilogue." *Indonesia*, no. 1 (April, 1966), pp. 131–204. Emphasis should be on the word *selected*, as the editors themselves note.

Shaplen, Robert. *Time Out of Hand: Revolution and Reaction in Southeast Asia*. New York: Harper & Row, 1969. One-third devoted to Indonesia, especially the September 30 Movement. First appeared, abridged, in *The New Yorker*.

Siagian, Toenggoel Papaloan. "The Operasi Karya." An unpublished paper on the involvement of the Indonesian Army in rural development.

Silent Slaughter, The. New York: Marzani & Munsell, 1966. A pamphlet produced by the Youth Against War and Fascism. Subtitled, "The Role of the United States in the Indonesian massacre."

Silverman, Jerry M. "Indonesianizing Marxism-Leninism: The Development and Consequences of Communist Polycentrism." Ph.D. thesis, Claremont College, 1967.

Simatupang, T. B. "Vietnam Dan Kita." Mimeographed. March 2, 1968.

Simon, Sheldon W. *The Broken Triangle: Peking, Djakarta and the PKI*. Baltimore: The Johns Hopkins Press, 1969. A solid, fine treatment of Sino-Indonesian relations during the Gestapu period.

Sjahrir, Sutan. *Nationalism and Internationalism*. 2d ed. Rangoon: Asian Socialist Conference, 1953.

———. *Sosialisme dan Marxisme*. Jakarta: Djambatan, 1967.

Sloan, Stephen. "A Case Study of the Indonesian Coup of 1965." Ph.D. thesis, New York University, 1967.

Soe, Hok Gie. "The Future of the Indonesian Communist Movement." *Solidarity* 3, no. 9 (September, 1968). Considers the prospect promising.

Straits Times, The. A daily newspaper published in Singapore with the largest English-language circulation in the region.

Sukarno: An Autobiography. As told to Cindy Adams. New York: Bobbs-Merrill, 1965. Sukarno demolishes himself.

Sutter, John O. "Two Faces of Konfrontasi: 'Crush Malaysia' and the *Gestapu*." *Asian Survey* 6, no. 10 (October, 1966).

Sutton, Horace. "Indonesia's Night of Terror." *Saturday Review*,

February 4, 1967. Subtitled: "Exclusive Report from Jakarta on the Red Purge."

Swianiewicz, S. *Forced Labor and Economic Development*. London: Oxford University Press, 1965. With references to Indonesia.

Taubinger, L. M. "Indonesia: The Plot That Failed." *National Review,* February 22, 1966.

Topping, Seymour. "Communists Emerging as Sukarno's Heirs." The *New York Times,* August 27, 1965. Last of three dispatches.

————. " '65 Uprising in Indonesia: Study in Red Blundering." *Ibid.* August 23, 1966.

Van der Kroef, Justus M. " 'Gestapu' in Indonesia." *Orbis* 10, no. 2 (Summer, 1966).

————. *The Sino-Indonesian Rupture.* New York: American-Asian Educational Exchange, 1968.

Vittachi, Tarzie. *The Fall of Sukarno.* New York: Praeger, 1967. A racy account by a Ceylonese journalist.

Warner, Denis. *Reporting South-East Asia.* Sydney: Angus & Robertson, Ltd., 1966. A collection of excellent articles during the period under review which first appeared in *The Reporter.* E.g., "The Peking-Djakarta Axis," September 23, 1965.

Wertheim, W. F. "Indonesia Before and After the Untung Coup." *Pacific Affairs* 39, nos. 1 and 2 (Spring–Summer, 1966).

Willner, Ann R. *Public Protest in Indonesia.* Papers in International Studies. Southeast Asia Series, no. 2. Athens, Ohio: Ohio University, 1968.

Wolters, O. W. *Early Indonesian Commerce: A Study of the Origins of Srivijaya.* Ithaca, N.Y.: Cornell University Press, 1967.

Index